CONTEMPORARY
SOCIAL AND
POLITICAL THEORY

CONTEMPORARY SOCIAL AND POLITICAL THEORY
AN INTRODUCTION

Fidelma Ashe
Alan Finlayson
Moya Lloyd
Iain MacKenzie
James Martin
Shane O'Neill

Open University Press
Buckingham · Philadelphia

Open University Press
Celtic Court
22 Ballmoor
Buckingham
MK18 1XW

email: enquiries@openup.co.uk
world wide web: http://www.openup.co.uk

and
325 Chestnut Street
Philadelphia, PA 19106, USA

First Published 1999

Copyright © Fidelma Ashe, Alan Finlayson, Moya Lloyd, Iain MacKenzie,
James Martin, Shane O'Neill, 1999

A catalogue record of this book is available from the British Library

ISBN   0 335 19624 1 (pb)   0 335 19625 X (hb)

Library of Congress Cataloging-in-Publication Data
Contemporary social and political theory: an introduction/Fidelma Ashe . . .
   [et al.].
       p. cm.
   Includes bibliographical references and index.
   ISBN 0-335-19625-X. – ISBN 0-335-19624-1 (pbk.)
   1. Social sciences – Philosophy. 2. Political science – Philosophy.
I. Ashe, Fidelma. 1965–
H61. 15. C65 1998
300' .1–dc21   98-19057
                                                                         CIP

Typeset by Type Study, Scarborough, North Yorkshire
Printed in Great Britain by Redwood Books, Trowbridge

CONTENTS

PREFACE

Social and political theory can be a daunting prospect for the student
new to the interrogation of ideas. The precise meaning and full import
of contemporary philosophies, the application of a concept or theory,
or the wider practical implications of a new way of thinking can be
difficult to grasp. Sometimes an idea can appear so defeatingly obscure
that it seems wiser to abandon the enterprise than pursue it further.
This attitude is both understandable and unfortunate, as theories and
concepts occupy centre-stage in the key discussions and disputes that
animate the social sciences and humanities. It is the purpose of this
book to provide an accessible introduction to contemporary social
and political theory that might guide those new to the field over
rough but rewarding terrain.

But what *is* theory and why is it so important? A theory might best
be understood as a conceptual framework that enables the organization and evaluation of social experience. A theory permits us to put
everyday experiences in context and to compare them, perhaps even
control them in some way. As conscious human beings we all think
theoretically in order to plan and order our lives, though usually we
do not think of ourselves as 'theorists'. Yet to complete even the most
banal of daily routines requires an implicit theoretical grasp of the
complex social rules, codes and behavioural regularities that we confront. Because everyday behaviour does not usually demand that we
make explicit our theoretical understanding of society, we tend to
treat our actions, and those of others, as mere 'common sense'. However, when certain forms of behaviour or particular social rules are not
adhered to – such as when someone is, we think, being offensive – we
invoke the rule that has been broken and consider the reasons for
having such a rule in the first place. It is on occasions like this, when
conventions and expectations are disrupted, that we must become
theorists of sorts. For it is then that we bring to mind the frameworks
that help us to order the world. We might even say that it is when such
conventions are broken, forcing us to address our habits anew so as to
reaffirm or change them, that we are being most social or even most
human. It is the conceptualization and evaluation of such habits, the

mental frameworks that inform and structure our social and political experiences, to which we attend in this book.

Even this kind of everyday theory is abstract, in that it stands at some distance from our immediate experience of the empirical world. Such abstraction helps us to bring together different experiences and allows us to compare them. In this sense, a theory functions like a 'conceptual map', helping us to plot our way through a complex world. Theories classify information and reduce real complexity to generalized conceptual associations. These conceptual associations help us not only to order our experience but also to ground expectations and to 'explain' certain phenomena according to these expectations. Without a theory of some sort, we would forever be at the mercy of the immediate flow of events, unable either to formulate or to classify our needs and preferences. As we have suggested already, we all make use of such theories all the time. We hold expectations of what the world will do and of how other people will behave, and we use these expectations to evaluate the likely outcome of a given situation and to plan new courses of action.

Social and political theory is not unlike such everyday theories, but it aims at a deeper level of understanding. It not only tries to grasp the world around us, and plot a course through it, but also examines the nature of intellectual activity itself. How can we be sure our expectations are well founded? Can we know if a proposed course of action will work out as intended? Are our ideas valid in all situations and at all times? Does the social world limit our outlook? Should we try in our thinking to transcend our cultural context? These are questions about the very nature of thinking, or the activity of reflecting on and criticizing our social world. Such questions are essential to the process of understanding both the way that world is and the ways in which we should try to change it.

But, like real maps, those of a conceptual variety can become outdated or insufficient for the exploration at hand. New lands can be discovered, quicker routes to interesting places may appear or someone might even point out we have been holding the map upside down. Such reversals are not unknown in science, philosophy or social and political theory. Sometimes it can seem as if we are somewhat disoriented and badly in need of a new map.

Many commentators now note the apparent decline of the intellectual certainties that have helped us to understand cultural and political change over the past two to three hundred years. These certainties included: a belief in the possibility of 'objective' knowledge and rational progress; an assumption that democratic forms of government brought about an increase in individual autonomy; and the idea that 'consensus' over major areas of social life was both possible and desirable in modern societies. These 'certainties' have shaped the dominant ideas about human society itself in the modern age; its basic underlying and distinctive characteristics; the foundation for theoretical knowledge about these characteristics; and the possibility of putting such theory into practice. Yet, for a variety of reasons, such assumptions are no longer so dominant in cultural and political debate. They are no longer immune from the critical interrogations of sceptics. Today, the optimism of the eighteenth and nineteenth centuries can seem excessive and even naive. In various aspects of intellectual life we have grown, if not cynical, then at least profoundly unsure that modern society can be understood clearly and directed purposefully for the better of all. The combined and accumulated impact of twentieth-century wars, economic and ecological crises and conflicts associated with cultural fragmentation has put paid to any unqualified hopes. This undermining of intellectual certainties throughout the Western world has placed attention increasingly on questions of theory and on the effort to draw up new conceptual maps that can orient us in our contemporary concerns.

In the past thirty to forty years, social and political theory has undergone a remarkable revival and expansion. The 'maps' inherited from the eighteenth and nineteenth centuries have been regarded as less and less reliable for guiding us through the experiences of the twentieth century. In the face of these experiences of war, conflict and crisis, social and political theorists have again been compelled to address basic questions, such as 'who are we?' and 'how are we best to live together?' In this climate, a variety of theoretical currents have powerfully challenged the 'mainstream' intellectual and political traditions inherited from earlier centuries, primarily the traditions of liberalism and Marxism. These challenges have often come from within these traditions themselves, but their impact has tended to go far beyond them. We might note, to take a few examples: the challenge of feminism to the masculine bases of social and political thought and institutions; the assault on the repressive features of programmes of social rationalization by continental thinkers such as Foucault, Derrida and Lyotard; and Habermas's reconceptualization of reason in communicative terms. None of these can be said to fit comfortably into any one of the ideological categories inherited from the past. Our point of departure in this book is the challenge that these thinkers have brought to the dominant traditions of social and political theory.

Students now have available to them a wide variety of introductory commentaries, as well as more specialized monographs on the theorists mentioned above. For this reason, we have avoided focusing exclusively on key thinkers alone. Instead, the volume offers a 'thematic' overview of contemporary debates. It takes as its starting point major concepts in the tradition of modern theory and it surveys the variety of challenges to, and transformations of, these concepts. Thus it is possible to consider the relevance of a wide range of theorists to debates *across* the spectrum of those disciplines that are rooted in the theoretical investigation of politics and society; from anthropology to sociology and political studies. There are eight chapters, each analysing debates around a particular concept.

'Rationality' (Chapter 1) is in many ways the key concept that has been at the foundation of dominant conceptions of modernity. Ideas about 'social criticism' (Chapter 2) have been significant, in that the impulse to criticize social and political arrangements has always been a central focus of theory. Theories about 'language' (Chapter 3) have been at the heart of much of the work which has undermined our belief in the triumph of reason, while no critical theory would be complete without a well developed conception of the operation of 'power' in society (Chapter 4). Another concept that was at the foundation of the modern project of rationalization is 'the subject', or individual human being (Chapter 5), while reflections on 'the body' (Chapter 6) have helped us to understand our experiences in a more concrete and contextually sensitive way. Theoretical ideas about 'culture' (Chapter 7) aim to investigate the ways in which our identities are constituted by social forces, and political theory has recently also had to grapple with the very nature of 'the political' and the way in which it is related to 'the social' (Chapter 8).

Of course, all these concepts are related to one another and, inevitably, there will be a degree of overlap in the chapters, since each concept is bound up with a similar history. However, each is sufficiently autonomous to justify separate consideration. In the various branches of the social sciences and humanities, different concepts have had differing weight attached to them. While readers may note the fact that the chapters cover comparable theoretical terrain at times, it is to be hoped that they also appreciate the different focus to each of these conceptual debates.

This book aims to provide a bridge between traditional social and political theory and current developments. The emphasis will be on theories that have not yet been taken into the mainstream of Anglo-American social science. We will be reflecting on the challenges to this mainstream that have been launched by thinkers working within the 'continental' approaches that have emerged in Western Europe, especially structuralism, poststructuralism and critical theory. Different theorists have been placed alongside each other and treated as contributors to debates rather than as isolated intellectuals. As such, the book will serve as a convenient starting point for students wishing to delve further into the ideas of particular thinkers, since it places these theorists in a wider context. Alternatively, it may function more generally as a guide to current debates within the social sciences and humanities. While the book may be read as a whole from start to finish, the chapters have been designed to stand on their own, and it should also be fruitful to begin with the concept that is of most interest to the reader and then to branch out from there. Cross-references to discussions in other chapters have been included where these might fill out an argument or concept.

Inevitably, a book of this variety will be selective in its choice of thinkers, debates and concepts. It cannot substitute for a closer analysis of the individual theorists whose ideas are discussed. Nor can it fill out in detail the wider historical context in which these debates occurred. As an introduction it can only invite the reader to appreciate the broad movement of ideas, deliberately leaving the finer details to other commentaries and specialist texts. At the end of each chapter we have added short guides to further reading to enable those who are interested to follow up on certain aspects of the chapter. We have also added, as an appendix, a 'glossary' of key terms. This gives brief definitions of certain frequently mentioned ideas that have begun to enter the vocabulary of contemporary theory.

An introduction to social and political theory cannot hope to expel all the fears that newcomers to the field might have. If we have managed to spark further interest or have assisted the reader in clarifying some difficult ideas then the book will have served its purpose. Despite common misgivings and some unfounded prejudices, social and political theory is above all a way of engaging with the real world. By sharpening our theoretical grasp of that world we hold open the possibility that we might continue to improve it.

Finally, we should like to thank our colleagues in the School of Politics at Queen's University for providing a friendly and scholarly environment within which to write this book. We would especially like to thank Bob Eccleshall, Vincent Geoghegan and Richard Jay for their consideration of and helpful comments on some of the individual contributions. Needless to say, we alone are responsible for what follows.

Fidelma Ashe
Alan Finlayson
Moya Lloyd
Iain MacKenzie
James Martin
Shane O'Neill

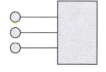

1 RATIONALITY
Shane O'Neill

INTRODUCTION

Philosophers often categorize human beings as rational animals, and they regard our potential for reason to be a distinctively human characteristic. Our capacity for rational action is also considered to be a vital source for the hope that social order and political justice can be reconciled with individual freedom. This hope is most particularly associated with the project of Enlightenment, a philosophically inspired movement that flourished among intellectual circles in eighteenth-century Europe. This project continues to provide the most fundamental orientation for modern ideas of progress.

The philosophers of Enlightenment argued that with the development of scientific method, human reason could illuminate the darker aspects of nature. Such advances in knowledge would provide us with the means to control both the natural world around us and the tendencies inherent in human nature that, left untamed, can lead to disorder and conflict. Rational inquiry would sweep aside unquestioning acceptance of religious or political dogma and usher forth a truly human age, where all could fulfil their potential for autonomous living.

This bold outlook has been the source of much controversy in recent social and political theory. The impulse to dominate nature that lies behind the Enlightenment conception of rationality has led some to attack its very foundations, while others have sought to reformulate the ideal so as to illuminate the darkness of our own times. The aim of this chapter is to outline some of the issues at stake in these controversies and critically to assess the extent to which it is possible to acquire knowledge that facilitates the rational control of nature and society.

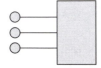

EMANCIPATION AND THE CONTROL OF NATURE

For Enlightenment thinkers rationality is the key to human emancipation. By the light of reason we can discover the laws which keep the natural and human worlds in motion. There is, in principle, no fundamental difference between the kind of knowledge we can have of the external world of nature and the inner world of human intellectual and moral experience. This assumption has played a vital role in the development of social and political theory. Later we will see that the attempt to model the social sciences on the natural sciences has some serious and troublesome consequences. For now we need to realize what first motivated these efforts. From the Enlightenment perspective, scientific knowledge liberates us from the shackles of dogma, leading us into a realm of freedom where we alone are in control of our destiny. No longer need we defer to the authority of a judgemental God who can condemn us at will to a tragic fate; nor need we have any superstitious reverence for the unfathomable mystery and insurmountable power of nature. There is no higher authority than the individual subject and it is on the basis of that subject's rights that a new emancipatory order is to be constructed (see also Chapter 5). That order will be characterized by social and economic progress, political justice and personal autonomy.

This is an exhilarating vision shot through with intoxicating optimism. One of its most remarkable expressions is found in the Marquis de Condorcet's *Sketch for a Historical Picture of the Progress of the Human Mind* (1795). This philosophical manifesto of the Enlightenment was written during one of the most turbulent periods of the French Revolution. Despite his optimism regarding the progress of the human mind, Condorcet had already fallen foul of the Jacobin administration. With cruel irony, he was executed less than a year after writing this impassioned hymn to the dawn of reason that the Revolution was thought to herald.

In the final chapter, Condorcet made a set of predictions, based on past experience of the ongoing triumph of reason, that outlines our imminent emancipation.

> The time will therefore come when the sun will shine only on free men who know no other master but their reason; when tyrants and slaves, priests and their stupid or hypocritical instruments will exist only in works of history and on the stage; and when we shall think of them only to pity their victims and their dupes; to maintain ourselves in a state of vigilance by thinking on their excesses; and to learn how to recognize and so to destroy, by force of reason, the seeds of tyranny and superstition, should they ever dare to reappear amongst us.
>
> (Condorcet 1955: 179)

Condorcet's supposedly well grounded prediction is exceedingly optimistic, not to say naively utopian. His hope that we were soon to realize such a rational form of life was sustained above all by confidence in the advances of scientific method that had transformed the intellectual landscape of Europe.

When reason is applied scientifically, it can yield knowledge of the truth about nature. A philosophical grounding for this enterprise had already been provided in the seventeenth century by Francis Bacon, one of the philosophers most admired by the Enlightenment thinkers. He maintained in *Novum Organum* (1620) that knowledge and power were one and the same thing, 'for where the cause is not known the effect cannot be produced' (Bacon 1955: 462). Bacon insisted that if we were to achieve *certain* knowledge of the true mechanisms of nature we would be able to control it, exert power over it and transform human life for the better. But how was such certain knowledge to be had? Bacon proposed two ways by which truth could be discovered: empirical induction and rationalist deduction. The former, which was preferred by Bacon, suggests that we begin by considering the world as it is experienced through our senses and then, 'rising by a gradual and unbroken ascent' (Bacon 1955: 465), we arrive at the most general of axioms. This, in the most simple terms, is the empiricist method of science.

According to the empiricist method, any knowledge we have about nature is given a firm foundation in self-evident truths to which we have immediate access through sense-perception. For example, I know that sulphur burns with a bright yellow flame because I have seen it do so. This is a basic fact about a singular phenomenon, or particular, that one can observe. If we observe this repeatedly, without exception, then we can infer that this phenomenon always occurs when the same conditions obtain – that sulphur always burns with a bright yellow flame. Thus we have arrived at a general axiom that can be tested by experiment. The kind of generalization involved here is warranted by a principle of induction that allows us to infer from past experience to the expectation of similar future experience. Hence we expect sulphur to continue to burn with a bright yellow flame. If we can identify such law-like regularities in the behaviour of particulars, then we will have grounds for claiming that we have discovered a universal truth about nature.

The second method for discovering truth, as identified by Bacon, is rationalist deduction. This begins with the most general axioms, 'the truth of which it takes for settled and immovable', and then proceeds by a process of logical deduction to a set of universal laws of nature that must hold by necessity. The name most immediately associated with this rationalist method is René Descartes. In his *Meditations on First Philosophy* (1641), Descartes provided an alternative foundation for certain knowledge. He began by doubting the truth of any knowledge derived from our sense-perception, thus immediately rejecting the empiricist's starting point in the quest for certain knowledge. My senses might deceive me, or I could be dreaming, or I may be under the power of a malicious demon. How can I be certain that the particulars I experience are true? After a good deal of tortuous agonizing, Descartes concluded that the proposition '*I am, I exist*, is necessarily true whenever it is put forward by me or conceived in my mind' (Descartes 1984: 17). The only possible foundation for certain knowledge, then, is that I myself exist. This is the one thing that cannot be doubted even if I am indeed under the power of a malicious demon in imagining that other particulars are true. Once we have this foundation of certainty we can, by the complex and often dubious logic of Descartes's theory of knowledge, go on to use our reason in working out the mathematical principles according to which the universe must conform. Thus, through a faculty of rational intuition, and prior to any observation of particulars, we can develop explanatory knowledge of the causal mechanisms that operate as universal laws of nature. By the light of reason we discover the truth of nature without relying on the untrustworthy evidence of our senses.

Of course, the Enlightenment vision goes well beyond the aim of guaranteeing certain knowledge of the laws of external nature. Condorcet also believed that we could have such knowledge about the progress of the human mind.

> The sole foundation for belief in the natural sciences is this idea, that the general laws directing the phenomena of the universe, known or unknown, are necessary and constant. Why should this principle be any less true for the development of the intellectual and moral faculties of man than for the other operations of nature?
>
> (Condorcet 1955: 173)

A historical study of the various stages of human society can yield knowledge of laws of intellectual and moral development that allow us both to explain the past and to predict the future. Reason, according to Condorcet, has been the driving force of history, and the development of our faculties has made possible ever more rapid progress towards a perfect form of human society – a life enlightened by human rationality at its highest stage. The more we know about the laws of human nature, the more happy and virtuous will we be. The age of reason will be the age of moral goodness, for we can be assured 'that nature has linked together in an unbreakable chain truth, happiness and virtue' (Condorcet 1955: 193).

The future, as predicted by Condorcet at the end of the eighteenth century, would see 'the abolition of inequality between nations, the progress of equality within each nation, and the true perfection of mankind' (Condorcet 1955: 173). There will be no cause for war, since rational actors will realize that the costs of war far outweigh any benefits. Once all nations have been enlightened, there will be agreement among them as to the moral principles that are to regulate international politics, and all national animosities will disappear. The main causes of inequality within society, differences in wealth, status and education, will diminish. This will occur through the abolition of privileges of birth, an increasing liberalization of economic markets and the introduction of welfare provision for the weaker members of society. Furthermore, if we act according to our rational faculties, we will manage to annihilate all the prejudices perpetuated by our reverence for tradition and custom. We will, for example, refuse to endorse any inequality of rights between the sexes. As inequality is overcome, between and within nations, all human beings will have the opportunity, through education and the free exercise of their reason, to perfect themselves and to achieve happiness. Thus society becomes more perfect, more virtuous and more rational.

Reason will reign in a society where all people can think for themselves. In public encounters, characterized by a free and open exchange of views among rational individuals, a spirit of tolerance and rational respect will emerge. Immanuel Kant, perhaps the greatest of all philosophers associated with the optimism of the late eighteenth century, understood the Enlightenment to represent 'man's emergence from his self-incurred immaturity' (Kant 1991: 54). We overcome this immaturity by having the courage and resolve to think for ourselves and by refusing to have others think for us. No clergyman, politician or teacher can really *think* for us. If we are to become mature, rationally autonomous human beings, we must be free to use our own understanding, particularly with regard to matters of religion. We are all to pursue our own happiness in whatever way we choose, once it is consistent with the principles of morality. For Kant, the only moral principles we should accept are those that could be accepted by every other rationally autonomous agent. In other words, each of us must accord to all others the same rights that we would seek for ourselves.

What more appealing vision could there be than a world without war, poverty or oppression; where equality, justice, tolerance, peace and happiness reign supreme; where all individuals are free to pursue, in a rationally autonomous manner, their own chosen life projects; where everyone respects the rights of each of their fellow human beings; and where an educated and virtuous public can deliberate over the common good by the light of a reason unfettered by the dogmas of tradition and prejudice? In that world, suffering and violent conflict would be minimized. We would use our knowledge of the external world to tame the dangers of nature, while our knowledge of human nature and society would allow us to bring about rapid progress in the improvement of humanity. Rationality is the key to such control of nature, and it offers us a direct path to human emancipation.

Vast resources have been spent developing the social sciences so as to investigate social and political life with a view to its amelioration. Most social scientific disciplines are still dominated by schools of thought sharing the Enlightenment assumption that we can discover universal laws of human behaviour. These laws are typically thought to serve as a foundation for theories that can help us to control social development for the better. This is a general characteristic of approaches as varied as behaviourism, utilitarianism, rational choice theory, functionalism, contemporary systems theory and some forms of Marxist analysis. Nevertheless, as we approach a new millennium we seem to be no nearer to a realization of Condorcet's vision. Our confidence in the ideal of a rationalized world has been shaken dramatically by the horrors of two world wars, the barbarism of genocide, the tyranny of totalitarianism and the threat of nuclear annihilation. Continuing famine, war, torture and degradation, as well as the shocking facts of destitution among large numbers of the world's population, remind us of the fact that we live in a world where injustice, oppression and misery are still widespread. Sexism, racism, sectarianism, homophobia and many other forms of prejudice are far from vanquished. Furthermore, we are now facing a potentially catastrophic ecological crisis that has been brought about by the ongoing destruction of the natural environment.

But what might disturb Condorcet most of all, were he miraculously to reappear among us, is the fact that the Enlightenment project itself is implicated in much of the misery that is around us. Think of the contributions that developments in the natural sciences have made to recent wars or to the ecological crisis. Or the fact that problems of poverty, famine, political oppression and social alienation appear more acute than ever in spite of, perhaps because of, the impulse rationally to control human nature. It could be argued, with some cogency, that the social and economic sciences have, more often than not, served to exacerbate inequalities by contributing to the efficiency of an unjust and oppressive global system. They have been used to protect mystifying state bureaucracies and rampant economic markets from the radical criticism that seeks to address such injustice and oppression. It would appear that the development of the sciences and the attempt to control nature have led to at least as much suffering as they have managed to alleviate. Perhaps rationality is not the key to emancipation, but the primary source of our misery.

The idea that modern societies are characterized primarily by dangerous processes of rationalization is the central theme of the work of Max Weber (1991). His account of social rationalization is one of the most influential analyses of modernity, and a founding moment of modern sociology. Weber argued that in modern societies we live in a disenchanted world, where all notions of the sacred, the magical, the mysterious or the religious have been exposed to the rational interrogations of the scientific worldview associated with the project of Enlightenment. He was keenly aware of the fact that this legacy of disenchantment is a double-edged sword. The process of rationalization may well provide us with a more efficiently organized form of life and a more objective means of regulating legal and social relations than would have been available to traditional societies. It might also leave us as individuals with more scope for autonomous action. But there are real dangers in the development of a rationally efficient bureaucratic system. The more control it achieves over social and economic life, the more alienated the individuals it is supposed to serve will become. If the system can cope with every eventuality then there will no longer be any need for democratic discussion or collective deliberation about the merits of one proposal or another. Individual freedom and human creativity would then be stifled, as we would find ourselves institutionalized and trapped within, as Weber put it, an 'iron cage of bureaucracy'.

While the Enlightenment conception of rationality, as the power to control nature, continues to animate much of the work in the social and political sciences, there has been, in the later decades of this century, a series of forceful theoretical challenges to the naive triumphalism of this project. In the remaining sections of this chapter, the sources of these intellectual challenges will be traced, first, by assessing some influential work in the history and philosophy of science and, second, by analysing the impact on the social sciences of the work of certain philosophers of language. The upshot of much of this work is to undermine not only the Enlightenment belief that the key to emancipation is the control of nature but also our confidence in human reason as a power that can provide certain knowledge of the laws that govern nature and society.

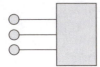

SCIENCE AS RATIONAL INQUIRY

Rational inquiry, from the perspective of the Enlightenment thinkers, is grounded in scientific method. One source of disquiet regarding the prospects for ever more rapid rational progress in our struggle with nature has emerged in a series of debates concerning scientific methodology. Perhaps the two most important thinkers who have contributed to these debates are Karl Popper (1994) and Thomas Kuhn (1970). In order to understand the significance of their contributions, we need, first, to consider once again the empiricist method of science.

Long before the beginning of the twentieth century, empiricism had held sway over rationalism as the dominant philosophical mode of grounding the scientific enterprise. It was generally thought that sense-perception was a more reliable foundation for certain knowledge than an assumed faculty of rational intuition that claimed immediate access to the laws of nature prior to experience. But serious doubts had also been raised about the logical coherence of the principle of induction on which the empiricist's claim to certain knowledge of the laws of nature had been based. This problem was given its most devastating formulation by David Hume (1978).

From an empiricist perspective, our only valid source of knowledge is sense-perception. If, through observation, we can identify law-like regularities, we can then infer, by the principle of induction, that we have arrived at a general axiom, or a truth of nature. Normally we take this to mean that we have discovered a necessary connection between a cause and its effect – such as the combustion of sulphur and the bright yellow flame with which it burns. Hume argued that we can have no such knowledge of causal necessities. Simply because we have, up to the present, always observed sulphur to burn with a bright yellow flame, we have no logical reason to claim that it *must* always do so in the future, or that it represents a necessity of nature. While we can have no knowledge of any unobservable mechanisms of natural necessity, this does not ruffle the feathers of a calm empiricist like Hume. We can, as he suggested, think of a cause merely as a regular correlation or a 'constant conjunction' between one event and another. Our expectations of future events are therefore not based on rational grounds but rather on habit or custom. Induction then yields only general correlations, but this is, according to a sceptical Hume, the only kind of knowledge we need, or can reasonably expect.

How then are we to account for the scientific status of a theory, or a set of generalizations that have been made on the basis of observation? How are we to test the truth of the claims that are made? The 'logical positivists', a group of hard-core philosophical empiricists working in Vienna in the 1930s, sought to formalize rational conditions according to which the truth of a generalization could inductively be justified. They insisted that the only valid test of truth would be the extent to which a theory could be verified by observation. Karl Popper rejected this reliance on verification and argued instead that empiricism could be better preserved if we were to accept fully the implications of the problem of induction by treating all scientific theories as tentative hypotheses. Hume's formulation of the problem makes it clear that the truth of all theories is contingent on matters of fact. A theory should be rejected if it is contradicted by facts that we can observe. We can then, on the basis of observation, show that a theory is not true. If it is contradicted by facts it has been shown to be false. So while one more piece of sulphur burning with a bright yellow flame could never guarantee the certainty of the claim that 'sulphur always burns with a bright yellow flame', one piece burning with a green flame would guarantee the falsity of that claim. There is no certain knowledge, no absolutely true theory. Scientific method depends not on verification but on falsification.

For Popper, science does not follow a path beginning with the observation of particulars, moving by way of the principle of induction, to a set of generalizations or laws. Rather, it begins with theories that seek to order our experience by offering tentative hypotheses as to the laws of nature. All theories are conjectures that invite refutation, and the bolder the conjecture the more interesting the truth that it promises. A genuinely scientific theory will make very clear the empirical tests according to which it might be falsified. Scientists do not seek confirming evidence to verify their hypotheses, but seek contradictory evidence so as to falsify them. This rules out certain theories that could claim to be confirmed by empirical evidence but that cannot underwrite their own falsifiability. Popper rejected such theories as being pseudo-scientific, and he included among them Marx's historical materialism and Freud's psychoanalytic theories. Since neither Marx nor Freud could show how their theories could be falsified by empirical evidence, they cannot even stand as conjectures that *might* be true. They are speculative theories that have no rational grounding, and so they cannot even enter the scientific domain.

Popper's primary concern is to overcome Hume's scepticism by proposing a view of how we can, on purely rational grounds, prefer some competing conjectures to others. What makes for a genuinely scientific theory, a conjecture that can be justified on the basis of rational argument, is the fact that it can survive severe tests. We prefer Newton's theory to Kepler's, and Einstein's to Newton's, because of the fact that the theory we prefer in each case has less contradictory empirical evidence standing against it. This critical rationalist perspective still allows for the growth of knowledge and so guarantees the progress of the scientific enterprise. We can through the rigorous testing of ever more adequate theories solve problems that impede our efforts to control nature. Our scientific knowledge is always open-ended, depending as it does on the critical reception of bold conjectures, but rational progress is still possible. This is as true of the social sciences as it is of the natural sciences. We can, in an open society, test social scientific hypotheses by trial and error and so engage in piecemeal social engineering by introducing reforms that will improve our condition. In this way, Popper's theory of scientific knowledge is related to his political defence of liberalism and to his critique of thinkers such as Plato, Hegel and Marx (Popper 1957). Progress is held to depend on a particular sort of 'open society' characterized by a limited government that seeks neither to impose judgements nor to plan society according to some elaborate scheme or principle.

Popper shares the Enlightenment conviction that rationality, as manifested in scientific knowledge, represents the key to progress. His conception of knowledge seeks to avoid the irrational consequences of Hume's effort to ground scientific method not on reason but on habit. He admits, however, that we can have no certain knowledge of absolute truths. Nor is there any immediate access to truth through sense-perception, since our theoretical conjectures will always inform our observations. But this claim is conveniently forgotten when Popper tries to show how one singular fact can falsify a theory. Is our observation of the falsifying fact not itself informed by a conflicting theory? Rather than pursue the highly questionable consistency of Popper's view on these matters, we can consider the way in which this claim, that facts are never innocent of theory, is given a much more radical twist in Thomas Kuhn's account of the history of science.

Kuhn's concept of the scientific 'paradigm' has had a remarkable impact on contemporary theory, with the consequence that our belief in the possibility of rational, scientific progress has been seriously undermined. For Kuhn, the history of science has not been one of steady progress in the accumulation of truth, either through inductive reasoning as positivists would have it, or by Popper's method of falsification. It has instead been characterized by a series of 'paradigms' punctuated by discontinuous ruptures, or revolutions, in scientific reasoning. The term paradigm is used in many different ways, even by Kuhn himself, but it has two particularly significant and related senses that are relevant here. First, it indicates the entire constellation of beliefs, values and techniques shared by the members of a scientific community. Second, it denotes one exemplary, concrete set of solutions to scientific problems that act, for that community, as a model for the solution of other puzzles. In the first sense, the paradigm operates as a 'disciplinary matrix'; in the second, as an 'exemplar'. Key exemplars in the history of science would include Copernican astronomy, which placed the sun at the centre of the universe, or Einstein's physics, which explained how predictions based on Newtonian mechanics could often be seriously mistaken. Copernicus and Einstein both provided model, or paradigmatic, solutions to a set of problems, and these solutions then became the focus of a new constellation of beliefs, or disciplinary matrix, around which a scientific community continued to operate for a sustained period.

In any given discipline, one paradigm of inquiry dominates at a particular historical period, and when this dominance is more or less unquestioned the community lives in a period of 'normal science'. The paradigm of research, such as Copernican astronomy or Einstein's physics, guides new generations of scientists in so far as it provides both a model set of solutions and a remaining set of puzzles that are still to be solved. During such a period of 'normal science', the basic assumptions that guide the research are taken for granted and so are immune from challenge. There will, however, be certain phenomena that the guiding theory cannot explain. Often adjustments can be made in order to deal with such anomalies. At a certain time in the history of a paradigm, the number of anomalies increases to such an extent that the basic assumptions of the theory can no longer be considered to be immune from challenge. This heralds the end of the period of normal science and the beginnings of a period of crisis, or revolution. At some stage, a rival theory will emerge, characterized by a set of assumptions that are not compatible, or are incommensurable, with those of the old paradigm. If two bodies of thought are incommensurable, it means that they cannot be measured against one another because no suitable standard of evaluation that could objectively be applied to both can be found. If the new rival theory can gain the allegiance of the more influential scientists of the day, then it will be in a position to set itself up as a new paradigm. Eventually, as successive generations of scientists are trained into this new constellation of beliefs, a new period of puzzle-solving normal science is institutionalized. This will continue until an increasing number of anomalies destabilizes the new paradigm, leading to yet another period of crisis and a revolutionary rupture in scientific thinking.

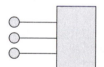

THE SPECTRE OF RELATIVISM AND THE POLITICS OF SCIENCE

There are at least two aspects of Kuhn's account of the history of science that have led indirectly, and often in spite of Kuhn's own intentions and hopes, to a radical questioning of the Enlightenment aspiration to a steady growth of rationally grounded scientific knowledge that would enable us to control nature and to emancipate ourselves from the causes of unnecessary suffering. First, there is the emphasis on the fact that paradigms are incommensurable. There can be no compromise between Copernican astronomy and the Ptolemaic paradigm it replaced. The sun could not be the centre of the universe if we assumed that the Earth was. What is involved is a radical transformation of thought akin to a religious conversion. Copernican astronomy did not build on the Ptolemaic model but shattered it. After such a revolution scientists see everything differently, and in this sense 'work in a different world' (Kuhn 1970: 135). So while a new paradigm can solve more problems than the one it replaces, it cannot show itself to be more true to the way the world *really is*. Since paradigmatic assumptions and methods differ so sharply, there are no rational criteria that would allow us to compare one paradigm with another. There is therefore no straightforward cumulative growth of knowledge, no way of closing in on the absolute truth of reality.

The implications of this view, that scientific paradigms are incommensurable, has led to a series of debates about the status of scientific method as a model of rational inquiry. If the most basic assumptions of any scientific outlook cannot themselves be rationally defended, how can any form of knowledge have secure foundations? Perhaps, as Paul Feyerabend (1993) suggests, there are no objective criteria of rational justification and the truth of any theory is relative to a particular view of the world. But if there are no rational criteria for choosing one paradigm over another, why not choose to continue to believe that the Earth is the centre of the universe, or that Newton's physics is preferable to Einstein's? Why not consider Marx's theory of history or Freudian psychoanalysis as incommensurable, but equally legitimate, paradigms that rival Popper's programme of falsificationism? Indeed, why should we invest more in medical science than in homeopathy, or prayer, or witchcraft? Should we not follow Feyerabend in adopting as our sole methodological principle the anarchistic motto: 'anything goes' (Feyerabend 1993: 296)?

Popper (1970) argued strenuously against the implied relativism of Kuhn's views about incommensurability, insisting that critical rational inquiry can provide a framework that allows comparison across paradigms. But Kuhn's main point was not that comparison across paradigms was impossible, but that there could be no shared rational scale according to which rival theories could decisively be ranked. Imre Lakatos (1970) offered a more sophisticated defence of falsificationism by drawing on many of the insights of Kuhn's work. He suggested that we should think of scientific inquiry as a series of research programmes that progress as long as they continue to make novel and interesting predictions. The core assumptions of the programme are protected by a belt of secondary or 'auxiliary' hypotheses, some of which could be rejected in the light of conflicting evidence. If the search for new auxiliary hypotheses becomes loose and arbitrary, then the research programme itself begins to degenerate. It is then time to abandon the core assumptions and to pursue an alternative research programme. Lakatos gives an insightful account of the standards according to which much scientific research is actually conducted, but he does not overcome the problem of showing how the core assumptions of research programmes could be ranked according to rational criteria.

An alternative conception of science that claims to offer an escape from relativism is the critical realist approach defended by Roy Bhaskar (1978). Realism opposes empiricism, in that it does not think the scientific enterprise to be primarily concerned with the search for law-like regularities. According to the realist, neither the positivist who seeks to verify the truth of a law of nature, nor the Popperian who seeks to falsify conjectures about truth, has an adequate account of explanation. In order to explain why sulphur burns with a bright yellow flame, it is not enough to insist that it always does so. We need to analyse the causality involved in terms of the nature of things and the way they interact or, in other words, with reference to the underlying structures and mechanisms of reality that generate observable phenomena. Such explanation often requires us to postulate the existence of non-observable entities, such as gravitational force. The onus on the scientist is to offer a description of reality that would allow us to explain events. Since the emphasis is not on regularities but on the complex interaction of causal tendencies within an open system, prediction is of secondary concern.

The realist can evade the charge of relativism more effectively than the empiricist by making a very clear distinction between ontology, the way things are in the world, and epistemology, the way we gain knowledge about the world. We must assume that things are the way they are whether or not we know about them. So the realist assumes that there are laws of nature to be discovered and that we have come closer to finding out the truth about nature with the development of the sciences. But the realist also accepts that there is no immediate access to knowledge of the laws of nature. Facts are never innocent of theory, and science itself is a social practice institutionalized within a particular cultural and historical context. What scientific theories offer are fallible explanations of real entities, and these theories must always be open to further elaboration or correction. So while our knowledge of nature is transitive, the world we seek to know is intransitive, in that it exists independently of our knowledge. Bhaskar (1986, 1988) has argued that realist principles also inform a critical social science that seeks to explain the way in which social structures can determine and constrain our activities. Such explanation of the obstacles to human development can facilitate programmes that might lead to the emancipatory transformation of those structures.

The second aspect of Kuhn's work that undermines the Enlightenment belief in science as the vehicle of rational progress is the stress he places on the institutional setting of scientific practice. New generations of scientists are socialized into the disciplinary matrix of a particular paradigm. They are trained to ask certain questions and to pursue their research according to specific methodological principles. Scientific inquiry is embedded in a social and political context, and research projects are dependent on their being funded. The vision of the isolated scientist investigating the laws of nature by the light of pure reason is a far cry from the reality of research funding competitions. Paradigms of research can be propped up with the support of social and political forces, governments, corporate bodies and private concerns that are far from disinterested observers of the laws of nature.

What Kuhn's work makes clear is that theories may not be chosen purely on the basis of logical reasoning or empirical evidence. We also have to consider factors such as conventional and political restrictions on research, conservative conformity to particular patterns of thought and the hierarchical structure of the scientific community. This has led to a proliferation of studies on the relation between science and social power, most notably the strong programme in the sociology of knowledge defended by Barry Barnes and David Bloor (1982). The guiding principle of this programme is the relativist view that there are no rational criteria that could justify the truth of a scientific theory. The decisive factor in the acceptance of one theory over another is the political struggle between the advocates of competing paradigms. A further implication of this relativist view is that there are no rational criteria according to which these political conflicts about scientific theories could themselves be objectively evaluated. Truth is the outcome of a power struggle.

Some feminist theorists, such as Helen Longino (1990) and Sandra Harding (1991), have also been inspired by this aspect of Kuhn's work. Since the notion of a paradigm reveals how certain unquestioned assumptions can shape and guide scientific research, it might be possible to show how gender bias enters surreptitiously into mainstream theory. Furthermore, since there are no criteria according to which the rational superiority of one paradigm could be demonstrated, it would seem legitimate for scientific inquiry to be inspired by a feminist worldview. According to Longino, we can be informed, in our interpretation of empirical data regarding sexual differences, by a set of values that favours egalitarian relations between the sexes. This egalitarian interpretive framework can challenge, on scientific grounds, the dominant *malestream* paradigm that is informed by patriarchal assumptions (see Chapter 6). If we are concerned to foster scientific practices that do not reproduce inequality and oppression, then we must advocate conceptions of scientific objectivity that challenge the external influences and background assumptions that members of the scientific community bring to their work. According to Harding, this means that the political standpoint of the scientist is a relevant consideration in the evaluation of scientific theories. Rigorous scientific scholarship can only take place under conditions where women and members of marginalized races and cultures have an opportunity to articulate their own standpoints. It would seem to be the case that, for Longino and Harding, as well as for Barnes and Bloor, scientific and political discourse are thought to interpenetrate in ways that would have horrified not only the Enlightenment thinkers but also Popper, and even Kuhn himself.

Conceptions of rational inquiry have also been influenced by recent developments, such as chaos theory, that challenge fundamental assumptions about the natural sciences. Furthermore, there has been a growing scepticism in society regarding the power of the sciences and their ability to provide us with rational control over nature. This has been illustrated very clearly, for example, in the crisis over British beef. Scientists seem to be unable to explain convincingly, let alone solve, the problem of BSE infection. Many members of the public think that scientists are so caught up in the political and commercial aspects of the crisis that so-called experts can now say nothing on the matter without adding to the confusion.

A related form of scepticism has been expressed theoretically in recent decades by a number of philosophers and social theorists who have refused to model human rationality on the scientific enterprise. If we are to conceive of rationality in a broader way, as these contextualist philosophers suggest, then we might be able to show why it is that science could not deliver on the promise of Enlightenment, particularly with regard to the aspirations of the social sciences. For these thinkers, any genuine understanding we might have of social and political life must be based on a rejection of the Enlightenment assumption that there are immutable laws of moral and intellectual development waiting to be discovered. We need to understand rationality in a less triumphalist way by breaking free of the Enlightenment obsession with foundations for certain knowledge. In other words, we need to emancipate ourselves from the illusions that have been generated through the impulse to control nature that drives the scientific enterprise.

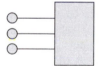

LANGUAGE AND CONTEXT

One of the key features of the Enlightenment's vindication of the effort to study social and political life on the model of the natural sciences was that its primary concern would be the explanation of human behaviour with reference to a set of law-like generalizations. According to the positivist research programme that has dominated the social sciences in the twentieth century, these generalizations would be grounded in the empiricist method of science, based on observation and inductive reasoning. This programme has been challenged by a number of philosophers who argue that the focus of the social sciences should not be the explanation of behaviour from the external perspective of a rationally disengaged observer. The focus should instead be the interpretation of social meanings within a particular cultural context. The social scientist must learn how to understand the meaning that action has in its context before the question of explanation could legitimately be considered. The shift of emphasis here from explanation to interpretation, from observation to participation, reflects a shift in the understanding of rationality. We should think of rationality not in terms of a discovery of laws of nature but in terms of the rules that give an action meaning in a particular context. The role of language is crucial here.

One of the most striking explanations of the need to adopt an interpretive approach to the social sciences is found in the work of Peter Winch (1990). Influenced by the philosopher Ludwig Wittgenstein, (1967), Winch argues that language offers us the only access we can have to reality. 'Our idea of what belongs to the realm of reality is given for us in the language that we use. The concepts we have settle for us the form of experience we have of the world' (Winch 1990: 15). There is no way we can get outside of language in our effort to grasp reality. We can only understand meaning if we know what it is to use words in a particular way. This understanding depends on our following the rules involved in the use of those words in their context, and this presupposes the idea that other people can also follow them. The rules of language are like the rules of a game. For example, unless I understood what it means to serve, to return serve, to award points and to keep score, I could not be playing tennis but, rather, I would be aimlessly hitting a ball with a racket. Similarly, if I was making noise with my vocal chords I could not be using language unless I understood that I was uttering words that carry a particular meaning. We can only use language if we know how to play the game involved, and we can only do that if we know the rules (see also Chapter 3).

For Winch, these rules constitute a 'form of life' into which we are integrated when we learn a language. There can be no private language, since we only learn what it is to follow a rule in a social context. It must be possible, in principle, for other people to grasp the rules of any language that I might, for whatever perverse reason, seek to invent for my own private use. As with any language game, all meaningful action is rule-governed. No way of life, be it that of the monk, the entrepreneur or the anarchist, would have any point if it were not constituted by rules. Human action is thus understood as the application of a set of rules. Similarly, all social institutions embody ideas, and social relations are 'expressions of ideas about reality' (Winch 1990: 23).

From this perspective, and in contrast with the natural scientist who seeks to discover causes, the social scientist tries to interpret meanings. There is no possibility of scientific prediction, since actors must decide for themselves how best to follow a rule, or to pursue a particular way of life, in new circumstances. Unlike burning pieces of sulphur, human beings are not causally conditioned. If we are to understand an action, we cannot provide explanations based on law-like generalizations; instead we must learn how people live in a particular way. We need to grasp the rule that is pursued by the actor. In other words, our understanding depends on our adopting the perspective of the people whose social action we are studying. In analysing social phenomena, we must begin to participate in a particular form of life. There are two important implications of Winch's application of Wittgenstein's later philosophy to the social sciences. First, the pre-eminent status of scientific knowledge is denied. Second, the possibility of our developing critical perspectives on other cultures and forms of life is undermined.

Science is denied pre-eminent status as a form of knowledge, in that it is thought of as one language game among others. It is inappropriate to apply the rules of the scientific language game to many aspects of social reality. In seeking to yield explanatory accounts of certain natural phenomena, science provides us with one mode of understanding reality. But the criteria of intelligibility that are employed in the practice of science are peculiar to science itself. They should not be thought to set critical standards to which other modes of understanding reality must aspire. Religion is one such alternative mode of understanding reality, and it too has a logic of its own. Again the question of incommensurability arises here. There are no criteria of intelligibility or logic, no rational standards according to which the games of science and religion, or art or politics, could all be evaluated critically. We should not judge a mystic's religious experience according to the criteria of a scientific outlook. Nor should we judge political action according to criteria appropriate to aesthetic appreciation. All criteria of logic are internal to a variety of ways of living or modes of social life, and it is this that leads Winch (1990: 102) to insist that 'reality has no key'. The great mistake of the Enlightenment thinkers was to reduce rationality to the criteria of logic associated with the discovery of the laws of nature. If we accept that science, no more than any other mode of inquiry, is not the key to reality, then we will have to adopt a broader conception of rationality. It will no longer suffice to think of rationality as a tool that can facilitate the control of nature.

Winch's concerns on this matter are not unlike those of Feyerabend, who, as we have already seen, seeks to undermine the pre-eminence of scientific reasoning in our culture. The dominance of science is a form of cultural imperialism that is underpinned by state support for scientific research. Science is not, *objectively*, any more legitimate a form of inquiry than mysticism, or witchcraft. Indeed, there is no objective point of view from which such a claim to pre-eminence could be made. If we still believe that science is the key to reality, then it is because of the way in which social power has operated by illegitimately enthroning science as the only logical mode of making sense of life. Like all other modes, such as religion, art or politics, its perspective is limited. We must be careful not to reason scientifically about activities and practices that have a different, and incommensurable, logic.

There are echoes of these sentiments in the postmodern attitude characterized by Jean-François Lyotard (1984) as an 'incredulity' towards all 'metanarratives', or grand theories that claim some universal significance. The Enlightenment's conception of scientific rationality as the key to continuous and universal progress in our struggle with nature is the ultimate metanarrative of modernity. The dominance of some such metanarrative will, Lyotard suggests, inevitably involve the subjugation of other discourses, or language games. Just as a religious experience could not be understood properly from a scientific perspective, neither can gender-based oppression be challenged effectively in a Marxist language of class struggle, nor can the interests of ethnic minorities be articulated within a discourse of national liberation. In order to overcome these forms of subjugation, or *differends* as Lyotard (1988) refers to them, we must introduce narratives whose effect is not to embellish a continuous, universal story, but rather to disrupt and to destabilize language games that illegitimately claim universal significance. Rather than thinking of rationality as the thread that holds together the story of human progress, we must stress the discontinuities and ruptures that inevitably ensue when one mode of rationality is illegitimately imposed on another. Politics, from this postmodern perspective, is the agonistic struggle of incommensurable forms of rationality. In this respect, Lyotard's theoretical interventions share many of the general assumptions that characterize the work of poststructuralists discussed elsewhere in this book: the genealogical inquiries of Foucault (see Chapters 2, 4, 5, 6 and 8), Derrida's project of deconstruction (Chapter 3), the interrogations of gendered identities by Butler (Chapters 5 and 6) and the conception of democratic politics in Laclau and Mouffe (Chapters 3 and 8). The stress these thinkers place on the need to destabilize dominant discourses is in tension with Winch's rather static understanding of forms of life. Poststructuralists draw on a rather different interpretation of the later Wittgenstein's views on language (see Chapter 3).

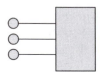

CULTURAL DIFFERENCE

The second implication of Winch's Wittgensteinian view that criteria of rationality are internal to particular language games is that the possibility of having a critical understanding of other cultures would appear to be undermined. From the perspective of Enlightenment rationalism, Western culture sets standards according to which the progress of other cultures could be assessed. The more rational, and therefore *advanced*, cultures were those that had apparently achieved some success in bringing human destiny under scientific control through the systematic domination of nature. From Winch's point of view, this involves the imposition of *our* standards of rationality on them and a failure on our part to recognize the extent to which *their* standards of rationality differ from ours. We will not understand the role that magic plays in certain African societies if we think of it as a mistaken form of science (Winch 1972). Such a judgement involves our failing to grasp the meaning of the social practice of magic in that context. Magic in those societies is an entirely different mode of understanding reality, one that is incommensurable with science since it does not seek to provide causal explanation. In contrast, magic addresses questions on which science has nothing to offer, such as the distribution of good or bad fortune. We have no hope of understanding other cultures if we do not learn how to participate in their form of life. We must grasp the rules of the language games they play, rather than seeking to judge them according to external standards of scientific rationality that are dominant in our culture but entirely inappropriate to the social practices we are hoping to explain.

The relativist implications here raise a number of concerns. If standards of rationality are internal, or relative, to social practices in particular cultural contexts, what is the scope for valid criticism of that form of life? Is it illegitimate for an external critic to challenge the validity of such social practices? Must we only learn how to participate in forms of life without ever having the opportunity to reject practices that appear to us to be unjustifiable? Take, for example, the caste system, the practice of female genital mutilation or the expression of racial prejudice. Is the point of social research merely to grasp the meaning of such practices by learning the rules of the game involved, or is it not also meant to offer a critical perspective on the moral justifiability of those practices? Is the need for criticism not all the more crucial if we bear in mind the fact that practices do not emerge only through the free use of language but also as a consequence of the operation of power? In fact, some social practices, including those mentioned above, may very well be produced by a set of power relations that systematically favour the members of some social groups over others (see Chapter 4).

All theorists who adopt a contextualist or interpretive framework are confronted by these problems, and there have been a number of significant responses to the charge of relativist conservatism. Richard Rorty (1990) maintains that an ethnocentric attitude, which is self-consciously rooted in a particular context, is inescapable, but that we should not worry about it. In Western societies we just happen to have come to identify ourselves with liberal political institutions that seek to ensure the avoidance of cruelty and the promotion of tolerance. We should defend these institutions, not because they embody some universally significant conception of human rationality, but simply because they are institutions that have helped us to cope with the reality of a modern pluralist world. Michael Walzer (1987, 1989a) argues that social criticism must be interpretive, since it involves the articulation of shared ideals that constitute the bonds holding political communities together. This does not imply that internal criticism cannot challenge current social practice. In fact, the point of criticism is to show how we often fail to live up to our own deepest shared convictions.

While the approaches of Rorty and Walzer may be able to show how some form of legitimate social criticism is possible within one form of life, or one tradition of inquiry, there is still a question as to how we might adjudicate between rival traditions. What if *our* standards of rationality demand that we condemn certain practices that seem central to *their* form of life? Alasdair MacIntyre (1988, 1990), who shares with Rorty, Walzer and Winch a scepticism about the possibility of a universally valid account of human rationality, does seek to show how a conflict between two rational traditions might be resolved. A rational solution can emerge only if one tradition can draw on aspects of the other to provide an enriched account of rationality that overcomes the conflict. For this to count as a rational solution, it must first show that it retains elements of continuity with both traditions. Second, it has to explain why neither of them were by themselves able to move in a coherent manner beyond the original problem of incommensurability. MacIntyre offers examples of resolutions of intellectual conflict in the history of philosophy (such as Thomas Aquinas's integration of the Aristotelian and Augustinian traditions of inquiry), but a similar type of analysis could be provided for conflicts of rationality involving cultural traditions.

In this respect, Charles Taylor (1985) invokes Hans-Georg Gadamer's (1989) notion of a 'fusion of horizons', the sharing of perspectives that we aspire to in our efforts to understand other cultures. While we are initially oriented in the encounter by an historically rooted account of rationality that constitutes our limited horizon of understanding, we must seek to achieve a fusion with the horizon of those 'others' we study. If we are genuinely to achieve an understanding of the rationality of the other, then we will change our own standards of rationality by revising them in the light of the insights that emerge from a critical exchange. In this sense, understanding something new is self-transformative to the extent that it involves a broadening of our own horizon. So, to return to Winch's example, while African tribes may have something to learn from Western researchers about the achievements of science, we may have much to learn from them about the best ways to attune ourselves to the natural environment. And of course the learning could also take place the other way around; we might learn some science and they might learn something about attunement to nature.

But doubt remains as to the adequacy of these contextualist solutions to the problem of criticism. There would appear to be no guarantee that the rationality embedded within particular traditions and practices will have the resources necessary to challenge effectively the ways in which systematic power can operate to the advantage of some social groups and to the disadvantage of others. This is the main reason why some contemporary critical theorists are determined not to give up on the possibility of reconstructing an account of human rationality that has universal significance. Only some such account of rationality could provide critical standards that would act effectively as a challenge to illegitimate power in all cultural contexts. The most influential theorist to pursue this project is Jürgen Habermas (1984, 1987a).

From Habermas's point of view, there is no possibility of a critical exchange across cultures unless there is some shared standard of rationality to facilitate mutual understanding. What makes for a rational solution to a conflict between two traditions is not just the possibility of a fusion of horizons, but the fact that there are certain criteria of rationality that all language games share (see Chapter 2 on some more general features of Habermas's critical theory). In Habermas's view, there is always the possibility of using language in an effort to reach understanding with another person or group in spite of the vast cultural differences that might be involved. This possibility is built into language as such. The ability to use language in a communicative way that facilitates mutual understanding is one of the key characteristics that distinguish human beings from other creatures. According to Habermas, the standards of rationality that constitute the communicative use of language are of universal significance. They are not internal to any particular culture, but universal, or, to put it another way, internal to all cultures. These standards of communicative rationality are the key to cross-cultural understanding, in that they create the conditions for the possibility of a rational solution to cultural conflict (see Chapter 8 on Habermas's views on justice). In this way, they might also provide a basis for cross-cultural criticism, in that they could yield an account of the social conditions that must obtain if rational solutions to potential conflicts are to be possible.

For example, the only way in which torture can be rejected as a legitimate social practice, with standards of rationality peculiar to itself, is to show how torture violates certain moral principles that must be upheld if social relations are to be built on mutual understanding rather than brute force and violence. If we are to minimize violence then we must seek to institutionalize a set of human rights that can be justified, not in relation to the aspirations of a particular culture, but on the grounds of an account of rationality that is universally valid. This formal universalism that Habermas reconstructs from our capacity to use language communicatively represents the most significant attempt to continue the Enlightenment project in a way that takes on board many, if not all, of the concerns of its contextualist critics.

CONCLUSIONS

We have seen how developments in the philosophy of the social sciences have combined with recent thinking on the history and philosophy of the natural sciences to undermine confidence in the emancipatory hopes of the Enlightenment project. In fact, the general thrust of most contemporary social and political theory leaves us with a very sobering view of what human rationality can achieve. The picture of the rational individual disengaged from nature, investigating the laws by which the natural and the social worlds are kept in motion, is simply not sustainable in the face of the critical concerns we have considered here. Human rationality must be thought of as being embedded within particular forms of life, and even the most abstract of the natural sciences is rooted historically in a particular institutional setting. There is no pure reason to enlighten us, only impure, historically bound forms of rationality.

It does not follow that the rationality embedded in particular practices does not have the capacity to direct us to a less violent and more just world. Current debates continue to rage regarding the possibility of reconstructing a conception of rationality that is both historically embedded and effectively critical. If it is possible to construct a universalist account of rationality by investigating the structure of the communicative use of language, as Habermas and others have tried to do, then perhaps it is also still possible to pursue, in a more sober and humble manner, the project of Enlightenment. If we cannot find a rational guide to minimize suffering and to overcome the causes of violence, then we are doomed to a fate where one system of repression simply replaces another. If the emancipatory project of Enlightenment is to have any future, it must be based on a conception of rationality that is no longer thought of primarily as a means of controlling nature, but rather as the means by which human beings can reach mutual understanding in spite of the social and cultural differences between them. Only some such rationally grounded understanding can allow us to live together in this multicultural world of late modernity without resorting to violence.

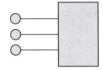

QUESTIONS

1 What are the main dangers involved in thinking of rationality as a means of controlling nature?

2 How can the objectivity of the scientific enterprise best be defended?

3 If we adopt a conception of rationality that views science as one language game among others, what implications does this have for social and political theory?

4 Can a universalist conception of rationality do justice to the reality of cultural pluralism?

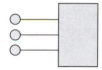

FURTHER READING

One of the best places to begin with an exploration of the legacy of the Enlightenment for contemporary social and political theory is the work of Richard Bernstein: the views of Kuhn, Winch, Gadamer, Habermas, Rorty and others are discussed at length in *The Restructuring of Social and Political Theory* (1976) and *Beyond Objectivism and Relativism* (1983), while *The New Constellation* (1991) engages with the radical critiques of reason offered from postmodern perspectives. More generally, the possibility of our gaining certain knowledge of the social world is typically the dominant theme in the many introductory works available on the philosophy of the social sciences. One of the most readable recent accounts is given by Hollis, *The Philosophy of Social Science: An Introduction* (1994) but see also Trigg, *Understanding Social Science* (1985) and Anderson *et al.*, *Philosophy and the Human Sciences* (1986). On Weber's work, see the editors' introduction by Gerth and Wright Mills to their collection of his writings, *From Max Weber: Essays in Sociology* (1991).

For a useful account of the philosophy of science, with extensive discussions of Popper, Kuhn, Lakatos and Feyerabend, see Chalmers, *What Is This Thing Called Science?* (1978), and for a more recent survey see Couvalis, *The Philosophy of Science: Science and Objectivity* (1997). The differences between Popper and Kuhn are explored in Lakatos and Musgrave (eds), *Criticism and the Growth of Knowledge* (1970). While Bhaskar is the most influential advocate of critical realism in the social sciences, useful introductions to this perspective include Keat and Urry, *Social Theory as Science*, 2nd edn (1982), Sayer, *Method in Social Science* (1984) and Outhwaite, *New Philosophies of Social Science* (1987). There are a number of collections of essays that gather together some influential feminist interventions in debates about science and objectivity: Harding (ed.), *Feminism and Methodology* (1987), Nicholson (ed.), *Feminism/Postmodernism* (1990) and Alcoff and Potter (eds), *Feminist Epistemologies* (1993).

Some of the key contributions in the debate about relativism that was stirred up by Winch's work are to be found in Wilson (ed.), *Rationality* (1970) and Hollis and Lukes (eds), *Rationality and Relativism* (1982). The concerns of many of the most significant contemporary contextualist thinkers, including Rorty, Walzer, MacIntyre and Taylor, are analysed in Mulhall and Swift, *Liberals and Communitarians*, 2nd edn (1996). On more recent developments in the debates about rationality that have been central to the controversies about post-modernity, see White, *Political Theory and Postmodernism* (1991), McCarthy, *Ideals and Illusions: On Reconstruction and Deconstruction in Contemporary Critical Theory* (1991) and the exchange between David Couzens Hoy and Thomas McCarthy in *Critical Theory* (1994). For readings relevant to the postmodern ideas discussed in this chapter (such as those of Lyotard), consult the further reading sections of the chapters that follow.

2 SOCIAL CRITICISM
Iain MacKenzie

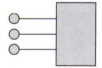

INTRODUCTION

The urge to criticize our social and political institutions is a funda-mental feature of humanity. Even though we may imagine homo-geneous and well ordered cultures where criticism no longer has a role, like waking from a dream the more we try to hold on to this vision the more it dissolves into the encroaching reality of morning. This is particularly true of the modern world. Since the daybreak of modernity, our social and political environment has become increas-ingly defined by, among other things, rapid technological change, the global spread of capitalist production, the mass movement and inter-mingling of populations and the renegotiation of state power and authority (see Chapter 8). The emergence of these modern phenom-ena rent asunder any unquestioned bonds that had been embedded within earlier social and political formations. In the modern world, the dream of a society where we accept our lot with pleasure and with-out question – a society where criticism has no role – is not just unre-alistic, it is the dream of tyrants.

The onset of modernity gave birth to a new form of criticism, one specific to the needs of a world where the old stable hierarchies of knowledge and authority no longer held sway, a world where social and political upheaval was the new certainty. Christened the Enlightenment on the grounds that the task of criticism at this time was to cast light on any dark shadows of superstition that still shrouded the modern world, it took as its *raison d'être* the need to build a society fit for the demands of the new epoch. Indeed, Enlightenment critics changed our understanding of what constitutes a good society. They cast doubt on the ancient Platonic idea that there is a single vision of the good life to be discovered by all, and argued instead that the only 'mature' form of social arrangement is one which actively encourages critical thought to flourish within the bounds set by our shared rationality (see Chapter 1). The Enlightenment, one might say, inscribed an ethic of rational interrogation on to the heart of modern social and political life. This ethic came to fruition in the steady rise of liberal institutions of government throughout the modern Western world. Only liberalism, it seemed could ensure the open society necessary for the full flowering of a mature, rational and critical attitude towards the organization of our public life.

The legacy of the Enlightenment, however, proved rather ambiguous. For all that it fostered a mature questioning attitude to our social arrangements, and for all that it helped to establish a free and open public sphere, it also bequeathed to the world deep class divisions, the unabated abuse of nature, the horrors of colonial domination, self-interested individualism and a belief in the inherent good of technological progress at any cost. Almost since its inception, the Enlightenment itself became the target of criticism. But a paradox emerged for those who sought to criticize this dark side to the Enlightenment's legacy. Given its commitment to mature critical reflection, it seemed impossible to criticize Enlightenment thinking without either confirming this commitment or being dismissed as an 'immature' defender of pre-modern superstitions. Increasingly, theorists wondered whether or not it was possible justifiably to criticize an epoch so thoroughly committed to an ethos of rational criticism. It is this problem that has led many contemporary social and political theorists to expend much of their intellectual energy reconceptualizing what is required in order to be a critic of (modern Enlightened) society. This chapter maps out how some of them have sought to traverse this difficult terrain.

As a guide through the maze of complex issues raised by this discussion, we may say from the outset that contemporary critics began to see themselves as social critics, or critics *in* society, rather than as Enlightenment critics, or critics *of* society. Borrowing Walzer's (1987, 1989a) terminology, Enlightenment critics hoped to *disconnect* themselves from everyday experiences so that they could pass judgement on life as if from a distance, whereas social critics aim to find the tools of criticism by *connecting* themselves to the world of everyday experience. The details and the ramifications of this distinction are best understood by beginning with the rise of social criticism in the writings of Karl Marx.

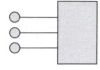

MARX: THE RISE OF SOCIAL CRITICISM

With the possible exception of Rousseau, Marx was the first critic of the Enlightenment who sought to construct a thoroughly immanent critique of its core beliefs; that is, a critique of the Enlightenment from within the horizon of Enlightenment thought itself. While his materialist analysis of the history of class division has inspired sociologists, anthropologists, literary critics, economists, historians and many others, it is sometimes forgotten that it also set in motion one of the most important theoretical questions of the twentieth century: what does it mean to be a social critic?

The roots of Marx's conception of social criticism can be found in his persistent rejection of idealism. Idealists, for Marx, were thinkers who placed more emphasis on the construction of a rigorous philosophical system than they did on the real social conditions which they sought to describe. The thinker who gave idealism 'its finest expression', as he put it, was Hegel. The job of real criticism, in contrast, was to 'revolt against the rule of thoughts' (Marx 1977: 159) and to get to grips with the material necessities of social life. The problem was not the logic of Hegel's philosophy as such (in fact, Marx adopted Hegel's dialectical approach to logic with gusto), but that Hegel's logical system was far too remote from the world of actually interacting human beings. To this extent, Hegelian criticism was no more than religion masquerading as philosophy, with no bearing on the material world of class division and oppression. We can see why Marx thought that 'the criticism of religion is the presupposition of all criticism' (Marx 1977: 63).

Despite this harsh judgement, Marx's embrace of Hegel's dialectical approach entailed the insight that a truly critical understanding of society must begin with an analysis of history. Not only did this enable Marx to distinguish his approach from rival versions of materialism (which tended to rob social relations of their dynamism), it also constituted the first element of his redefinition of what it means to be a social critic. Marx challenged the traditional conception of the Enlightenment critic as someone who meditates on social relations upon the basis of supposedly timeless truths about humanity. Kant (1993), for example, argued that the critic could transcend their specific historical circumstances through the correct use of reason, and thereby attain an insight into the human condition which would serve as a touchstone for the critique of irrational and culturally specific illusions. The point of the Enlightenment project, in other words, was to find a universal basis for criticism that was unsullied by the contingencies of historical circumstance. For Marx, on the contrary, those very contingencies of history were the starting point for social criticism. He believed that the first task for social critics should be to embed themselves in the course of human history rather than try to rise above it. In order to avoid the idealizing tendencies of traditional historians, however, the materialist historian must begin with certain basic facts about human needs. In *The German Ideology* (1844), Marx and Engels claimed that humans 'begin to distinguish themselves from animals as soon as they begin to produce their means of subsistence, a step which is conditioned by their physical organisation' (Marx 1977: 160). The history of humanity, in other words, begins with the first act of production to satisfy human need. This insight led Marx and Engels to the idea that 'the nature of individuals thus depends on the material conditions determining their production' (Marx 1977: 161). Within the bounds set by the basic human needs for food and shelter, therefore, human nature should be understood as varying in relation to the extent that our means of production vary. This 'materialist conception of history' displaces the Enlightenment's preoccupation with abstract or ahistorical features of humanity. The social critic, we may say, develops a theory of human nature on the basis of an engagement with history, whereas the Enlightenment critic attempts to transcend history with an abstract philosophical thought-experiment.

This first aspect of social criticism quickly gives rise to a second. If social critics in Marx's view must chart the history of human production, they must be aware of the mode of production in which they themselves are embedded. A proper analysis of history must also include a detailed analysis of the present. In this respect, Marx's analyses of the machinations of the destructive effects of the market economy in *Capital* (1867) not only exposed the deep class divisions that characterized modern, enlightened, liberal society, but also helped to provide Marx with a crucial element in his redefinition of critical inquiry (Marx 1977). Adapting the distinction mentioned earlier, we may say that Marx's thorough investigation and critique of the capitalist economy enabled him to be a critic *in* history rather than simply a critic *of* history. The second prerequisite of social criticism, therefore, is that critics understand their role in the unfolding historical drama of human interaction.

As long as criticism was thought to be an individual act, where only supreme critical minds could dive to the depths of the human condition, a properly social form of social criticism could not emerge. Marx understood that the idea of an individual critic reflecting maturely upon the issues of the day in rational dialogue with other similar individuals had to be revised in order to generate a new model of criticism capable of challenging the Enlightenment ideal. For a dialectician like Marx, this meant connecting the object of critical reflection with the subject doing the criticism. It is well known that Marx challenged accounts of society that prioritized the behaviour of individuals and focused his critical gaze on the dynamics of the class system instead. The result of this was a devastating account of the ever increasing immiseration of those who sold their labour power in exchange for money. It was an analysis that had a profound effect on generations of sociologists. As Giddens (1971) has pointed out, even Weber and Durkheim, who disagreed quite considerably with the Marxist analysis of society, can be said to share the idea that sociology should concern itself first and foremost with the analysis of capitalism. After Marx, one could no longer simply assume that the object of criticism was the behaviour of individuals.

When formulating a theory of social criticism, however, changing the object of criticism is not enough. One must also construct a new sense of the subject that engages in critical activity. Given this, the working class in Marx's analysis not only emerge as a new social phenomena to be described or catalogued, they also emerge as critics in their own right. The essence of his position was summed up in an early response to Hegel's *Philosophy of Right* (1821): 'the weapon of criticism cannot, of course, supplant the criticism of weapons; the material force must be overthrown by material force. But theory, too, will become material force as soon as it seizes the masses' (Marx 1977: 69). Marx's analysis of the class struggles that keep the motor of history running led him to conclude that the proletariat had supplanted the rational individual as the standard-bearer of critical activity. The proletariat, he argued, are so alienated from their humanity by capitalism that they have a real interest in bringing Marx's theoretical analysis into the practical sphere of human action. This bold move marked the decisive break with Enlightenment criticism. In keeping with his call to 'revolt against the rule of thoughts', the Enlightenment ideal of mature individuals rationally debating the legitimacy of social organizations in an open public sphere was shattered by Marx's insistence that the public sphere was dominated not by the opinions of individual consciences but by a nascent *class* consciousness on the verge of realizing its world historical role – the emancipation of humanity from class division.

Just as Marx acknowledged that the criticism of history demanded a critic situated in history, so the realization of the proletariat's class consciousness would only come to fruition as they came to know the source of their present oppression. It is the job not only of intellectuals like Marx to carry out critical analyses of capitalist society; the proletariat must themselves become conscious of the workings of the capitalist economy with the aid of these analyses. That said, the proletariat can only really become conscious of its role as the practical embodiment of critical thought through the revolutionary act of changing the social and political world for the better. We can think of this as the last postulate of Marx's reconceptualization of social criticism, a postulate summed up in the famous eleventh thesis of his *Theses on Feuerbach* (1845): 'The philosophers have only interpreted the world, in various ways; the point is to change it' (Marx 1977: 158).

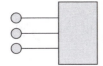

MARXISM: THE FALL OF SOCIAL CRITICISM

The task of developing Marx's account of social criticism fell to the interpreters of his work. Ironically, the more they tried to build on his ideas, the more they exposed the cracks in his critical edifice. We may say that Marx gave birth to social criticism, but Marxism and its off-spring unwittingly exposed the weaknesses of Marx's own vision.

For a growing body of recent commentators, it was Engels's attempt to ascribe an overly scientific quality to Marx's ideas, especially after Marx's death, that constituted the first Marxist turn away from Marx (Engels 1978). While Marx's analyses often contained scientific or quasi-scientific reference points, it is said that Engels sought to legitimate Marx's revolutionary project by arguing that its validity was on a par with the validity of laws about the physical universe. This set in motion a problem that has dogged Marxism to this day: if it is a law of history and social development that the proletariat will inevitably come to rise up against the forces of capital, then how does Marxism explain the lack of revolutionary zeal so clearly displayed by the masses? Lenin (1973) was one of the first to tackle this problem head-on. He focused on the need for a highly centralized revolutionary party that would guide the masses along the emancipatory path until they realized their full historical role for themselves. His emphasis on the need for an elite troop of revolutionaries was no doubt fuelled by the practical demands of generating a revolutionary force in an agrarian society such as tsarist Russia. But Lenin's practical approach raised two theoretical problems for Marxist social critics. First, could the conditions ever be right for a communist revolution without the presence of a mass proletariat to embody Marx's critique of capitalism? This question has haunted twentieth-century Marxism, particularly those Marxists who want to understand the revolutionary movements of the post-colonial world. Second, was the existence of a strong centralized party structure a necessary prerequisite of revolutionary activity, or did it stifle the flowering of revolutionary consciousness? The idea that Leninism would block the flow of radical politics was well expressed by Rosa Luxembourg: 'The ultra-centrism asked by Lenin is full of the sterile spirit of the overseer. It is not the positive and creative spirit' (quoted in Kearney and Rainwater 1996: 168). Her prescient warnings, years before the October Revolution, exposed the conservative impulse that accompanied the revolutionary movement in Russia.

One of the reasons why Marx's analysis lent itself to a Leninist agenda is that it tended to over-stress the role of economic relations in the functioning of society. As argued by Gramsci (1971), if Marxism is to account for the lack of revolutionary zeal among the proletariat, then it must provide a more thorough analysis of the ideological mechanisms that cajole the masses into thinking that their own oppression is legitimate. It was just such an analysis that led Gramsci to reformulate the concept 'hegemony' to describe the relationship between power, ideology and culture in modern societies. Hegemonic processes have only a distant relationship to economic factors, as they function primarily through the social and political apparatuses of modern life, such as the arts, government, schools, the family and so on. The ruling class maintains power by convincing the masses that their downtrodden position is natural and unchanging. The task of Marxist criticism, on this account, is not only about encouraging the masses to realize their historical role; it is also about the need for 'organic intellectuals' – intellectuals who come from the oppressed class – to expose the arbitrariness of the assumptions supporting the dominant ideology. This approach has been very influential for critics in media and cultural studies seeking to understand the relationship between class, culture and domination (see Chapter 7). Recently, Laclau and Mouffe (1985) have argued that Gramsci's analysis of hegemony greatly helps our understanding of the contingent yet legitimating function of the discursive structures that operate throughout the social and political world (see Chapters 3 and 8).

For some of his other interpreters, Marx under-theorized the nature of history. Notably, Benjamin commented on the need to view history less as an unbroken line progressing towards an emancipated future and more as a series of fragments with no deep underlying logic. The real task of Marxist historical materialism, he suggested, is not to reduce history to a homogeneous mass of 'empty time' – time robbed of its ability to give birth to novelty – but instead to 'blast open the continuum of history' (quoted in Kearney and Rainwater 1996: 222). Only once this is done will the revolutionary potential of the 'now', the potential of the present to be other than it is, be able to emerge. Interestingly, this theme is picked up by Derrida (1994) in his deconstructionist reading of Marx. This emphasis upon the unknowability of the future and the radical potential of the present, therefore, has come to play a large role in many non-Marxist, even anti-Marxist, accounts of social criticism (for example, Baudrillard 1975).

Despite attempts to rethink Marxism within the context of feminism (for example, Barrett 1980) the main problem with Marx for his feminist interpreters is the masculine bias implicit within his conception of social criticism. Although Marx redefined the idea of criticism such that the critic was no longer an apparently enlightened male reflecting maturely on the issues of the day, his image of the hard-working proletarian as the practical embodiment of theoretical criticism rising up against the forces of capital was still unavoidably masculine. Little was said about the role of women in the march of history towards *human* emancipation. One reason for this is that Marx dwelt heavily on the social and political nature of economic production, but failed to see the social and political basis of human reproduction. Radical feminists such as Firestone (1970) have tried to redress this imbalance in Marx's theories by stressing the fundamental nature of sex class as opposed to economic class. For other feminists, such as Elshtain (1981) and Jaggar (1983), Marxism has proved itself ill-equipped to address the complex nature of family relations, child-rearing and reproductive activity.

Ironically, therefore, Marx's interpreters have slowly but surely exposed the limits of Marx's concept of social criticism, such that contemporary theorists have had to look elsewhere for a response to the paradox of the Enlightenment. While acknowledging that Marx's emphasis on the economic basis of society brought the nature of critical activity clearly into view, contemporary theorists recognize the need to look beyond strictly economic factors to the less tangible but more multifaceted domain of power if they are to secure Marx's own aim of grounding criticism within the social and political world.

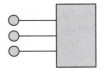

SOCIAL CRITICISM AND POWER

Marx developed a new conception of social criticism by assuming that the nature of society is 'fundamentally conditioned' by economic relations. The fact that the proletariat has proven to be so stubbornly recalcitrant when it comes to fulfilling its revolutionary role, however, points to the existence of powers at work in the social world that Marx's economic analysis does not adequately understand or explain. Indeed, the complexity of human society is poorly served if it is ultimately reduced to the impulse to produce. Social critics must account for the complexity of other forces that motivate and shape people's lives if they want to ground their critical agenda completely *within* the social and political sphere. One of the most compelling social forces of the modern world is the desire for power. For this reason, the work of Nietzsche is of the utmost importance, as he gave full, if somewhat idiosyncratic, expression to the many subtle ways in which power not only envelops all social relations but, as he saw it, helps to construct these relations in the first place.

For all that Marx and Nietzsche have come to represent almost diametrically opposed approaches to contemporary political life – the dinosaur of modernity and the proto-postmodernist, respectively – we should not forget their common desire to revolutionize our

understanding of criticism. As with Marx, Nietzsche saw that the first
step in this process was the critique of religion. If religion was smashed
by the hammer of criticism, then the whole of speculative philosophy
would crumble in its wake. Moreover, Marx and Nietzsche shared the
view that the only sure way to ward off the dangers of idealism is to
give philosophy a historical sense: 'lack of historical sense is the
hereditary defect of all philosophers . . . what is needed from now on
is historical philosophising' (Nietzsche 1994: section 2), or what he
also called 'genealogy' (Nietzsche 1969). Where Marx ultimately subordinated history to economy, however, Nietzsche saw in history the
operation of a force more mysterious than the economic transactions
of humankind. He called this force the will to power. The will to power
is the desire that has as its chief end the aim of exercising more power.
This is not only power in the sense of the social or political powers
that control our lives, it is also the power that actually *constructs* our
social and political lives. At a metaphysical level, therefore, the will to
power is an underlying condition of social existence: 'to impose upon
becoming the character of being – that is the supreme will to power'
(Nietzsche 1968: section 617). This power does not reside in the conscience of an individual or in the mentality of any particular group; it
is, rather, an impersonal desire located in the undertow of the stream
of social life. At a practical level, Nietzsche argues that we can discern
the will to power in all our social and political relations, transactions,
organizations and institutions. The aim of historical philosophizing,
from a Nietzschean perspective, is to chart the course of this will to
power through the history of society. This Nietzschean analysis was
developed by Foucault, particularly through his work on punishment
and sexuality (see also Chapters 4, 5, 6 and 8).

The consequences of this view for our understanding of the
Enlightenment are dramatic. Although the express aim of the Enlightenment was to challenge the dogmatic authority of religion, from
the perspective of the impersonal will to power the Enlightenment
simply replaced established religion with a new religion of its own:
humanism. Humanism is the presumption that human beings are at
the centre of the social and political world and that we are the sole
judge of all that is valuable in that world. The Enlightenment shunted
God to the margins of the social and political world and 'Man', this
new rational creature able to transcend and judge the world of experience, assumed the mantle of the divine. While the mass of humanity,
according to Nietzsche, gladly bowed before this new god, he believed
that we had sloughed off the shackles of religious dogma only to bind
ourselves anew with the chains of 'Man'. From this perspective, the
Enlightenment is no better or worse than the pre-modern religious
superstitions it replaced. Both established religion and the new
religion of humanism function in fundamentally the same way: they
constrain the creative energies of life by subordinating them to illusions of the human mind.

Interestingly, Marx is implicated in this new religion of humanism. Marx's history of human productive activity, a history that culminates in a triumphant image of human emancipation, elevates humanity into the role of divine creator. The working 'Man' will eventually construct a perfect world, albeit as much by revolutionary class struggle as by mature rational reflection. From a Nietzschean perspective, Marx's critique of religion is much like the Enlightenment critique; it only expels religion from its worldview to allow it in again through the back door of humanism. We might note, however, that some Marxists, such as Althusser (1971), have tried to excise this humanism from Marxist theory.

Despite the fact that he developed such a radically anti-humanist perspective, Nietzsche shared Marx's strategy of side-stepping the paradox of the Enlightenment by creating a new form of social criticism. How is it possible, though, to construct a version of social criticism that does not rest on humanist assumptions? As we have seen, Nietzsche sought a historical method of philosophizing that would reveal the multifarious insinuations of the will to power across the whole social terrain. Wherever traditional philosophy thought it had located an abstract, universal claim about the human condition, Nietzsche traced the history of this claim back to its sordid beginnings in the arena of social and political conflict. From a genealogical perspective, the very idea that there are 'truths' about the human condition which it is philosophy's task to unearth is dangerously misleading. Indeed, for Nietzsche (1954: 47), 'truths are illusions which we have forgotten are illusions.' The genealogist's task is to uncover the social and political processes that have made us believe that certain claims about humanity are universally and at all times true. The ultimate task, of course, is to expose the deep-seated desire that motivates our belief in truth itself.

This genealogical technique is at its most finely tuned whenever Nietzsche criticizes morality. His most scathing attacks are saved for those philosophers who claim to have refined moral laws that they believe ought to govern our lives. Whenever philosophers (or, indeed, anyone) lay down such moral laws, Nietzsche presumes that they are trying to constrain whatever remains of the creative energy of our lives: 'the essential and invaluable element in every morality is that it is a protracted constraint' (Nietzsche 1972: 92). The moral life is not one to which we should all aspire. Rather, it is that which constrains life's diversity and subordinates the creative energy of life to the service of the will to power. This savage attack on the nature of morality was inspired by Nietzsche's diagnosis of the disease afflicting his own society. He felt that the Enlightenment spirit of critique had become twisted and deformed into a spirit of slavish or reactive morality that preached obedience to new dogmas. One of the jobs of genealogical criticism is to set the energies of life into motion by releasing them from the constraining desire to obey contemporary norms of behaviour. Like Marx, therefore, Nietzsche saw that the need for an historical approach to social criticism will always be found in the politics of the present.

With his critique of the debilitating effects of Enlightenment humanism on the life of his contemporaries, Nietzsche opened the door to a strange world of the future beyond the world of the human. In part prediction and part proclamation, Nietzsche (1909) hailed the death of 'Man' and heralded the birth of the 'overman'. This has proven to be one of Nietzsche's most controversial ideas. For some early commentators, Nietzsche's prediction was chillingly portentous. They saw in Nietzsche's overman the precursor to the Nazi idea of an Aryan race of perfect beings. This is a view which still has some resonance to this day, typically among his Anglo-American interpreters, though few now would accuse Nietzsche's writings of being *essentially* fascist in outlook. In contrast, the French reception of Nietzsche in the 1960s, through the likes of Deleuze, Klossowski and Foucault (all of whom had a hand in compiling the French version of Nietzsche's collected works), saw the overman as an attempt to overcome the philosophy of humanism. As such, the overman does not represent an ideal type of human, but instead a compelling metaphor for the destruction of human-centred philosophy and the birth of a philosophy which looks beyond 'Man' and towards the impersonal yet creative forces of life. Regardless of these differing interpretations, from the point of view of social criticism, Nietzsche's aim was to wrestle the torch of criticism out of the hands of the enlightened rational individual. Just as Marx thought that the proletariat would become the real social critics, Nietzsche conjures up the image of an overman to embody the new spirit of criticism he believes will resolve the paradox of the Enlightenment. Of course, as Marx's proletariat must begin the process of emancipation in order to realize their historical role, so Nietzsche's overman can only come into existence with a celebration of the life that exceeds Man; a celebration of becoming (life) in the face of being (the will to power).

But can this call to embrace the forces of life really be called social criticism? While Nietzsche may have encapsulated a profound element of our sense of the human condition, is it not the case that his conception of social criticism is too far removed from what we recognize as the social and political world? Moreover, the kind of celebration of life Nietzsche evokes as a basis for social criticism calls for an aesthetic response to our social condition, rather than a response based on rational standards; one may celebrate life by painting a picture, but it is not immediately obvious how this constitutes an act of social criticism. There is no doubt that Nietzsche's analysis of the will to power sheds light on the nature of modern social and political life by exposing the role of power in constructing our social relations and the fact that our pursuit of the 'good life' is often nothing more than the pursuit of more power. But what is lacking in Nietzsche's analysis is a *detailed* account of how these forces and desires come to construct the social and political world. That had to wait for Foucault's analysis of regimes of power/knowledge.

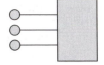

SOCIAL CRITICISM AS TRANSGRESSION

The Nietzschean revival in France during the 1960s has deeply marked the world of contemporary social and political theory, as many of the chapters in this book demonstrate. The resurgence of interest, however, did not mean a simple reiteration of Nietzschean themes. Social theory had moved on, and there was a new strain of anti-humanism emerging from anthropology and linguistics, called structuralism. Structuralism argues against the idea that society is best understood as the sum total of a complex series of individual actions. It proposes instead that society should be thought of as the background structure which actually gives shape and meaning to our individual actions. For Lévi-Strauss (1963), perhaps the most ardent advocate of structuralist analysis, all our social relations and activities are structured by a series of conceptual oppositions that shape the way we view the world: culture/nature, human/animal, man/woman and so on (see also Chapters 3 and 7). Analysing culture in terms of these oppositions can, for Lévi-Strauss, provide a way of understanding the unconscious foundations of a world we ourselves have created. However, the problem with structuralism is that it lacks a critical edge. Its synchronic approach to the study of society (that is, the way it analyses societies without reference to their historical formation) tends to legitimate whatever social structures are in operation at the time. The aim of *post*structuralism is to retain the anti-humanist insights of structuralism while modifying the theory to account for social change. Poststructuralists like Foucault found in Nietzsche, among others, the necessary tools with which to turn structuralism into a historical and critical theory. But where Nietzsche helped to give structuralism a critical edge, structuralism helped to give Nietzscheanism the theory of society that it lacked if it was to become a convincing account of social criticism. We can see how this altered the nature of Nietzschean social criticism by looking at Foucault's relation to structuralism, his version of genealogical critique and his analysis of the project of Enlightenment.

Typically, commentators have thought Foucault's early writings to be closely associated with structuralism (though he expressly resisted the label). His concern in these early works is to see how specific social institutions, like psychiatry and medicine, function to generate bodies of knowledge that gain legitimacy within society. In *Madness and Civilisation* (1965), his first major work, he charts the course of competing definitions of madness to expose the mechanisms by which we (the majority of society) come to understand ourselves as rational and sane. His conclusion is as startling today as it was then. For the majority of any society to know themselves as a rational majority they must exclude others whom they deem to be irrational. The different ways in which we have excluded the irrational from society, either by casting them adrift on the ship of fools or by incarcerating them in sanatoriums, reveals the different ways we have thought of ourselves as rational. Foucault's argument is premised, therefore, on the belief that there is no universal or ahistorical conception of rationality that transcends social conditions of exclusion; a conclusion that flies in the face of the Enlightenment's understanding of reason and its conditions.

In *The Order of Things* (1970) and *The Archaeology of Knowledge* (1972) Foucault tried to generalize his findings about the constitution of particular forms of knowledge by uncovering the general role played by the human sciences in constructing the idea of 'Man' as both the subject and object of social inquiry. It was these analyses that generated discussion of the role played by 'discourses' in the human sciences. The term 'discourse' refers to the fundamental assumptions of the human sciences that give meaning to 'Man's' analysis of 'Man'. It was Foucault's insight, though, that the activity of reflecting on who we are is always accompanied by the activity of excluding others from society. In other words, knowledge about ourselves is not based on rational reflection upon our shared human condition but on political acts of exclusion at various methodological and social levels.

Although his early works contain large doses of Nietzscheanism, Foucault's analysis of the discursive construction of our self-knowledge was ultimately bereft of insight into the nature of power in the social and political world. If he was to develop his argument further he had to find new tools to aid his interrogation of the politics of exclusion. In a crucial article, 'Nietzsche, genealogy, history' (1984), Foucault began this process by exposing the 'will to knowledge' at work whenever one undertakes a historical analysis. Rather than finding the deep truth of history, the hidden motor that propels us through time, Foucault's genealogist unmasks history's contingencies in order to expose the dubious nature of the motivation to search for an underlying truth in the first place. The genealogist, we may say, recovers the vicissitudes of history to undermine those historians who look for grand narratives of human development among the archives.

This genealogical task inevitably involves an analysis of the present conditions of power within society, because it requires that we uncover the reasons why society requires historians to produce the great stories of our society's rise to maturity. What powers are at work in our search for the truth of who we are? Foucault (1980) came to formulate the genealogical task as the excavation of the 'regimes of power/knowledge' that make us think we have an accurate understanding of how we have become who we are. It is important to dwell for a moment on why Foucault feels it is necessary to conjoin power and knowledge in the new term power/knowledge. The problem Foucault faced with his discourse analysis of the human sciences is that he did not conceptualize his role as a practitioner of the very human sciences he was examining. If the genealogical task of exposing the operation of power in our constructions of history was to be fulfilled, Foucault realized that he had to unmask his own position of power as an analyst of social and political phenomena. Only then could he become a critic *in* society rather than a critic *of* society. After all,

> each society has its regime of truth, its general politics of truth: that is, the types of discourse which it accepts and makes function as true; the mechanisms and instances which enable one to distinguish true and false statements, the means by which each is sanctioned; the techniques and procedures accorded value in the acquisition of truth; the status of those who are charged with saying what counts as true.
>
> (Foucault 1980: 131)

By interlocking the operation of power with the construction of knowledge in such a way that the generation of knowledge is not possible without an already existing operation of power, Foucault deliberately problematized his own status as an analyst. His investigations of the human sciences and social institutions were now to be seen as strategic interventions into the social and political life of his day, rather than distanced reflections on the underlying assumptions of the human sciences. Foucault, we may say, took the Nietzschean turn when he conceptualized his work as a political assault on the social institutions of contemporary society. The two books that most obviously encapsulate this form of analysis are *Discipline and Punish* (1977) and Volume 1 of *The History of Sexuality* (1978). In these books, Foucault charts the complex construction of different kinds of penal and medical/sexual knowledge and the ways in which these forms of knowledge are implicated with changing relations of power within society. The result is a strident intervention into contemporary social and political life; one that calls into question our sense of the natural or rational superiority of present day penal institutions and sexual mores. As with Nietzsche, Foucault's account of social criticism demands a historical look at the present and embraces the perspective of the present in order to examine history.

From the point of view of social criticism, however, this genealogical method is not unproblematic. According to Habermas (1987b) and Taylor (1989), for example, Foucault tends to trip himself up with his own analysis. The essence of the problem is that his critics do not accept that Foucault can make claims, which we must take as truth claims, about the relationship between power and knowledge, given his stated assumption that all claims to knowledge or truth are inextricably embroiled within operations of power. In other words, Foucault's attempt to develop the social character of a Nietzschean account of social criticism does not actually resolve the primary problem of Nietzscheanism: its inability to deal with the paradox of the Enlightenment. Either Foucault is for the Enlightenment, in which case he must accept that his perspective on society is ultimately subject to the demands of reason, and his claim regarding the inextricable bond between power and all forms of knowledge is mistaken. Or he is against the Enlightenment, in which case his analysis of the social and political world must be thought of as irrational, or at least arational.

Feminist critics of Foucault have raised related problems. If Foucault denies the possibility of knowing the truth about our condition in terms devoid of power relations, then his work seems to paralyse the political impulse of contemporary feminism towards the liberation of women from patriarchal oppression (for example, Hartsock 1990). For many feminists, this implication of Foucault's work means that he strayed too far from the Enlightenment ideal of rational liberation from oppressive superstitions and power structures (for example, Benhabib 1992). While a growing body of feminist thinkers disagree with this negative assessment of Foucault's politics (for example, Butler 1990; Lloyd 1996), the central problem remains: how can Foucault achieve a critique of the Enlightenment from within the remit of the Enlightenment? On what basis is it possible to ground a Foucauldian conception of social criticism?

The most direct answers to these questions can be found in Foucault's late essay, 'What is Enlightenment?' In this essay, Foucault surprised his critics and admirers alike by seeming to come out in favour of the Enlightenment project. But it was a very specific version of Enlightenment that Foucault had in mind. Whereas Nietzsche had sought to condemn the Enlightenment on the grounds that it was based on the new religion of humanism, Foucault invited us to dissociate the Enlightenment from the doctrine of humanism. If we do this, he argues, then we can salvage a conception of Enlightenment fit for the demands of contemporary social and political life. In particular, the critical attitude of the Enlightenment could be reinvigorated by refusing the dogma of humanism, a dogma that is at the heart of the politics of exclusion, and by conjuring up in its place the spirit of resistance which resides within all social relations (even though it is a spirit which Foucault acknowledges is rarely expressed). This mobilization of resistance, for Foucault, can form the basis of an ethos which could overcome the contingent limits placed on our identity by the framework of Enlightenment thought, and begin the process of criticizing the Enlightenment from within. For this to happen, critics must locate the limits of Enlightenment thought and then embrace activities which take us beyond these limits. We may call this an ethos of transgression; an ethos that steps beyond the limitations of the present and that experiments with the endless possibilities inherent in the future.

But does this provide Foucault with a coherent, social critical response to the Enlightenment? While this issue is still hotly debated (Hoy and McCarthy 1994; Kelly 1994), we can say that Foucault grounds social criticism in the endless process of critical engagement, whereas the Enlightenment always subsumed criticism under the banner of human reason. For Enlightenment thinkers, criticism had to be rational first and foremost. For Foucault, all that is worth saving from the Enlightenment is its total commitment to criticism, which means that its commitment to both humanism and rationalism must not be free from critical interrogation. The baseline of Foucault's account of social criticism, therefore, is a permanent commitment to the criticism of all social and political institutions and norms. Is this really *social* criticism? As the next section will make clear, there are still many advocates of social criticism who think Foucault's version is prey to the criticisms made against Nietzsche's account – that it over-emphasizes the aesthetic element of criticism to the detriment of a rational interrogation of the social and political world. But how can we salvage reason, given the ways in which it can be used to exclude those we do not want to be members of our society? This question had already been taken up in the early part of the twentieth century by the neo-Marxist theorists associated with the Institute for Social Research at Frankfurt.

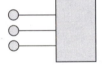

SOCIAL CRITICISM AND REASON

One of the significant features of the critical theory of the so-called Frankfurt School was that it halted the trend towards dogmatism within Marxism. While many Marxists tended to characterize Marx's contribution as a decisive break away from traditional philosophical concerns, and therefore tried to set in stone what it was that made Marx's ideas so unique, thinkers like Adorno and Horkheimer emphasized the continuous thread between Hegel and Marx and, through this link, connected Marx back to the canon of Western thought. It was this philosophical reading of Marx that gave them a unique insight into the ambiguous legacy of the Enlightenment.

Enlightenment thinkers saw themselves as the harbingers of a great victory of reason over superstition and science over myth. According to Adorno and Horkheimer (1972), this self-image soon became 'engulfed' by its own 'mythology'. Reason, in the guise of abstract, mathematical and scientific method, was portrayed as the saviour of humanity brought down to earth by the minds of great individuals. Reason, it seemed, could not be questioned in any sphere of life. But for all that the Enlightenment freed modern society from the darkness of superstition, it also blinded us all with the all-pervasive light of reason. Under the influence of Weber (1947, 1978), Adorno and Horkheimer recognized that this new myth of the omnipotent status of Enlightenment reason was having profound and momentous effects on every aspect of society, but not in the way envisaged by the Enlightenment thinkers themselves. In our haste to make social and political life more rational, Weber saw that we were trapping ourselves in an 'iron cage' of bureaucracy and state machinery. At its worst, the drive towards a rational society was the spring that fed the flood of totalitarianism that dominated world affairs in the early part of the twentieth century. Far from fulfilling its promise of human emancipation, therefore, the Enlightenment ideal seemed to be ensnaring us as cogs in the wheels of rationally efficient systems, with no discussion of whether or not such rationalization was necessarily part and parcel of a good life. The legacy of the Enlightenment, on this account, is the idea that reason is an instrument for the efficient ordering of society rather than a way of evaluating what counts as a good society. But whereas Weber was sceptical about our ability to free ourselves from the increasingly virulent progress of rationalization, the Frankfurt School theorists still clung, however tentatively, to the Marxist hope of human emancipation. The question they faced was how to criticize the deleterious effects of the Enlightenment's conception of instrumental reason and open the door to an emancipated future without falling prey to the ever present forces of irrationalism. It is this question that has motivated the work of the Frankfurt School's foremost successor, Habermas (see also Chapter 1).

Habermas's main contribution to contemporary social and political theory is his assiduous attempt to articulate an alternative conception of rationality that can be used as a basis from which to criticize the distorting effects of instrumental reason in the modern world. As such, Habermas aims to reconstruct the Enlightenment project of rational criticism while warding off the dangers inherent in an abstract and formal conception of reason as an instrument of order. The importance of his project, we may say, is that he attempts a rationalist critique of instrumental reason. As *The Philosophical Discourse of Modernity* (1987b) and *Postmetaphysical Thinking* (1992) make clear, this places his work firmly within the remit of social criticism: that is, the criticism of the Enlightenment project from within its own parameters. Where he differs from the thinkers mentioned already is that he is more sympathetic to the general thrust of the Enlightenment project and to the internal critique of it advanced by Marx. In contrast to Marx, he sees a reconstructed conception of universal reason as a necessary corrective to an account of social and historical development that is focused on the mode of material production. While he endorses the general point that it is the task of social critics to try to understand the evolution of a given society, this must be done in a way that 'free[s] historical materialism from its philosophical ballast'

(Habermas 1987a: 383). Once the more crude forms of historical materialism are rejected, Habermas argues that the critical relevance of an adequate account of socio-historical evolution must be under-pinned by a reconstructed theory of reason. Without an account of reason, he argues, historical philosophizing becomes inconsistent and susceptible to the dangers of moral relativism. The relationship between Habermas's evolutionary account of social development and his reconstruction of reason is explored in the debate between Hoy and McCarthy (1994). It is more pertinent in this context to get to grips with Habermas's reconstruction of the Enlightenment's commit-ment to reason and the role this plays in his account of social criticism.

The key moment in Habermas's reconstruction of social criticism is his attack on all subject-centred philosophy and his advocacy of an intersubjective alternative. The Kantian vision of philosophy, for example, has at its heart the image of a rational individual ruminat-ing on the nature of life in isolation. For all that Kant (1991) argued for active deliberation in the public sphere, the reasoning process was always fundamentally the task of individuals. For Habermas, if we are to salvage what was worthwhile in the Enlightenment ideal but avoid its worst excesses, we must conceive of reason in terms of intersubjec-tive relations rather than view it as a capacity of individual minds. The place Habermas chose to look for such a conception of reason was in the way we communicate with each other through language.

Although it is a very complex idea in its details, the basics of Haber-mas's communicative conception of reason are fairly straightforward. We know that language is often the site of conflict and power (see Chapter 3), a fact that might suggest that it is the wrong place to look for an account of universal reason. But for Habermas (1984, 1987a), we also know what it is to use language in a way that is oriented to mutual understanding. This must be the case, as otherwise we would never be able to understand everyday language use to be vulnerable to the distorting effects of social power in the first place. We know, for example, when language is being used for the pursuit of particular goals irrespective of the wishes of others (when a politician plays with words to promote their own popularity rather than to promote what is, say, morally justifiable). Similarly, argues Habermas, we know that undistorted language use is based on using language for the pursuit of ends that can be shared by all. In such a case, the force of the better argument – rather than, say, power, money, habit, custom or fashion – is all that is at work, and any agreement reached can be said to be a communicatively achieved consensus. This consensus is rationally justifiable by virtue of its being agreeable to all without coercion. In contrast, a proposal is instrumentally or strategically rational when the speaker is aiming to promote their own ends. Any agreement reached on the basis of one participant imposing their own ends on others is to be thought of as a *de facto* accord rather than a communi-catively achieved consensus.

The reason why Habermas makes so much of this distinction is that it provides the tools with which he is able to shape a response to the paradox of the Enlightenment. Habermas avoids the problem of criticizing reason in a circular manner by constructing a critique of the Enlightenment dogma of *instrumental* reason from the universal standpoint of *communicative* reason. The most immediate benefit of this dual conception of reason for a theory of social criticism, according to Habermas, is that it resists the relativizing, aestheticizing and irrationalist tendencies of the Nietzschean and Foucauldian critiques we have looked at above. In stark contrast to Foucault, Habermas believes that all valid social criticism will justify itself according to certain standards that are built into language itself. We can reconstruct this universal conception of reason such that it can act as a standard against which to judge one-sided, instrumental accounts of reason, as well as straightforward irrationalism in all aspects of social and political life. Habermas's version of social criticism, we may say, is a critique of reason from within the domain of reason itself, rather than from the perspective of reason's allegedly sordid genealogy. But this raises a problem. Is Habermas's approach really a version of social criticism at all, or is it just the old Enlightenment ideal of rationality dressed up in new clothes? While there are many different ways of answering this question, if we look at how his theory of communicative rationality informs his approach to moral norms then we will go some way towards clarifying the issues at stake.

If language use points towards a general theory of rationality, then there is reason to believe that it may also help out when it comes to the adjudication of moral claims (Habermas 1989). If, under conditions of undistorted communication, we all agree that 'x is the right thing to do', then, according to Habermas, we can say that x is normatively justified. The central point here is that claims regarding the right thing to do cannot be justifiably validated by reference to an individual's preference, or to the preferences of some section of society. 'I will do x because it is the right thing for me (some of us) to do' does not count as a good reason to accept x as a universally valid norm. If everyone affected by x could agree in an uncoerced dialogue that it is the right thing to do, then, and only then, does it make sense to talk of x being normatively justified (see Chapter 1). On the face of it, this all sounds very similar to Kant's Enlightenment approach to moral criticism. While Kant (1964) sought to justify moral norms in the non-contradictory universalization of an individual's moral conscience, Habermas recognizes that such abstraction from actual dialogue is prey to the Hegelian charge that the norms generated are meaningless and empty of moral substance. In response to this, Habermas argues that moral norms are only justified to the extent that they can be willed by all affected by them in an intersubjective agreement (and not simply by an isolated rational individual). It is the way in which Habermas conceptualizes the embeddedness of human action within a 'communicative context' that avoids the abstract and formal qualities of the Kantian approach.

This account of his moral theory illustrates Habermas's awareness of the need to generate the grounds of criticism from within the social and political world in which we live; in other words, his aim to embed his own theory within the core concerns of social criticism. But for all that, it is obvious that Habermas has adopted a rather different way of approaching the fundamentals of social criticism. His explicit return to a discussion of reason and his desire to build a moral and ethical framework on the basis of this reconstructed rationalism connect his work with more traditional forms of criticism within sociological and political theory. In political theory, for example, Habermas's most recent work has shown strong similarities with Rawls's attempt to delineate a theory of justice (see Rawls 1993; Habermas 1996). For many, this proves the strength and novelty of Habermas's approach. It is his ability to straddle the world of social criticism, criticism from within, and the world of traditional criticism, criticism from above, that makes his contribution so telling (for example, McCarthy 1991). For the more sceptical, especially those of a feminist hue, there may be rewards in reading Habermas, but there are also dangers in his dalliance with more traditional Enlightenment modes of criticism (Meehan 1995). For those with a more straightforwardly dismissive attitude to traditional varieties of criticism, Habermas has increasingly forsaken the tasks of social criticism and succumbed to the temptations of the old Enlightenment dogmas of rationalism and humanism (for example, Lyotard 1984). The key issues, it would appear, are whether or not Habermas is successful in developing a genuinely intersubjective approach to philosophy, and even whether or not intersubjectivity is really an appropriate ground upon which to build a theory of social criticism.

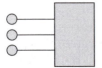

CONCLUSIONS: THE PROMISE OF FEMINIST SOCIAL CRITICISM

So far not much has been said about feminist social criticism. In part, this is because many feminist social critics take their lead from the kind of debates already mentioned. But more importantly, there are some feminist social critics involved in the construction of such innovative attempts at defining the tasks of social criticism that it is hard to place them on the map of ideas outlined above. What they all share is the belief that a truly embedded form of social criticism cannot come into existence until the body is theorized as a site of creativity and contestation rather than as a lump of raw matter. For all that the Nietzschean and Foucauldian versions of social criticism helped to generate discussion about the body, it is contemporary feminist writers who have done most to bring the body into view as a new terrain of (and for) social criticism (see Chapter 6).

The importance of focusing on the body from the point of view of social criticism is twofold. First, the idea of a socially constituted and active body is not easily placed within the traditional categories of critical thought. Varieties of social criticism that emphasize these aspects of the body, therefore, are typically less in thrall to the canon of Western philosophy and less inclined to the formal abstractions that accompany disembodied accounts of subjectivity (see Chapter 5). Second, once the body has been liberated from its role as the servant of the mind, social criticism itself is typically given a new lease of life. It tends to place more emphasis on the promise of new forms of critical activity; forms moved by creativity, inspired by new technologies and propelled by the desire to write as much with literary flair as with philosophical rigour. For this very reason, many feminist critics leave their masculinist counterparts cold and unable to decipher the new conceptual terrain which they are creating.

Butler (1990, 1993), Haraway (1991) and Cixous (1980a) (to take an indicative sample) all aim to go beyond the pitfalls and traps of Enlightenment thinking by conjuring up a new terrain of thought based on novel understandings of the body. For all the differences between these theorists, each has helped to bring the body into the field of the social in ways that impact on how we are to understand the tasks of social criticism. The promise of the ideas outlined by these theorists is that social criticism can be taken beyond its preoccupation with the paradox of the Enlightenment. Only once we are far into the new millennium will we be able to judge whether or not this promise can be fulfilled.

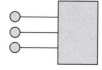

QUESTIONS

1 What elements must a theory possess to be considered a theory of social criticism?

2 Can theories of social criticism that reject humanism retain a genuinely critical dimension?

3 How do you think theories of social criticism will develop into the new millennium?

4 To what extent do theories of social criticism help us to justify political action?

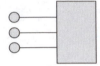

FURTHER READING

Those interested in pursuing the idea of social criticism would do well to familiarize themselves with the outlines of contemporary continental thought since Kant. This can be done by looking at David West, *An Introduction to Continental Philosophy* (1996), and this could be usefully supplemented with Kearney and Rainwater (eds), *The Continental Philosophy Reader* (1996). The literature on Marx is huge, but for a good account of the way Marx challenged the traditional conception of the relationship between theory and practice, see Avineri, *The Social and Political Thought of Karl Marx* (1968). A more recent collection with many useful assessments of Marx's ideas is Carver (ed.), *The Cambridge Companion to Marx* (1991). Aside from the primary texts, students of Nietzsche would do well to start with Sedgwick (ed.), *Nietzsche: A Critical Reader* (1996) and Conway, *Nietzsche and the Political* (1996). Those interested in Foucault could start with Rabinow (ed.), *The Foucault Reader* (1984), Dreyfus and Rabinow, *Michel Foucault: Beyond Structuralism and Hermeneutics* (1982), Deleuze, *Foucault* (1988) and Simons, *Foucault and the Political* (1995). The student of Habermas could begin with Outhwaite (ed.), *The Habermas Reader* (1996) and supplement this with McCarthy, *The Critical Theory of Jürgen Habermas* (1984), White, *The Recent Work of Jürgen Habermas: Reason, Justice and Modernity* (1988), Baynes, *The Normative Grounds of Social Criticism: Kant, Rawls, Habermas* (1992) and O'Neill, *Impartiality in Context: Grounding Justice in a Pluralist World* (1997). Finally, there are a number of journals that should be consulted, such as *Philosophy and Social Criticism*, *Radical Philosophy*, *Constellations* and *Thesis Eleven*.

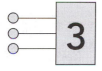

3 LANGUAGE
Alan Finlayson

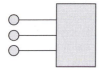

INTRODUCTION

There cannot be a social theory that does not seriously attempt to comprehend the nature of language. Language enables the establishment of a complex social order, allowing people to interact with each other, to formulate principles and practices and to maintain them over time. Without this sort of complex, shared, communicative order there is no culture, no history, no society. It is the possibilities for complex behaviour created by our use of language that make us different from many other animals.

Yet it does not follow from this that understanding language is straightforward. The phenomenon of language is not one that can simply be placed alongside others, for it is something that makes possible, and arguably defines, all other social phenomena. For this reason, language has come to occupy centre-stage in contemporary social thought, and has been a preoccupation within disciplines as diverse as psychology, philosophy, anthropology, sociology and history.

Despite all the attention given to language, and by so many scholars, no consensus about how to understand it has developed. Theoretical perspectives on language have been used both to ground and to undermine the key concepts of Western social and political thought. Approaches and theories vary widely, and are the object of sometimes vitriolic dispute. For a theorist such as Habermas, the fact of linguistic communication necessarily entails the possibility of mutual understanding providing resources that allow for the resolution of disputes by means of rational discourse between citizens (see Chapters 1, 2 and 8). Yet for others the analysis of language suggests that our social world has no basis to it other than arbitrary fictions produced by social conventions. This latter view forms the basis for a critique of traditional conceptions of such core theoretical concepts as rationality, subjectivity, knowledge, power and the political.

In many respects, these two contrasting perspectives mark out a major fault line in contemporary social and political thought. Students of social theory, before coming to any decision as to where to stand in current debates, must first decide how they will understand language. It is to aid in such an assessment that this chapter illustrates some of the arguments and diverse applications made of theories of language in contemporary social and political thought.

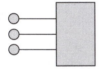

LANGUAGE, THOUGHT AND MEANING

We tend to imagine that our minds develop thoughts about the world which are then turned into words that can in turn be understood by others. Something like this assumption has underpinned much of Western philosophy. Aristotle, for example, saw an equivalence between a verbal expression, a thought and the substance or entity on which that thought was focused. In the twentieth century, a number of schools of thought have problematized such a schema and suggested instead that, rather than being a simple vehicle for the transmission of thought, language actually structures our thinking. Wittgenstein, for example, was sceptical of any assumption that the concepts 'proposition, language, thought, world, stand in line one behind the other, each equivalent to each' (1967: proposition 96). From his perspective, language is not a neutral communicative mechanism reflecting meaning, but produces or constitutes meaning. This has quite profound implications. It implies that meaning is not simply 'out there' waiting for us to find it, but that it is the result of human creative activity. This is not to say that there is no 'real world', but that what that world means to us, how we interpret it, how we understand it, depends on language.

Such a view was advanced by the linguist and anthropologist Edward Sapir (1949), and his colleague Benjamin Lee Whorf (1954). The so-called Sapir–Whorf hypothesis argued that language determined the way we think, that each language was unique and that the way one language divided up the world would not be found in any other. Before we label the world, make it comprehensible through language, it has no order, only a 'kaleidoscopic flux'. It is through naming and categorizing that conceptual order is imposed on the world.

For Sapir and Whorf, it is not simply words but structures of language that shape our comprehension of the world. Rather than understanding language as determining the culture or thought of a community, we may think of it as structuring that culture. As such, the idea of our having easy access to an objective 'real world' is made somewhat problematic. As Sapir put it:

> Human beings do not live in the objective world alone, nor alone in the world of social activity as ordinarily understood, but are very much at the mercy of the particular language which has become the medium of expression for their society. The fact of the matter is that the 'real world' is to a large extent built upon the language habits of the group . . . We see and hear and otherwise experience very largely as we do because the language habits of our community predispose certain choices of interpretation.
>
> (Sapir 1949: 162)

Think, for example, of the way in which languages classify words by gender and how terms are organized into synonyms and antonyms. A language groups events, objects, experiences and so on into different categories, and produces a sense of the way things interrelate. Sapir and Whorf give the example of the Hopi Indian language. In Hopi, the one word *masa'ytaka* refers to everything that flies, be it a bird, an insect or an aeroplane. Furthermore, they do not have tenses as in English; instead there are forms of speech that denote various durations. Thus, they argue, the Hopi have a different worldview, since their language entails a different system of classification of the objects they encounter, as well as a different conception of time and space. These are fundamental organizational principles through which we interpret the world. In this way we may understand that linguistic systems might influence thought by first making intelligible the world we are thinking about. Rather than understanding language as determining thought, we should perhaps think of it as determining what we think about – as setting, in some sense, a limit to our world, a framework within which we operate.

If we are going to follow this route we need to deal with some difficult questions. If meaning is constituted in language, and not derived from the objective world, we need to explain, first, how meaning is at all possible, and, second, how language works to produce, reproduce and change meaning. Sapir and Whorf tend to assume homogeneity within a language. The language somehow evolves as if it is the mystical product of the community, the chosen repository for a unique view of the world. An account of the interaction between language as a cognitive system and language as a practical tool that evolves through usage in complex, perhaps conflictual, social circumstances is also required. There are several approaches to these sorts of question, but one of the most influential thinkers on these matters predates Sapir and Whorf: the Swiss linguist Ferdinand de Saussure. His work had an enormous influence on twentieth-century social theory and philosophy, especially in continental Europe.

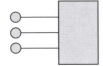

LANGUAGE AND STRUCTURE

In thinking about language, Saussure was influenced by the idea that there are underlying structures to social life, in particular Durkheim's sociological work on the ways in which things acquire meaning for people. Meaning had to be related to the social framework in which we live. Thus Saussure became interested in the connection between language, meaning and social frameworks. Between 1907 and 1911, while Professor of Linguistics at Geneva, he delivered three courses that addressed these questions and developed a novel conceptualization of language. After his death, these lectures were reconstructed from the notes taken by students and were published in 1916 as the *Course in General Linguistics*.

Saussure regards language as being made up of signs. The basic components of language, the elements that carry and signify meaning are these signs. Just as road signs, such as a red triangle, signify danger or a skull and crossbones signifies poison, so the marks on a page that make up words and the verbal utterances of speech can be thought of as signs – and like signs these are representations that have to be decoded.

The linguistic sign is made up of two parts: the sound-image itself and the concept it carries. Saussure calls these the signifier and the signified, respectively. We tend to think of a sign as simply the image or sound in question, but a sign is only a sign if it carries a concept or meaning with it – any mark that did not have a concept attached to it would not be a sign. This means that concepts are not merely floating around, pre-existing our creation of a language to express them. Rather, they are embedded within language and its usage.

To clarify this, let us follow one of Saussure's examples (1960: 65–7). If you are shown a drawing of a tree, however schematic, and asked what it is, you will most probably reply that it is a tree. That of course would be wrong. It is not a tree, it is a mark on a page or canvas, a mark that happens to form a sign which connotes the concept tree. For the same reason, 'TREE', is not a tree either, but black marks on the page of a book. You understand these marks as being the sign for what we think of as a tree. It is not the thing itself, but a representation which we come to understand as signifying the idea of the things with leaves that make up woods. If we accept this, then we have a new question. Why does this sign signify what it signifies, why is a tree called a tree? This brings us to a fundamental principle of Saussure's linguistics – the arbitrary nature of the sign.

For Saussure, the linkage between a signifier and a signified must be understood as arbitrary. There is no intrinsic or natural connection between the things that make up forests and the sign 'TREE'. This should be perfectly obvious, since we know that in France the word is *arbre* and in Germany it is *baum*. People can get by perfectly well referring to what we call a tree as *arbre* or *baum* or something else within linguistic systems other than English. Perhaps then, in theory at least, trees could have been called 'seats', or 'freds'. It is just that the term tree has come to be used in English, and by custom and practice we use it and know what it means. This is true for all signs. 'In fact', argues Saussure (1960: 68), 'every means of expression used in society is based, in principle, on collective behaviour or – what amounts to the same thing – on convention.'

By declaring the linguistic sign arbitrary, Saussure does not mean to suggest that the choice of signifier is left entirely to the speaker at any one moment (if I did start calling trees 'seats' you would not understand me), but simply, yet momentously, that there is no natural connection whatsoever between signs and signifiers. Consequently, meaning must be understood as a matter of socially produced convention, operating within a language system. This builds up into a specific and comprehensive, but none the less arbitrary, way of organizing, comprehending and experiencing the world.

Now, to understand the systemic nature of language, we need to make a further conceptual refinement and distinguish between what Saussure called *langue* and *parole*. By *parole* is meant the actual 'speech' act, the occasion of signifying. *Langue* is the structure that makes this act possible, the underlying framework. As Saussure says, 'it is the social product whose existence permits the individual to exercise his linguistic faculty.' It is *langue* in which Saussure is primarily interested, since meaning must be understood in the context of the system that comprises language. It does not need to refer 'outside' itself for the production of meaning – it produces meaning by its own internal rules and relationships. Terms, or signs, derive meaning from their place within the system, by their position relative to other terms and not from anything inherent in the terms themselves. As Saussure (1960: 117) puts it,

> in all cases we then discover not ideas given in advance but values emanating from the system. When we say that the values correspond to concepts it is understood that these concepts are purely differential, not positively defined by their content but

negatively defined by their relations with other terms in the system. Their most precise characterisation is that they are what the others are not.

This can be difficult to grasp so let us follow another of Saussure's examples (1960: 108–9). Imagine a train – the 8.25 Geneva to Paris train. Every day the same train, the 8.25, leaves Geneva station. The passengers on the train, the railway staff and so on are different every day, but it is still the 8.25 Geneva to Paris train. The coaches may change every day, even the engine, but it is still the 8.25 Geneva to Paris train. This is so because the train occupies a place in a system of meaning – the train timetable. Within this system, the 8.25 occupies a unique position, and this position, relative to all the other trains, gives it an identity. Even if the train is late and leaves at 8.30, even if it is always late, it will still be the 8.25 because of the position it occupies within the system. The system differentiates elements, and on the basis of this differentiation it is able to assign a structured position and hence a meaning to these elements. There is nothing about the 'train-ness' or '8.25-ness' of the train that gives it such meaning – only the system can do that.

In a similar way, you might think of the pieces of a chess board (Saussure 1960: 110). If you lose one of the knights you can substitute anything for it, the dog from your *Monopoly* game or Mrs Peacock from *Cluedo*, and play just as well as long as the piece you substitute is different from the others on the board. You could change all the pieces and, as long as they were to fit into the system that distinguishes chess pieces, you could play the game just as well.

This clarifies Saussure's conception of the linguistic system and the assignment of meaning within it. We must not think of a term, or sign, as simply the fusion of a particular sound-image with a particular concept. Instead, 'language is a system of interdependent terms in which the value of each term results solely from the simultaneous presence of the others' (Saussure 1960: 114). For any clarity of definition, or linguistic value, to emerge, a thing must be related, first, to a dissimilar thing for which it can be exchanged, and, second, to a similar thing with which it can be compared. We might think of money: before we can know the worth of a coin we need to know, first, what it can be exchanged for or what it will buy, and, second, what it is worth in relation to similar things (other coins). Think about how you judge the value of a currency with which you are not familiar. You see how much your ten franc note will buy you and relate that note to the lesser coinage and the greater notes. Probably you convert the francs back into a currency with which you are familiar and judge it from this comparison.

Now how does this relate to words? Saussure offers the example of 'sheep' in English and 'mouton' in French (Saussure 1960: 115–16). On one level, these two terms signify the same thing. But in English there is also the word mutton, which refers solely to sheep that is made ready to eat. The French language does not have this term. As a consequence, the English word 'sheep' has a different value to the French 'mouton', even though it has the same signification. It means something that is of a certain order – a type of animal as opposed to something you can eat. The terms only have these meanings because of their differential nature. One could think of terms like dread and fear. The meaning is different but if the word dread were not available then any content it might have would belong to the word fear. Again, it is their differentiation that matters, and not anything that adheres inherently to the terms. Is it possible to specify the precise meaning of 'happiness' without resorting to distinguishing between it and 'joy', 'pleasure' and 'contentment', or indeed 'pain' and 'suffering'? Thus, a term is meaningful only because of its context or environment. That context is the system of language, the system of all other possible meanings, and it is this system, this structure, that determines the meanings and values of the elements.

This is a model of language as a closed structure made up of elements defined by their differential position within a system. The system determines the form of the utterances that may be made, and it functions because of its purely conventional nature. This system structures our thought and our experience of the world. 'Without language, thought is a vague uncharted nebula. There are no pre-existing ideas, and nothing is distinct before the appearance of language' (Saussure 1960: 112). Language provides the signifiers needed by thought, the way of distinguishing between different ideas or sets of ideas. Without language, thought would be indistinct and jumbled, while without thought, sounds would be meaningless. But the bond between them produces a system that marks off meaning and makes communication possible.

The Saussurean system suggests that for a term to mean anything, all other possibilities of meaning must be excluded. This could be an important way to think about politics and ideology. It is one thing when the word is a fairly banal one such as 'tree' or 'sheep'. It is quite another if the word is 'freedom', 'equality' or even 'politics'. These terms are crucial signifiers but their meaning is imprecise. The fixing of meaning for such terms could be thought to be a matter of social and political argument or struggle. Freedom could mean the absence of any restraint on an individual or the possibility that one can carry out certain actions. In order to have a clear meaning, other possible meanings must be excluded.

A very significant example might be the terms 'male' and 'female'. For each to contain a clear and precise definition, other possible definitions must be excluded. The two terms become opposites to the extent that we understand female to mean not-male and male to mean not-female. This leads to a way of organizing the world based on systematic differentiation and exclusion.

Saussure's description makes the linguistic system into a kind of hidden reservoir upon which we all must draw, yet of which we are not aware, a system that determines the possible patterns of our speech and thought. While subject to change and transformation, this system can lead us to certain conservative conclusions about our interpretation of the world. The system is self-defining, and it regulates itself internally without appeal to any external reality. Indeed, the system may be said to constitute its own reality.

For many investigators in the social and human sciences, language has become a useful paradigm for conceptualizing and analysing social formations. Saussure saw his work as the foundation for a new science of the sign – semiotics. Saussurean linguistics has provided a model of how a culture might work, and he has provided a focus on meaning production or signification that has proved fruitful for many theorists. In particular, the structuralist cultural theories of Claude Lévi-Strauss (1963) in anthropology and the early work of Roland Barthes (1983) in literary and cultural theory have been marked by his influence. These theorists focus on culture as itself a language, a system of signs deriving meaning from their position within a totality.

However, Saussure's influence has not been entirely benign. Like Sapir and Whorf, Saussure tends to assume the homogeneity and uniformity of a language system. By separating the system of *langue* from *parole*, Saussure hoped to create a viable object of scientific inquiry that could initially be examined 'synchronically' (in terms of its own systematicity) rather than 'diachronically' (in terms of its development over time). This downplays the vagaries and varieties of language use and its deployment within social and political contexts. If this homogeneity were considered to be a merely apparent uniformity, dependent on social factors for its maintenance, then the linguistic system would look more unstable, more actively politicized. In a sense, where Sapir and Whorf tended to make language seem as if it were the mystical product of the community, Saussure can make the community sound like the mystical product of language. For social or political theory, this is not helpful. Not only does this draw one into unhelpfully abstract realms, but it also makes it possible for theorists to conceive of social and political action as simply a branch of literary practice. There may be a value to such a perspective, but we do not want to reduce social action and thought to language systems, since those systems also have to be understood in terms of social action and context. However, such reductionism is not the only route out of Saussurean thought, especially if one understands the relations of difference within the system to be hierarchical relations that are permanently in political tension with one another.

THE 'LINGUISTIC TURN'

It is important to note that the ideas of Saussure, as well as those of Sapir and Whorf, are only part of a much larger 'linguistic turn' in philosophy and social thought that occurred initially towards the end of the nineteenth century and that extends well into the twentieth. Anglo-American philosophy focused on language as both the source of and the remedy to philosophical problems of logic. Perhaps most influential in the present context is Ludwig Wittgenstein. Wittgenstein's early work, as represented by the *Tractatus Logico-philosophicus* (1921), attempts to specify the precise logical structure of linguistic propositions, famously claiming that the 'limits of my language mean the limits of my world' (Wittgenstein 1994: proposition 5. 6). But his later work, primarily the *Philosophical Investigations* (1953), shifts perspective, recognizing that language is not uniform, but complex and multiplicitous. Wittgenstein uses the term 'language-games' to refer to patterns of linguistic practice, thus drawing attention to the way language works according to rules, just as in various games. The rules of a game determine what 'moves' are and are not allowed. In order to participate in a game you have to abide by the rules. If you don't, the game cannot be played. Each game has specific rules that allow it to function and to which everyone has to submit in order to play. Rules from one game are not applicable in any other – people playing different games with different rules cannot play with each other. Thus, Wittgenstein argues, to use language means to follow a rule and to follow a rule is to participate in a 'form of life'. The concept of 'language-games' draws attention to the fact that 'the speaking of language is part of an activity, or of a form of life' (Wittgenstein 1967: proposition 23).

There are language games in philosophy, in mathematics, within and between various groups – there are countless numbers and types, each with resemblances to others but each also quite specific and rule-bound. Interaction between them is not straightforward. We do not follow the rules because we choose to, we follow them, Wittgenstein says, 'blindly'. We may try to justify the way we follow a rule, but 'if I have exhausted the justifications I have reached bedrock and the spade is turned. Then I am inclined to say "This is simply what I do" ' (Wittgenstein 1967: proposition 217). Wittgenstein has been taken here to be suggesting that inhabiting a language involves our abiding by rules that constitute a specific form of life. That form of life is incommensurable with others, in that there are no external criteria according to which differing forms of life could rationally be ranked. This connection between language-games and 'forms of life' has had a significant impact on the social sciences, in that the investigation of a social order could be taken to require analysis of a 'form of life', understood as the sets of rule-bound practices people engage in. By allying this perspective to the Weberian notion that the object of social inquiry is meaning, or the meanings actions and events have for the people involved, Peter Winch aimed to find a methodological basis for the social sciences (see Chapter 1).

Wittgenstein's arguments have preoccupied Anglo-American traditions of philosophy. According to one interpretation, these arguments endorse a view of tradition as a necessary yet inexplicable part of human life. To live is to inhabit a specific tradition which gives meaning to existence. The justification for this tradition lies outside our remit, inaccessible to us within our closed language games. We might think of this as the conservative Wittgenstein. But Wittgenstein's work has also been given a more radical turn. In confining meaningful discourse within language-games, Wittgenstein develops a position sceptical of transcendent, universal claims to rationality or truth. If each language-game has its own set of rules (its own logic or rationality), then language-games, or different forms of life, constitute the world in a unique way. While this view reminds us of aspects of the Sapir–Whorf hypothesis, or indeed Saussure, unlike them Wittgenstein does not focus on supposedly uniform, overall linguistic systems, but on the multiplicitous nature of language-games. This significant difference of emphasis is often underestimated. In contrast with Winch's account, one could read the later Wittgenstein to be unsettling the very idea of a fixed rule by reformulating the relationship between language, thought and action (Staten 1985: 20).

Wittgenstein has been put to a wide range of uses in contemporary thought. For example, Lyotard (1984) has used the idea of language-games to launch a postmodernist attack on the very foundations of knowledge. Richard Rorty (1989) has adapted Wittgensteinian arguments to his version of philosophical, and political, pragmatism. Rorty tries to dismiss philosophical attempts rationally to explain the natural world or to justify social and political arrangements. Rationality is, for him, always bounded within a particular context. We should, he suggests, abandon the philosophical enterprise in favour of an exploration of the edifying possibilities of language. The language used in great literature, for example, can forge bonds of solidarity among particular groups of people. Literature can move and inspire us in pursuing the liberal aim of minimizing cruelty in our social relations. Neither Lyotard nor Rorty views language as a set of fixed rules that constitute our form of life. On the contrary, they highlight the disruptive possibilities that language offers. These theorists show us how language can be used to transform or to undermine the way we think about our social world.

It is in part these more radical uses of Wittgenstein's philosophy that have led to many of the most significant disputes in contemporary social and political thought. Now not only do we have arguments about what truth, justice, freedom or rationality are, but we also argue whether or not these are useful concepts at all. We must confront the possibility that we are confined within systems of meaning constituted by a language that we do not speak but that, rather, speaks us. If this is the case, can we really find out what truth or justice are in themselves? Is there any way for us to transcend the particular contexts of our language so that we might glimpse the universal truths of human life? (See also the section on language and context in Chapter 1 for a discussion of the questions concerning relativism and universalism that are raised here).

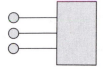

LANGUAGE AND SOCIAL POWER

Thus far, our discussion of language has operated at a rather abstract level. We have been concerned to conceptualize in a general sense the form and function of language and to relate this, broadly speaking, to epistemological concerns about the nature of human knowledge. Yet language contains nuances, and it is highly variable and specific in its usage. An investigation of language that operated only at a high level of abstraction, ignoring the concrete practices of language usage, would be seriously inadequate. Words can have differing effects depending on how we say them, where and when we say them and, indeed, who it is actually doing the saying. We judge people by the way they use language, by their articulacy, accent, phrasing and so forth, making fine distinctions as to their background, lifestyle or education.

While philosophers have tended to occupy the abstract level, sociologists and sociolinguists have focused on the concrete level of language usage, and a range of methods and approaches have been developed. For example, Schutz (1972) used language as a way of developing a phenomenological approach to sociology, seeking out the ways in which people in a society order their experience. Garfinkel's (1967) ethnomethodology is concerned with the everyday, basic level of social interaction, and it studies the 'indexicals' or suppositions of such discourse so as to uncover the way in which the social world is constructed and interpreted by social actors.

Sociolinguistics looks at the relations of language to education, to social class, to gender and so forth, mapping the distinctions of usage and the way such distinctions may be mechanisms of social control or the reproduction of social inequality (see Bernstein 1990). This is an important political issue in the context of curriculum development in schools (Crowley 1991). Linguists themselves have turned the precise tools of their art to unpicking the way written and spoken discourse can function ideologically in the form of bias found, for example, in news accounts. They show how these accounts can privilege certain points of view or interpretations (see Hodge and Kress 1993; Simpson

1993). But there is a danger here that a focus on the empirical and technical level of language usage can neglect the wider theoretical concerns that can connect this to a more general theory of social life. We need to match up grand theories of the social world with an analysis of this empirical level of usage. The work of Pierre Bourdieu is instructive here.

In opposition to the Saussurean paradigm, Bourdieu has stressed the need to understand language as not only a system but a particular kind of social practice. This entails looking at language in its social-historical context and not, as Bourdieu believes Lévi-Strauss to have done, considering it as an abstract system. Saussurean linguistics, according to Bourdieu, has been too easily transferred into other areas of study, and in this, language, culture and society have been turned into a theoretical construct, to the detriment of appreciating the social and historical nature of language and culture. In transferring the linguistic model into social science, theorists have introduced 'a Trojan horse', which separates the system from its usage (*langue* from *parole*) and so leads analysts to 'unexpected and sometimes preposterous reinterpretations' (Bourdieu 1991: 33). This has an ideological effect, to the extent that any effort to turn the language system into a fixed object of study separates it from its social conditions of production. It makes contingent products of history appear as unchanging structures of nature. Bourdieu's break with linguistic structuralism aims to reintroduce to the study of the symbolic domain questions of social power.

Bourdieu reminds us that there is no such thing as a homogeneous language system, and wherever there appears to be one, this signals the domination of one linguistic system. The establishment of a uniform language is the result of much political and physical struggle. The obvious example for Bourdieu is the enforced standardization of French after the Revolution, but the same process can be observed in numerous instances. Industrialization, the growth of nation states with national education systems and the changing division of labour necessitated the development of languages that would be both standardized and formalized. In colonial situations this has sometimes meant the violent eradication of traditional languages. This suggests that the dominance of forms of language is intimately related to the power structure of society, and this is precisely what Bourdieu wants us to understand.

Bourdieu's analysis of language and social power is embedded in, and informs, his theory of social practice. This is not the place to rehearse fully Bourdieu's theory, but it is important to have some sense of it here. In order to deal with the problematic duality of agency and structure, Bourdieu introduces the concept of 'habitus'. Habitus is the term he uses for 'systems of durable, transposable dispositions . . . principles which generate and organise practices and representations' (Bourdieu 1990: 52). In other words social action occurs within a framework which orients and directs. The habitus is both a field making social action possible and a product of social-historical practices. These practices generate a set of dispositions, habits and orientations made manifest by the social bodies inscribed within the habitus. We are all embedded in a habitus, and this leads us in certain directions and away from others. We are inculcated into a habitus from childhood as we learn the codes and rituals of our culture, not least in the way our bodies are trained to move in certain ways, to make certain appropriate gestures and so forth (see Chapter 6). For Bourdieu, language is not the model for understanding habitus, but one aspect of it, the rules of language usage themselves being subject to social-historical practices.

With this methodological and conceptual orientation Bourdieu looks at the practical usage of language, asking what governs judgements of the appropriateness of speech. Within one habitus there may be one 'correct' way of speaking, and in others a different one. Bourdieu relates this to social power and hierarchy. Public discourse is structured in certain ways, the ways of the bourgeoisie, that we learn in school and university. Within this framework, those who speak within the habitus of working-class culture will find it harder to act, will feel that their voice is not appropriate.

In the present context, we might think Bourdieu to be closer to Wittgenstein than to Saussure. While Saussure was concerned with developing a science of the structure of language, Wittgenstein, along with the so-called British 'ordinary language' philosophers, started from the empirical level of language usage. But Bourdieu is interested in making specific sociological analyses rather than developing a general and speculative philosophy of language. This difference is clear from Bourdieu's engagement with the 'speech-acts' theory of Austin (1962), one of the most important of these 'ordinary language' philosophers. Austin introduced the idea of linguistic 'performatives'. This refers to linguistic actions, not merely comments or observations on the world but actions in themselves. Austin offers the examples of saying 'I do' in a marriage ceremony or 'I name this ship . . .'. These uses of particular words are themselves action, not comments on other actions. In saying that you are naming a ship, you have already completed the act of naming it. Austin argues that for such a speech act to be effective, or 'felicitous', it must be part of some ritual that sanctions its appropriateness – saying 'I do' is effective only within a proper marriage ceremony. While Austin is most interested in what this means for language, Bourdieu regards this observation as a recognition of the way language is governed by certain social 'institutions', or rules of practice, that confer legitimacy on certain usages of language. Thus, 'the use of language, the manner as much as the substance of discourse, depends on the social position of the speaker, which governs the access he can have to the language of the institution, that is, to the official, orthodox and legitimate speech'

(Bourdieu 1991: 109). One must be socially authorized to say such things effectively even as one reproduces authority in the saying. For Bourdieu, one cannot find in language the principles of its own governance or the power of its manifestations. Authority comes to language from the outside; language 'at most represents this authority, manifests and symbolises it' (Bourdieu 1991: 109).

When describing the operations that go on within the social field, Bourdieu often uses the language of economics. There is a linguistic 'market', and utterances (or ways of uttering) have variable 'values'. Within the education habitus, certain ways of speaking and writing, the 'official' language code, have a higher value than more colloquial ways of articulating. This can be exchanged for status, qualifications and consequently high-paid employment and social power. Speakers may thus be said to have different amounts of linguistic 'capital'. This prejudices the market against those with working-class speech patterns or on the basis of ethnicity or gender. Hierarchy is inscribed within language and reproduced by it, but is not reducible to it. This leads to a theory of symbolic power and symbolic violence. Bourdieu can analyse the way power relations are made and sustained in disguise through symbolic form, and the way they circulate within and around a social formation. In turn, he relates this to a theory of the political 'field' and the structuring of political discourses, slogans, programmes and so forth.

Bourdieu's work allies sophisticated theory to revealing empirical observation, and it has focused on a wide range of phenomena. Within this work, his critique of Saussure is a necessary corrective to excessive and/or indulgent appropriations. Bourdieu restates the significance of the social conditions of language usage for theories of society and social power. Such a restatement refers us back to the classic dichotomy of social theory – that of structure and agency. In theories of society, how much weight should we give to the 'free' actions of individuals and how much to the determining effects of social structures? Language-based social theories pose this dilemma rather starkly. Post-Saussurean structuralism has tended to be seen as over-emphasizing the effects of structure. But those accounts that focus solely on individual agency have to respond to the problem of structure or run the risk of lapsing into a simple voluntarism that naively renders social theory redundant.

Thus Bourdieu attempts to find a way between the two poles of structure and agency. A similar effort has been the core preoccupation of Anthony Giddens in developing his concept of 'structuration'. Where language-based philosophies tend to think of rules as abstracted, structured principles that determine social action, Giddens has tried to elucidate the mutual dependence of structure and agency. He argues that structure can only be understood in terms of rules that are themselves reaffirmed only in the act of their being followed. Structure is a medium for the constitution of social practices, and as such is enabling as well as constraining. Furthermore, structures are dependent on their reproduction by being acted upon. In other words, social agents act on the basis of structured rules but those rules only exist because they shape social actions. Thus, 'structural properties of social systems are both the medium and the outcome of the practices that constitute those systems' (Giddens 1979: 69). By setting structure and agency in this mutually dependent and reflexive context, Giddens is able to stress the potential fluidity of social rules and the need to understand them in a broader context than that of abstract structures. Crucially, he focuses on the reproduction of social systems. This emphasis on thinking of social structures in terms of their usage and reproduction means paying attention to the effects of time and space and to the forms of power and domination that shape (and are shaped by) them. Here power is understood as the capacity to transform social situations, and as such it is intrinsic to society (see Chapter 4).

Giddens, then, like Bourdieu, seeks to rethink the relationship between structure and agency. Both, particularly in terms of the linguistic paradigm of social investigation, show that it is necessary to think about language (or social structures) in terms of its manifestations within, or as, social practice as well as in terms of abstract systems. But we need not conclude that language systems must be collapsed into a methodological individualism. Language and other social structures certainly do have a conditioning effect on social thought and practice. Bourdieu's methodological critique of Saussureanism has merits, as does Giddens's critique of Lévi-Strauss's structuralism. Both emphasize the need to focus not only on deep structures but also on the practical nature of social actions or linguistic utterances in the context of social power.

Giddens's theory of structuration takes us beyond the narrow realm of theories of language. But there are other linguistic approaches to social theory that focus on both language systems and social practice, and these have also tried to link such a theoretical framework to an understanding power. It is to an exploration of these theories that we now turn, from language and 'habitus' to discourse.

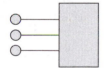

FROM LANGUAGE TO DISCOURSE

Recent social and political theory has shifted from a focus on language, narrowly conceived, to utilize the broader concept of discourse. The term 'discourse' is used in a number of different ways by contemporary theorists. Often it refers simply to language as it is used and to the way language is shaped into larger units consisting of connected sets of propositions or statements. Our concern here is with the use of the concept as a way of broadening out theories of language to make them more generally applicable to the social and political world, taking account of the 'empirical' level without losing sight of necessary theoretical issues. In this context, 'discourse' refers both to the way language systematically organizes concepts, knowledge and experience and to the way in which it excludes alternative forms of organization. Thus, the boundaries between language, social action, knowledge and power are blurred.

This has made discourse a crucial concept for social and political analysis. Laclau and Mouffe (1985) interpret the fixing of discursive structures as part of the process of securing hegemony (see Chapters 7 and 8). That is to say, domination may be secured or legitimated by establishing a particular system of meaning as being universally applicable. In a similar way to Saussure, when he argued that meaning derives from difference, Laclau and Mouffe argue that a political discourse fixes itself against a difference in the form of an oppositional antagonism. For example, we might say that the political conflict in Northern Ireland is structured around mutually antagonistic discourses that define, and limit, the identities of Protestant and Catholic. Thus the social identities are established on the basis of their differentiation. To explain such a conflict, discourse theory connects linguistic philosophy to theories of culture and identity or subjectivity (see Chapters 5 and 7).

Discourse theories, such as that of Laclau and Mouffe, derive in part from the early work of Foucault, who understood discourse to be constitutive of social subjects, organizing social relationships into conceptual frameworks. For him, discourse analysis is concerned with investigating the variable 'discursive formations' which make it possible for certain statements to be made and attitudes to be held, while others are excluded (see Chapter 2). A discursive formation is a 'set of rules' by which objects, subjects and strategies are formed, and the concern of analysis is with the relationships between 'institutions, economic and social processes, behavioural patterns, systems of norms, techniques, types of classification, modes of characterisation' (Foucault 1972: 45).

Discourse theory is especially dependent on the work of Jacques Derrida. As we have seen, Wittgenstein argued against his own initial proposition that language could delineate the fundamental logical principles of the world, and instead proposed that there is a multiplicity of language games. Derrida advances a similar theoretical approach. He criticizes structuralist theories (such as that of Saussure but also Lévi-Strauss), stressing that language is not a closed monolithic structure: 'more than one language' he declares, 'no more of one language' (Derrida 1986: 15). For Derrida there cannot be a universal language, theory cannot make itself applicable across all contexts. Meaning is intrinsically unstable and marked by what he terms *différance*. This is a term with a double meaning. It means both difference and deferral (the 'a' he inserts into the term is silent in spoken

French), indicating that meaning is both established by differentiation and deferred, or never quite lined up behind the term that is meant to refer to it.

Derrida's aim here is to query the certainty of the Western philosophical tradition by questioning how concepts can be understood free from their linguistic context. He argues that philosophers have tried to suppress the problem of language so that their concepts can appear neatly lined up with thought and true reality. For example, Derrida shows how philosophers have consistently privileged the act of speech over that of writing. Speech is treated as offering the moment of authentic unity between the word, the thought and the world. Writing, by contrast, is conceived as a secondary form, always suspect and prone to contamination, since it is severed from the original moment of enunciation (perhaps this is why we expect witness testimony in law courts to be delivered vocally and in person, or academics to deliver their lectures even when they are simply reading out an already written set of notes). Somehow we think that what is said is more true or authentic if it is actually being said by someone we can see saying it. We think that speech offers transparent and unified meaning, whereas writing must be secondary, since it cannot offer such certainty.

For Derrida, this derives from the kind of metaphysics advanced by Aristotle, where speech, thought and the real world all line up neatly and harmoniously. Derrida argues against such a perspective, which he calls a 'metaphysics of presence', the idea that language, thought and meaning could be directly present to one another, giving us a pure and unmediated access to the world. For Derrida, such a view actually limits our view of the world, since it posits some sort of perfect ground of unity or wholeness outside of our immediate experience but to which all thought must ultimately conform. This ground might be the source of universal and ultimate truth guaranteed by God or, in modernity, by the idea of 'Man' as the centre of the universe. Such a perspective is maintained only through a kind of violence which gives a concept or term fixity through the suppression of its opposite. We have seen how Saussure argued that meaning derives from difference within a system. Lévi-Strauss attempted to establish fundamental binary oppositions (man/woman, raw/cooked and so on) that structured culture and perception. For Derrida, these oppositions (like that of speech/writing) are maintained in a hierarchical form, but they do not correspond to necessary, universal truths. To understand this we must move beyond structuralism, which tends to regard the movement of meaning as restricted and fixed by some sort of centre. Instead we should recognize that structures are 'decentred' and that the unity, or 'presence', of a system is constantly disrupted by the 'play' of signifiers.

Feminist writers such as Cixous (1980b) have adapted Derrida to show how women are systematically oppressed or excluded by phallocentric systems of meaning. A series of oppositions (such as male/female, culture/nature, active/passive, head/heart) structure our culture, lending authority and power to the first term while subordinating the second, making it impossible for women (or woman) to be thought of in a way that abstracts them from their subjugation. The challenge, then, is to develop a way of writing, and thinking, that utilizes the tendency of 'play' to undermine the structure and open up new possibilities.

The Derridean approach presupposes a multiplicity of meanings that undermines the possibility of ever fixing the meaning of the world once and for all. But we do not live as if there is no secure meaning to our social world, we live as if things can be understood as fixed or given. Derrida shows how meaning can appear to be fixed through oppositions and exclusions, but the first term in a binary opposition can never be completely stable or secure, since it is dependent on that which is excluded. Derrida's philosophy, sometimes called deconstruction, aims to challenge this not by abolishing the division or simply reversing the hierarchy. The ultimate aim is instead to dismantle the hierarchy by showing how philosophical discourse which is structured around such oppositions, and which allows them to establish the illusion of transparency or presence, must at certain points fall apart because it is dependent on what it excludes. Derrida thus reads philosophical texts by searching out the points where this dependency is inadvertently revealed.

Intrinsic to the political concept of discourse that derives from Derrida is the claim that such structures are thoroughly contingent. That is to say, they arise out of specific circumstances, and while they may come to dominate our thinking at a particular time, it could always have been otherwise. This is related to Saussure's argument about the arbitrary nature of the sign, but the concept of contingency also stresses the instability of signification, the ever contested nature of meaning. Discourses produce an apparent necessity to meaning, they make things look natural and obvious, but such necessity or objectivity emerges only within a discursive structure. Indeed, discursive structures may be understood as attempts to fix meaning and to obscure contingency. This enables us to establish a relationship between theories of discourse and the study of ideology (although the traditional Marxist conception of ideology is problematized by discourse theory). We can look at the ways in which meaning and symbolic practices function to maintain a status quo or to render the domination of some over others an apparently natural fact, bearing in mind that our conceptual organization of the world is never finally fixed or closed.

This is what Laclau and Mouffe (1985) attempt to do with their theory of hegemony. They show how politics is structured around notions of collective identity such as class, nation, gender and so forth. But for Laclau and Mouffe, this identity does not derive from anything necessarily intrinsic to social experience, and such identities do not have any automatically given primacy. They are derived from the play of discourses that attempt to establish an identity as fixed or given. Politics is then understood by discourse theory as the process of establishing such identities and exclusions. But this must be grasped as a process that is never complete. Identities are always unstable, and they may give way to other, newer, forms of social identity.

Although Laclau and Mouffe use the concept of discourse, it is important to realize that discourse, in their usage, does not refer just to language. They, like Foucault, see discourse as also giving rise to definite forms of social experience or institutions that perpetuate and add to the legitimacy or appearance of fixity of a discourse. For example, think of national identity. We believe in national identity because of the apparent fixity both of the discourses that establish what it is and of that to which it refers. This is done in part by opposing one national identity (say Englishness) to others (say Frenchness). An English national identity can then be defined by opposition to the French. This discourse can work on all sorts of things in a culture. English manners, food, religion, values and so on can all be opposed to French, so as to make Englishness seem like a definite and fixed category. This notion of Englishness may also be used to define certain groups (such as ethnic minorities or lesbians and gay men) as behaving in a way, or having values, opposed to this sense of Englishness. But this level of discourse will also give rise to institutions that perpetuate it – we will have a nationally based education system, a nationally based media network and so forth, and these will lend credence to the sense of a specific and inviolable 'Englishness'.

It is important to realize that Laclau and Mouffe are not turning everything into language and forgetting about the real world. Rather, they argue that meaning and action are not strictly speaking separable, that the division of 'the social' and 'the discursive' is not clear cut. They argue that 'every identity or discursive object is constituted in the context of an action' (Laclau and Mouffe 1990: 103). As such, nothing can be justified by an appeal to its being natural or pre-social. For Laclau and Mouffe, 'natural facts are also discursive facts . . . the idea of nature . . . is itself the result of a slow and complex historical and social construction' (*ibid.*). This does not mean that things don't exist, but that they exist for us, as social and linguistic creatures, through our discourses that order them and make them accessible to us as objects which we then act upon. As they put it:

> this does not put into question the fact that this entity which we call a stone exists, in the sense of being present here and now, independently of my will . . . its being a stone depends on a way of classifying objects that is historical and contingent. If there were no human beings on earth, those objects that we call stones would be there nonetheless; but they would not be 'stones',

because there would be neither mineralogy nor a language capable of classifying them and distinguishing them from other objects.

(Laclau and Mouffe 1990: 103)

It is not Laclau and Mouffe's point that something, say 'Englishness' to follow my example, does not really exist, or that there is a real or true identity simply obscured by ideological discourse. The identity exists because of discourse and is not external to it. As it can never be totally fixed or closed, it will fall into moments of crisis (where the contradictions of the discourse are exposed) and will be challenged, perhaps by other identities or other versions of 'Englishness'. Such a discourse attempts to fix meaning and deny the possibility that our social world could be ordered differently.

Discourse theory certainly suggests the possibility of adequately matching up theories of language and semiotics with an understanding of social processes so that we can make specific analyses of a social, political situation. It entails a broadening out of the concept of language to include non-linguistic elements, and thus blurs the boundaries separating concepts such as language, thought and action. This latter claim, while clearly part of the twentieth-century tradition of social theory, also poses a challenge to the dualism of structure and agency which informs much of sociological theory and method. In political theory, the ideas of discourse theory have been very useful in analysing politics, and have been turned to the study of diverse phenomena such as Thatcherism (Hall 1988), the politics of race and sexuality (Smith 1994) and South Africa (Norval 1996).

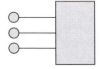

CONCLUSIONS

Reflection on language has had a significant place in twentieth-century social and political theory. This chapter has touched on only a part of that significance. Other chapters in this book show the way in which an analysis of language can interweave with other preoccupations, thus generating new insights and posing new challenges. Students new to social theory must assess for themselves the perspective, or combination of perspectives, they find most convincing: the anthropological linguistic determinism of Sapir and Whorf; Saussure's innovative but limiting structuralism (or the appropriations of Saussure's thought by Lévi-Strauss or Barthes); the British tradition of linguistic philosophy, especially Wittgenstein's imaginative meditations; or the French tradition that leads to Derridean deconstruction. On another side, there is Bourdieu's detailed attention to language in societies of unequal power, or the linguists and sociolinguists with their range of detailed analyses. The field is huge and varied. This is a testament to the importance we now place on the problematic nature of articulation, signification and meaning in contemporary societies.

Such inquiry into language is motivated by the best of theoretical intentions – a concern as to how human beings come to be social, how they come to make sense of, and to share, the world around them. With that comes a second, no less important concern, as to whether or not we are making the best sense of the world we can. This raises the possibility that the world is made to make sense one way rather than another because it suits the interests of some for it to do so. There is a hard political edge to even the most abstract of linguistic theories, an edge which, in some cases at least, forms the basis for a demand that the intrinsically political nature of meaning be recognized. Any democratic form of politics must in turn acknowledge the inherent multiplicity of the political and social world. With this in mind, it seems appropriate to conclude with another quotation from Saussure:

> In the lives of individuals and societies, language is a factor of greater importance than any other. For the study of language to remain solely the business of a handful of specialists would be a quite unacceptable state of affairs.
>
> (Saussure, cited in Crowley 1991: ii)

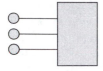

QUESTIONS

1 Do you think the shape of our language influences the shape of our thinking?

2 What are the key points for social and political theory in Saussure's theory of language?

3 How important is it to understand language primarily in its social context?

4 Do theories about the relationship between power and discourse help us to think about the politics of language?

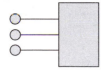

FURTHER READING

This is a large and difficult area of study, but there are some useful introductory guides. The student new to the field should be wary, since the field of linguistic philosophy and analysis is very varied and not all concepts have uncontroversial meanings or interpretations. You may find that a concept used in one way by political theorists crops up in a different context when used by literary theorists.

A useful summary of the structuralism of Saussure and Lévi-Strauss (including some material on the Sapir–Whorf hypothesis and a brief explanation of Derrida) is Hawkes, *Structuralism and Semiotics* (1977). Another good introduction is Culler's *Saussure* (1985). A particularly user-friendly introduction to this field is Stuart Hall's 'The work of representation', available as the first chapter of Hall (ed.), *Representation: Cultural Representation and Signifying Practices* (1997). This volume also contains analyses of cultural forms which might illuminate some of the perspectives sketched out in this and other chapters. In the same series, Woodward (ed.), *Identity and Difference* (1997) contains an introductory chapter by the editor covering concepts such as difference as well as Lévi-Strauss's model of structuralism and other relevant themes. Johnson, *Derrida* (1997) is a useful short introduction and is easier going than Norris, *Derrida* (1987). The latter has more depth but it does seek to confine Derrida to a philosophical context. Further introductory material on Lévi-Strauss and Derrida can be found in Skinner (ed.), *The Return of Grand Theory in the Human Sciences* (1985).

Richard Jenkins's short text on Bourdieu is a useful general introduction to his work, and it should help to place his account of language in its broader context. There are good introductory and analytical essays on Bourdieu in Thompson, *Studies in the Theory of Ideology* (1984). The concept of discourse and its application to political analysis is introduced in an accessible manner by David Howarth in his contribution to Marsh and Stoker (eds), *Theory and Method in Political Science* (1995). None of these can adequately substitute for the original texts of original thinkers, which, although difficult and challenging, can, if taken slowly, introduce readers to the giddy pleasures of contemporary social and political theory.

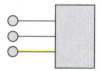

4 POWER

Iain MacKenzie

INTRODUCTION

Everyone has a sense of what it means to be powerful or powerless. We say people are powerful when they can wield influence over others. This may be because they have positions of prominence within society, such as in government, or because they are wealthy, charismatic or 'went to the right school'. The powerless, whom we typically think of as the majority of any society, are those without all such advantages of money, rank or circumstance. Just as 'cold' is defined as the absence of 'heat', so powerlessness is defined as the absence of power. This implies that we know what power is and that we can unproblematically describe and categorize its various manifestations. However, the whole drift of contemporary social and political theory is in the other direction. Power is an 'essentially contested concept' (Gallie 1955/6; Connolly 1983), one whose meaning and application is inherently disputed. There is no consensus among theorists regarding the nature of power, the way it operates in the social and political world, the manner in which it relates to associated concepts (such as authority, domination, resistance and empowerment) or its usefulness in the construction of a critical perspective on the legacy of modernity and the Enlightenment.

Once our common-sense ideas about power are put to the test, we find that they are much less coherent and persuasive than we might expect. One of the central tasks of contemporary theory is to explore the complex world of power relations that suffuses our everyday experience. As we shall see, it has exposed multifaceted operations of power in aspects of our lives that everyday definitions do not, and could not, illuminate. That there is no agreement about the exact nature of social and political power has not prevented the emergence of insightful and innovative work. Indeed, it may be that a little conceptual fuzziness aids interrogation of the social and political world.

Beside such analytical problems, discussions about power must also grapple with a sense of the historical development of the concept within the changing social and political world. Although it has always been one of political theory's primary concerns, the rise of modern governmental institutions (see Chapter 8) gave new life to debates about power. With the birth of liberal democracies came the need to analyse exactly where governments got their power from, how it was maintained and whether or not it was used to dominate people rather than serve them. The classics of liberal political theory are of crucial importance, therefore, in discussion of the nature and domains of power. For this reason, the chapter begins with a very brief account of Hobbes's definition of power. Alongside the rise of modern governments, the Enlightenment pursuit of a rationally ordered social and political sphere gave new impetus to debates about power. One of reason's main tasks was to expose the traditional hierarchies of power that fuelled dogmatic obedience to others, so that individuals could gain a new maturity and exercise their capacity for free and critical thought (Kant 1991). This project raised new questions. What is the relationship between power and reason? When, if ever, can the use of power be justified rationally? As we shall see, these questions resonate in contemporary debates between feminists, poststructuralists and critical theorists.

The huge social and political changes that have rocked the world since the early modern and Enlightenment periods have radically altered the context in which these questions are asked. It is no longer the case that reason and modernity are always seen as victorious in the battle with power. The modern legacy of elite domination of liberal institutions, invidious individualism, class division, patriarchal domination and colonial oppression means that contemporary thinkers are as likely to use a theory of power to criticize rationalization processes as they are to use a theory of rationality to criticize the detrimental effects of power in society. This will become increasingly evident as we progress through the different accounts of power below.

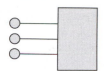

THE CLASSICAL DEFINITION

In *Leviathan* (1651), Hobbes presented one of the first systematic definitions of human power. He wrote: 'The Power of a Man, (to take it Universally) is his present means, to obtain some future apparent Good. And is either Original, or Instrumental' (Hobbes 1991: 62). 'Original' power, which Hobbes also calls 'Natural' power, designates the 'eminence' of an individual's 'body or mind' over other individuals. The examples he gives are 'extraordinary Strength, Form, Prudence, Arts, Eloquence, Liberality, Nobility'. 'Instrumental' powers are those acquired through the exercise of original power (or, as Hobbes adds, by fortune) and are a means to the end of acquiring more power. Under this category Hobbes lists 'Riches, Reputation, Friends and the secret working of God, which men call good luck'. There are three elements of this definition worth highlighting. First, Hobbes defines power as a capacity of individuals, in both its 'Natural' and 'Instrumental' forms. Second, power is the *potential* to obtain that which the individual desires. This does not require the fulfilment of desires; rather, it represents the means by which desires may be obtained. Lastly, power is relative. The 'eminence' of an individual's power depends upon the extent to which it exceeds the power of other individuals. Thus, for one person to have power others must lack it.

The merit of Hobbes's account is the insight it gives into the different ways power is manifest in society – through strength and friendship, eloquence and money, even prudence and good luck. Yet by defining power as a relative capacity or potential to attain that which an individual desires, Hobbes opens the flood gates to a myriad of competing and contradictory phenomena that muddy the waters of his account. Power is reduced to a list of faculties and capacities that have too little in common to form a useful conceptual category. This is a problem for many accounts of power, and is especially manifest in Hobbes's own work.

Hobbes's own definition of power is a crucial contribution to his overall thesis that people without a source of authority to bind them together will dissolve into a chaotic, warring mass of individuals all striving for a power that none can hold absolutely. This grave situation is avoided to the extent that individuals institute a Sovereign power, 'the Leviathan', to rule over them. This is achieved by agreeing with each other to give up their power and authorize the Leviathan to be their representative, with the sole aim of making sure by all necessary means that there is no return to the terrors of the 'state of nature'. 'The greatest of human powers, is that which is compounded of the powers of most men, united by consent, in one person, Natural, or Civil, that has the use of all their powers, depending on his will: such is the power of the common-wealth' (Hobbes 1991: 62).

There are two main problems raised by this account. First, it is hard to imagine how the Sovereign authority is instituted, given the diverse list of capacities, potentials and natural gifts that Hobbes includes as powers to be surrendered. As Hindess (1996: 38) puts it, 'It is far from clear that the eloquence of one person, the strength of another, and the reputation of a third, can be added together to form a power greater than any one of them.' Indeed, the nature of powers such as a natural gift for eloquence, artistry or even 'good luck' make it hard to imagine how these could be 'given up' at all. Second, while Hobbes provides a list of the attributes of powerful individuals, this does not adequately capture the more complex notion of collective power and its subsidiary, governmental power. Hobbes mistakenly construes the power of the commonwealth over the individual contractors to be equivalent to the power one individual has over another. This gives an implausible picture of the forms of power specific to the machinations of government – for example, military, bureaucratic and state-economic power.

Retaining the broad outline of Hobbes's theory (though he added that people only have power when they are able to carry out their own will), Weber (1947) recognized that a general definition of human power must be augmented by a discussion of the particular ways in which power is manifest in society. Although Weber believed that it was beyond the remit of sociology to assess the power of 'the social relations in a drawing room', the sociologist could, and should, assess generalized 'forms of domination' within society. He conceived of domination in terms of two 'ideal types': 'domination by virtue of a constellation of interests' (especially, domination by economic monopolization) and 'domination by virtue of authority' (the 'purest type' of such domination being 'patriarchal, magisterial or princely power'). Each type of domination could be legitimate or illegitimate. Of particular interest is Weber's account of the three sources of *legitimate* domination or 'authority' – traditional, charismatic and legal-rational – each of which supports claims to the *rightful* exercise of power over others. Traditional authority is based on the authority of deeply embedded social customs. Charismatic authority rests upon the power of an individual's personality to persuade, coax and influence others. Legal-rational authority derives from the respect people have for the formal qualities of the 'rule of law'. This last source of authority is preferred by Weber as the basis for state power, as it takes authority away from individuals and places it in formal procedures and roles. That said, Weber also perceived the dangers involved in an increasingly 'bureaucratic society' that placed the rational drive for greater efficiency above the dangers of increasing estrangement from the organizations that run our lives. His analysis of the 'iron cage' of bureaucracy created by the increasingly legal-rational justification of authority in modern political regimes gives the classical Hobbesian definition a more contemporary sceptical and ambiguous twist, as well as informing much of twentieth-century social and political theory. In particular, Weber's analysis of state power and the link he makes between this and broader processes of social bureaucratization has provided the framework within which contemporary debates about the nature of the state have taken place (see, for example, Pierson 1996).

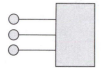

POWER AND INDIVIDUALS

A rather different approach to the nature of power in democratic societies, though one retaining the idea that power operates essentially through individuals, emerged within American political science. Robert Dahl (1957) embraced the techniques of behaviourist social science to analyse the operation of power in American society. What he calls his 'intuitive idea of power' is the claim that 'A has power over B to the extent that A can get B to do something that B would not otherwise do.' Dahl defines power in this way so that it is amenable to social scientific measurement. If measurement is possible, then it is also possible to compare distributions of power operating within, or between, given political communities. For Dahl, this meant that the social scientist could understand the operation of power within nation states like the USA by comparing the nature of 'decision-making' within political communities and by examining who has a say in making decisions, how often and how successfully. Conducting such research in New Haven, Connecticut, Dahl (1961) concluded that the operation of power throughout the USA was not concentrated in the hands of one elite but was dispersed across a plurality of elite groups (hence the label 'pluralist' for his conception of American politics and society). While each of these elite groups wielded power in relation to decisions regarding one particular set of issues, none of them held sway on all issues.

While Dahl's behaviourist definition of power continues to be influential within political science, modifications of it have been proposed. Most notably, Bachrach and Baratz (1962) argued that Dahl took account of only one 'face' of power. They contended that in addition to the power of decision-making, Dahl should also have considered the power of limiting decisions, or agenda-setting. To Dahl's definition of power they added the idea that power also involved 'the practice of limiting the scope of actual decision-making to "safe" issues by manipulating the dominant community values, myths, and political institutions and procedures' (Bachrach and Baratz 1963: 632). This 'second face' of power is an important development for understanding how dominant social and cultural groups may subtly wield power in society over and above the power of actual decision-making, by the mobilization and institutionalization of bias within decision-making bodies (see also Schattscheider 1960). An insightful and often cited application of this model of power to the politics of air pollution can be found in Crenson (1971).

That said, behaviourist definitions of power, like those of Dahl and Bachrach and Baratz, are prey to the general problems of behaviourism. First, it is difficult to imagine what exactly counts as a 'change of behaviour' and how exactly this is to be measured. Can we really measure how much agents or agencies have 'done what they would not otherwise have done' or how much their choices are limited by bias? Second, not all changes in behaviour are due to the effects of power. Many changes of behaviour could more sensibly be put down to discussion, advice, revelation and so on. The most telling criticism of behaviourism also applies to the definitions offered by Hobbes and Weber. As Steven Lukes (1974) has argued, both classical and behaviourist definitions of power are based upon the problematic claims of 'methodological individualism'. Methodological individualism is a procedure of social inquiry that privileges the will and intentions of individuals when examining society and gives no credence to the idea that social structures and social forces may exist autonomously from these individual wills. This assumption raises two problems, each of which has appeared in the discussion so far. First, an individualistic premise misses the point when talking of collective power: 'collectivities and organisations are made up of individuals – but the power they exercise cannot be simply conceptualised in terms of individuals' decisions or behaviour' (Lukes 1974: 22). While all the authors mentioned try to understand the power of governments, organizations and collectivities, they tend to conceive of these agencies as reducible to the actions of key individuals or as if they were actually individual agents with a recognizable will of their own. Second, the assumption that power arises as a result of individual desires ignores the way power shapes our sense of what we desire. Lukes argues that we cannot understand power if we do not understand the way it operates to block our true desires, which he labels our 'real objective interests'.

This gives rise to the following definition: 'A exercises power over B when A affects B in a manner contrary to B's interests' (Lukes 1974: 34). The reason Lukes calls this view of power a 'radical' one is that it depends upon the evaluation of interests in the social and political world. Where the behaviourists were concerned only with outcomes, Lukes links outcomes to interests, such that any given outcome must be *evaluated* to see if it is in the interest of the agent or not. This has some profound consequences for what actually counts as a power relationship. For example, two sides to a dispute may come to an agreement about the best policy proposals to adopt. For the traditional liberal and behaviourist view, this agreement should be viewed as a mutually acceptable arrangement among rational actors that does not involve the operation of power. As Lukes points out, though, if the agreement works against the real interests of one party, even if that party is unaware of this, then it should be thought of as an example of a power relation. Where Dahl's one-dimensional view of power takes people 'as they are', and the two-dimensional view of Bachrach and Baratz accepts that people's desires may be 'submerged or concealed', the radical three-dimensional view of power 'maintains that men's wants may themselves be the product of a system which works against their interests' (Lukes 1974: 34).

While Lukes's definition of power in terms of interests is a useful rejoinder to the behaviourist concern with outcome, it only raises new problems of its own. Precisely because of the evaluative element now built into the definition of power, it is not clear that it could ever be used as a tool for the social scientific analysis of power. Of course, this is only a problem if one is concerned to adopt a model of social research that apes the methods of the physical sciences (see Chapter 1). Leaving that to one side, the idea of 'real, objective interests' was never properly developed within Lukes's framework. Another problem with this account of power is the unresolved tension regarding the extent to which structural features of the social sphere determine our interests. While Lukes's radical view pointed towards background determining structures, he was keen to maintain a sense of active human agency, so as not to relinquish the idea of moral responsibility. The upshot of this tension, as Clegg (1989: 103) puts it, is that 'agency and structure are not dialectically synthesised. Agency remains predominant and structure has been marginalised.'

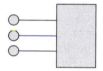

POWER AND SOCIETY

While Lukes struggled to unify structure and agency in his work, other contemporary theorists tended towards accounts of power devoid of reference to individual interests or intentions. In this section, we will examine the work of two very different approaches to power that none the less share the idea that it must be understood, first and foremost, as a feature of social systems. The first is the functionalist account of power developed by Talcott Parsons, while the second is the Marxist account outlined by Nicos Poulantzas.

Parsons (1990) shifted the emphasis of sociological research away from the study of how people act in society to the study of how society structures the way people act. Correspondingly, his account of power does not feature a theory of individual intentions or capacities. 'Power', as Parsons (1990: 265–6) saw it

> is a generalised facility or resource in the society . . . It is the capacity to mobilise the resources of the society for the attainment of goals for which a general 'public' commitment has been

made, or may be made. It is mobilisation, above all, of the action of persons and groups, which is binding on them by virtue of their position in the society.

We can clarify this in three ways. First, to say that power is generalized is to imply that it is a property of social systems, not a property of individuals or groups within society acting as if they were individuals. Importantly, this challenges the (Hobbesian) view that power in one individual or group is relative to the lack of power in another. For Parsons (1963), such 'constant-sum' approaches – where the amount of power in a given society is constant and therefore the distribution of that power must be relative – fail to see that power is a 'variable-sum' phenomenon, whereby power may increase or decrease within society as a whole. Second, and echoing Weber, Parsons sees power as closely allied to authority. In contrast to Weber, though, power is the right to pursue the *collective* interests of the social system, not just the interest of one *section* of society. This distances Parsons from the Weberian concern to link power to forms of domination. Third, Parsons's conception of power as a capacity to mobilize 'public commitments' develops the link between power and empowerment, to be discussed in the next section with reference to the work of Arendt and Habermas.

There is merit in Parsons's account of power as a social reservoir from which individuals, groups and governments draw to benefit the whole social system. Parsons is right, at least to some extent, when he suggests that power is the medium of social and political transactions in a manner directly analogous to the way money is the medium of economic transactions. Given this analogy, however, it is impossible to make a distinction between the legitimate and the illegitimate use of power. For this reason, his conception of power serves to reinforce established inequities and divisions within society. Although Parsons recognizes the counter-intuitive character of his approach, it is difficult to shake the strong sense that we lose something if we situate power too far away from domination. As Giddens puts it, Parsons defines out of existence 'two obvious facts': that decisions by collectively authorized governments may none the less serve 'sectional' interests (the interests of one group over another), and that 'the most radical conflicts in society stem from struggles for power' (Giddens 1968: 265). As with the behaviourists, the problems with Parsons's account of power derive from the image he has of society as a whole (see, for example, Habermas 1987a). By conceiving of power as a resource that sustains the functioning of society, he does not do justice to the idea that power is often the key factor in disturbing, not sustaining, social systems.

A rather different societal interpretation of power, but one especially concerned to highlight the way power serves sectional interests, can be found in the work of Poulantzas. In *Political Power and Social*

Classes, Poulantzas develops a specifically Marxist theory of power based on a class analysis of social and political life. 'Power', he says, 'is the capacity of a social class to realise its specific objective interests' (Poulantzas 1973: 104).

For Poulantzas, 'the frame of reference' of power is the class struggle in society. In this way, he distinguishes the structural features of power in society from what he calls instances of interpersonal 'might', such as may arise 'between members of a sports club'. Poulantzas argues that the capacities or motivations of individuals must be distinguished from the 'objective coordinates that determine the distribution of agents into social classes and the contradictions between those classes' (Poulantzas 1972: 242). Individuals are merely the conduit for the operation of economically structured power relations, which themselves operate through relatively autonomous social and political forms, like the state. Echoing earlier formulations, Poulantzas does define power as a capacity, but one of classes, not individuals. As with Hobbes, this capacity is relative to that of others. The capacity of the ruling class to maximize its interests depends on its minimizing the ability of the ruled to realize theirs.

An important element in Poulantzas's definition of power relates to the previous discussion of Lukes's notion of 'objective interests'. While liberals tend to assume that interests are defined by the agent exercising power, others argue that such interests are defined by position in a social structure. Clearly, then, for Poulantzas, class position is the key determinant of 'objective' interests. Ideology is then understood as a mechanism for the transmission of false interests. Indeed, according to Poulantzas, 'ideology . . . can give rise to numerous forms of illusion'.

Within this perspective, Poulantzas seems to confine agents to the restricted positions of either their economically derived class position or that which ideology imposes upon them. According to Miliband (1972: 259), Poulantzas turns the decision-makers of any given society into 'functionaries and executants of policies imposed upon them by "the system"'. The problem with Poulantzas's account, he argues, is that it appears to take power out of the hands of individuals and groups altogether. This flies in the face of our intuitions about power, and is based upon an untenable dichotomy between social structures and individual motivations. As Lukes (1974) points out, in contrast to Poulantzas, research into power relations must clearly examine 'the complex interrelations' between the objective structural coordinates of power and the way it is shaped by individual motivations. While it is true that individuals wield power within the bounds of structural limitations, the fact that we feel very strongly about it is, according to Lukes, enough to suggest that we retain an element of individual intention and motivation. As we saw, though, this only raises the further issue of how Lukes is able to straddle the theoretical divide between power as a structural determinant and power as a capacity of individuals (or groups acting as if they were individuals). For many contemporary sociologists, Giddens's (1977, 1979, 1984) work on 'structuration theory' is the best place to look for a way of overcoming this dichotomy.

Poulantzas appears to take on board certain traditional features of the study of power and turn them to the service of Marxist analysis. He recognizes, however, that power in society takes many forms, which are only 'in the last instance' structured by modes of economic production. He argues, in contrast to more traditional or dogmatic Marxists, that political power is not the 'simple expression' of economic relations. This takes Poulantzas away from traditional Marxism (see also Althusser and Balibar 1970), and it helps to pave the way for the poststructuralist discussion of power developed by Michel Foucault.

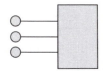

POWER AND EMPOWERMENT

It would seem that debates about power always lead to debates about the relation between structure and agency. Similarly, they always also lead to debates about whether power is best understood as 'power over' or 'power to'. Traditional liberal and Marxist accounts argue that power is best understood as something exercised over individuals or classes such that it constrains freedom. Other theorists, as we glimpsed above with Parsons, argue that power is best thought of as the capacity to enhance people's lives, such that, in this sense, it is a necessary condition of social and political life. We can look in more detail at the issues raised by this latter conception of power through the work of Arendt and the criticisms made of her work by Habermas (1986).

In her book *On Violence* (1970), Arendt reflects upon the differences between violence, strength, force, authority and power. She is concerned that these terms are all too often confused:

> it is . . . a rather sad reflection on the present state of political science that our terminology does not distinguish among such key words . . . all of which refer to distinct, different phenomena and would hardly exist unless they did.
>
> (Arendt 1970: 43)

In particular, political science has tended to conceive of power relations in terms of 'command' and 'obedience'. But always thinking of power as the ability to command obedience from others, she argues, reduces the complex world of governance to the simple 'business of dominion'. Such reductive accounts of political life present an impoverished picture of the 'realm of human affairs' – a realm that must be understood in all its 'authentic diversity'. As a way of combating such reductionism, Arendt invokes the republican tradition in the history of political thought. In contrast to the individualism of liberals like Hobbes, the republican tradition conceptualizes power as a form of collective empowerment. Understood in this way, power is viewed as the basis on which sound government should rest, rather than the capacity of government simply to command obedience from its citizens. As Arendt puts it:

> power corresponds to the human ability not just to act but to act in concert. Power is never the property of an individual; it belongs to a group and remains in existence as long as the group keeps together. When we say of somebody that he is 'in power' we actually refer to his being empowered by a certain number of people to act in their name.

(Arendt 1970: 44)

In defining power as the empowerment of 'the people', Arendt's position is close to that of Parsons. The difference between them is that Parsons sees power as that which sustains social systems, whereas Arendt sees power as that which legitimates governance and the rule of law. Parsons's understanding is *systemic*, whereas Arendt's is a *collective* conception of power. The distinction means that Arendt's approach does not fall prey to the charge of conservatism as easily as does Parsons's functionalism. Her focus on empowerment, rather than on the functioning of society, enables her to distinguish power from violence. 'Power and violence are opposites; where the one rules absolutely, the other is absent. Violence appears where power is in jeopardy, but left to its own course it ends in power's disappearance' (1970: 56). Power is always legitimate power because it depends upon the concerted action of the people over which rule will be exercised. Violence cannot be legitimate because it is only ever the instrumental means to some other end. And while the end may be *legitimate*, says Arendt, violence itself can only ever be *justifiable* by appeal to that legitimate end. In and of itself, violence is never 'legitimate'. Given this distinction, Arendt retains the Parsonian sense of power as a reservoir from which society may sustain itself, but she adds a critical edge missing in Parsons by assigning to power, among other things, the role of empowerment in the face of violence.

There is still a problem, though, in that the 'common-sense' notion of power includes the idea that power itself may be illegitimate. This issue, among others, is investigated by Habermas (1986), who develops some of Arendt's ideas with the aim of transcending the limitations of her theory. Habermas finds Arendt's distinction between power and violence initially to be very illuminating. He sees in this distinction a way of expressing the communal bonds that empower people when they act together without the distorting influences of, for example, the market. He is sympathetic to the idea that legitimate social and political institutions gain their power by virtue of the extent to which they empower the people whose lives they govern. Habermas also agrees with Arendt that the full realization of such empowerment requires a free and open public sphere.

Despite this general agreement, Habermas (1986) disagrees with Arendt's claim that power can only be empowering. He argues that Arendt narrows our sense of power and its role in political life in ways that lead to absurdities. Her discussion of politics, he contends, grafts the republican ideal of the Greek *polis* on to the modern world of politics. As a result, her republicanism does not adequately comprehend the ways in which modern political life is systematically embroiled with market economies and state bureaucracies. This means that many of the dichotomies that underpinned the Greek world – the division between public and private life, for example – are no longer sustainable. As a result, Arendt's view of politics as an autonomous sphere of empowerment 'screens out' the competition for power in social and political systems. Her conception is thus too one-sided for Habermas, as it does not allow for the distorting effects of modern systems of power on the communicatively generated bonds of society.

Habermas draws on Weber's analysis of the 'iron cage of bureaucracy', and argues that the distorting effects of social and political power have become such an 'institutionalized' part of politics that the struggle for power is now a 'normal component of the political system'. Thus, Habermas credits Arendt with the insight that legitimate power arises from a world of unimpaired interaction and the recognition that 'dominant theories of power' are insensitive to this phenomenon. But he criticizes Arendt for over-emphasizing empowerment, to the detriment of an analysis of the ways in which political power functions to undermine the very conditions that generate such legitimate power in the first place. He summarizes his position as follows:

> the concept of the political must extend to the strategic competition for political power and to the employment of power within the political system . . . Conversely the dominant theory narrows this concept to phenomena of political competition [and] does not do justice to the real phenomenon of the generation of power.
>
> (Habermas 1986: 87)

The merit of Habermas's critique is that it emphasizes power both as empowerment and as a form of distortion or domination. But there is another important issue that has not been adequately addressed by Arendt. Nor, it might be suggested, has Habermas made much progress on this matter. Neither theorist has been concerned to discuss the nature of power's constitutive role in the construction of individual and collective identities. This aspect of the operation of power in society has been most fruitfully developed by feminist and poststructuralist theorists.

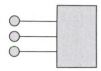

POWER AND IDENTITIES

We have already seen that many theories of power include an account of how it constructs an agent's interests. Feminist and poststructuralist approaches often take this a step further. While agreeing that power constructs our sense of what we desire, they add that power also constructs our sense of who we are as social and political beings. Power, on this account, reaches into the deepest layers of our identity. Whereas Enlightenment theorists argued that every individual is fundamentally rational and autonomous (see Chapter 5), many feminists and poststructuralists question this assumption by exposing the operations of power that make us think of ourselves as rational and autonomous beings. We shall begin with feminist approaches to the discussion. Feminism covers such a diverse set of social and political agendas that it is not easy to discern a shared conception of power. Feminists may, for example, locate themselves in relation to established definitions of power. Liberal feminists may assume a broadly individualist and conflictual model of power relations, while socialist or Marxist feminists may stress the role of class and economic domination. There are, however, certain general features of the discussion of power that most feminists would agree upon, and we shall dwell here on four of them.

First, feminists tend to stress that relations between men and women are shaped, at least in part, by relations of power. Historically, social and political theory has paid scant attention to relations between the sexes, treating them as beyond the scope or remit of conceptual analysis. Feminists have not only stressed this omission, but have also tried to construct theories that place sexual relations squarely on the conceptual map.

Second, many feminists agree that definitions of power that focus on 'interests' must consider the gendered nature of those interests. For example, that many women *want* to become housewives may reflect the insidious operations of male power in society, which construct and reinforce the notion that 'a woman's rightful place is in the kitchen'. Any interests-based conception of power must, therefore, include an account of the gendered nature of those interests.

Third, feminists agree that throughout history women have been denied social and political power, however it is defined. Leaving to one side possible anthropological counter-examples, one cannot dispute the claim that women have been excluded from power in Western societies. Indeed, feminists tend to share the view that the source of women's exclusion and oppression over the years is the patriarchal system of male domination. Sustained and systematic oppression of women by men in nearly all areas of life has been a hallmark of Western civilization since its inception. Understanding the nature of this power and how it has been exercised is a core concern of contemporary feminism.

Fourth, it is the exclusion and oppression of women that motivates feminists to consider power in the context of emancipation: 'as an emancipatory movement which seeks to end a particular kind of power relationship, feminism is deeply concerned with issues of how power should be conceived and understood' (Yeatman 1997: 144). That said, and despite tabloid caricatures to the contrary, feminists on the whole do not conceive of women's liberation as the domination of men by women. Instead of replicating the structure of patriarchal power, feminists tend to stress that power must be linked not to domination but to empowerment. Flammang (1990: 207) puts it well: 'Feminists recognise that women have been denied power, but insist that women do not want power if what that means is business as usual ... a zero-sum game where one person's gain is another's loss.' Ackelsberg (1997: 172) agrees that the task of contemporary feminist politics is to 'create new, more mutualist, expressions of power'. However, the difficulties involved in creating new structures of power within society are evident in Elshtain's comment that 'the challenge for women at this fateful juncture is to keep alive memories of vulnerability as they struggle to overcome structurally sanctioned inefficacy and to reaffirm rather than repudiate interdependencies as they seek a measure of institutional legitimacy' (Elshtain 1992: 122). Whatever the difficulties, though, feminists agree that it is a core task of feminist theory and practice to reconceptualize what is meant by power and to reconstruct the way it operates in society.

Feminist interventions heighten our awareness of the way power constructs our sense of ourselves as gendered beings. They call into question the way power is deployed within the social and political world to mobilize the exclusion of women. There is little doubt that feminist theories of power provide a useful corrective to the tacit assumption in traditional discussions that political power is a public capacity that manifests itself in masculine forms. The problem facing feminists is the construction of a conception of power markedly different from traditional, masculine approaches. For this reason, some feminists have turned to Foucault's understanding of the nature of power.

Poststructuralist theorists, like Foucault, tend to view all aspects of our identity, not just our gendered identity, as products of power relations. *The History of Sexuality* (1978) gives the clearest exposition of Foucault's general account of power: 'power is not an institution, and not a structure; neither is it a certain strength we are endowed with; it is the name that one attributes to a complex strategical situation in a given society' (Foucault 1978: 93). On the basis of this definition, we can usefully situate Foucault's account of power in relation to those discussed above. In contrast to Dahl, Foucault does not locate power in 'decision-making' individuals or institutions. For Foucault, the idea that power is the ability of A to direct the action of B is too impoverished an account of what he sees as the 'multidirectional' nature of power. In line with the functionalism of Parsons and the structuralism of Poulantzas, Foucault distances his account from liberal conceptions of power by arguing that it is not a commodity of individuals, or groups acting as if they were individuals.

Power, for Foucault, is an essentially social phenomenon that structures our sense of who we are and how we relate to others in society. In contrast to Weber, Foucault does not believe that power is necessarily linked to domination, and in this respect he would agree with Arendt's claim that operations of social and political power should not be reduced to the 'command–obedience' relation. As Foucault put it, power does not operate in only a 'top-down' manner. Bearing in mind Habermas's critique of Arendt, however, Foucault accepts that domination is one of the primary manifestations of power in society. Foucault also accepts that this domination may take the form of class domination, as in Poulantzas. What he does not accept is the idea that the complex workings of power are reducible to the single determinant of class relations. In general, Foucault rejects any attempt to locate the source of power in any one part of society, be it the state, the people or social classes. As such, he conceives of power as globally dispersed throughout the social and political arena, but argues, none the less, that it only ever manifests itself as a 'local' phenomenon. All social and political relations may be power relations, but each particular relationship (between the people and the state, between doctors and patients, between prisoners and warders and so on) must be understood on its own terms, without reducing it to an instance of, say, bourgeois oppression, state authority, collective empowerment or whatever.

Of course, for all that each particular power relationship must be analysed on its own terms, the social theorist must not forget to examine the connections that may have been established over time between, say, doctors and the state. The examination of the way certain relationships of power have become embroiled with the social and political world Foucault calls, following Nietzsche, genealogy (see Chapter 2 for a fuller account). We may summarize this complex position by saying that power is a feature of all social relations but it is not a unifying feature of 'the social'. This distinguishes Foucault from the work of Parsons and Poulantzas. For Foucault, each specific social relation will manifest a specific operation of power that forms a loose network with other relations of power rather than a coherently functioning social system or structured framework of class conflict. From the perspective of feminism, it is not immediately apparent how Foucault's conception of power is linked to the politics of emancipation. Given that all social relations are relations of power there is apparently little room for the idea of resisting domination. For Foucault, however, resistance and emancipation are not equivalent concepts. He persistently argued that 'where there is power there is resistance', but he saw no place for the idea that resistance is the fore-runner of emancipation from relations of power. Resistance, for Foucault, is a shift in the balance of existing power relations, whereas emancipation promises an existence liberated from the effects of power. Given his claim that all social relations are relations of power, Foucault could see no point in striving for emancipation. Indeed, the promise of emancipation, according to Foucault (1978), is itself a ruse of power. As many feminists (McNay 1992) and others (McCarthy 1991) have pointed out, it is by no means clear that Foucault can sustain this distinction between resistance to domination and the impulse to emancipate oneself, while retaining the critical impact of his work.

These general elements of Foucault's approach to power give an insight into the particular analyses of power in modern societies that he discusses in, for example, *Discipline and Punish* (1977). Through an investigation of the changing nature of punishment (from 'public tor-ture' to 'humanist reform' to 'normalizing detention'), he develops an account of the way power operates in modern societies and how it has changed over the past two hundred years. The emphasis of Foucault's work on punishment (and his later work on government and sexu-ality) is not to discover, therefore, the ways in which the penal system has been 'distorted' by power, but how power functions through a variety of penal institutions and social relations to produce the idea of 'the prisoner', 'the deviant', 'the normal citizen' and so on. In short, Foucault is concerned with how power functions to produce cat-egories of identification; more simply, identities or our sense of who we are. In other words, power shapes our social relations in a way which enables us to have 'knowledge' of our own identity and our social and political world; hence Foucault's notoriously tricky concept 'power/knowledge'. Foucault conjoins power and knowledge because he sees that the way we generate knowledge about ourselves and the way power operates in society are inextricably linked. It is one of the chief mistakes of social and political theory, according to Foucault, to think that we can have knowledge of who we are and what the social and political world is like, without becoming caught in relations of power.

To sum up, Foucault presents us with a view of power as a shifting and contestable network of relations co-extensive with the social and political world. Moreover, power has a constitutive role in the for-mation of identities, and as such is part and parcel of the formation of knowledge about the social and political world. As Foucault (1978: 92) puts it, power is 'the multiplicity of force relations immanent in the sphere in which they operate and which constitute their own organ-isation.' For all the philosophical density of this quote, it neatly en-capsulates the various elements of Foucault's account of power as outlined above.

Another approach to the relationship between power and identity has been elaborated by Bourdieu (1977, 1990). Following on from Weber's assessment of modernity as the increasing rationalization of the social and political world, Bourdieu develops an account of the way contemporary social and political practices are increasingly siphoned off into autonomous symbolic spheres. The paradigm case is the market, where economic transactions are now founded almost solely on the symbolic value of the bits of paper and metal (or the bits of information on computer screens) that we call money. The realm of economic production, we may say, is separated from its symbolic representation. But, according to Bourdieu, this is not happening only in the economic sphere. The cultural sphere is also becoming increasingly differentiated, both from other areas of life and within itself. This has led to a new breed of specialist that now dominates the cultural scene. According to Bourdieu, modern society is characterized by a 'market' of competing cultural transactions, where artists, scientists, politicians and the like vie with each other to produce the dominant, most convincing account of what the social world is like and how it should be organized. The medium through which these cultural struggles operate, the cultural 'money' that gets passed around, Bourdieu (1991) calls 'symbolic power'. Symbolic power refers to the way actual relations of power are transmitted in a social world already defined by embedded positions of authority and influence. Much of Bourdieu's work on art, education or law focuses on the way symbolic power operates in society. Cronin (1996: 70) gives a very neat and pertinent example:

> social scientists, such as economists and sociologists, wield symbolic power over how lay people and other professionals view the social world in virtue of the symbolic capital of reputation and personal authority they have acquired through symbolic struggles in the scientific field.

Symbolic power is founded on the construction of certain identities in the social and political world: for example, the identity of social scientists as people equipped and trained to speak about the social world with authority. The merit of this account is its emphasis on the way power can flow through symbolic media as well as through material relations, bodies, classes, the state and so on. On the other hand, Bourdieu's account may over-stress the economic nature of symbolic interaction in much the same way that Parsons's model of power also relied too heavily on the paradigm case of an economic transaction in its understanding of the way power is distributed through the social and political world.

CONCLUSIONS

We have travelled a long way from common-sense definitions of power. On the journey we have considered questions of agency and structure, domination and liberation, empowerment and identity. All these issues are at the heart of debates about the nature of power. One further issue, however, has yet to be brought to the fore – that is, the relationship between theories of power and theories of social criticism (see Chapter 2). It is an odd fact about theories of power that the more they seek to describe all social relations as power relations the less equipped they are to provide a critique of the very relations of power they describe. But it is a similarly odd fact about theories of social criticism that the more they try to demarcate an area of social life devoid of power relations the less convincing they are as theories that supposedly come from within the social and political world. This conundrum forms the core of many of the debates within contemporary theory. We can be sure that this tension will help to keep the motor of theory running well into the new millennium. What is more, it will always remind us that there is a constant need to interrogate our common-sense ideas of power if we want to criticize the way our social and political world operates.

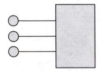

QUESTIONS

1 If theories of power are to prove convincing then what kinds of social and political relationship must they address?

2 Is there a payoff between plausibility and clarity as regards theories of power?

3 Are there any forms of social interaction that are untouched by relations of power?

4 To what extent, if any, do theories of power illuminate the workings of contemporary politics?

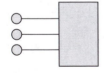

FURTHER READING

While they are not for the faint-hearted, the student of power would do well to start with the three volumes of *Power: Critical Concepts* (1994) edited by John Scott. Not only does this contain some of the classical articles and extracts discussed above, it also has clearly put together sections for the student interested in 'power, interests and agency', 'elites and community power', 'power and the nation state' and so on. A useful supplement to these massive volumes is the rather more manageable collection edited by Lukes, *Power* (1986).

Commentaries to read alongside these texts are: Hindess, *Discourses of Power* (1996); Barnes, *The Nature of Power* (1988); Boulding, *Three Faces of Power* (1989); and Clegg, *Frameworks of Power* (1989). They all provide comprehensive and readable accounts of competing definitions of power as well as offering interesting angles in their own right. For reasons of space, many influential conceptions of power were not examined above. See, for example, Russell, *Power: A New Social Analysis* (1938), Wrong, *Power: Its Forms, Bases and Uses* (1979) and Laclau and Mouffe, *Hegemony and Socialist Strategy* (1985). For those interested in the literature surrounding Dahl's intervention into the debates about power, a good place to start is Bell *et al.* (eds), *Political Power: A Reader in Theory and Research* (1969). The growing body of literature on feminist conceptions of power can be glimpsed in Davis *et al.* (eds), *The Gender of Power* (1991) and Radtke and Stam (eds), *Power/Gender: Social Relations in Theory* (1994).

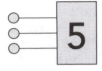

5 THE SUBJECT
Fidelma Ashe

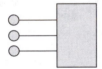

INTRODUCTION

A common-sense view of human beings sees them as rational, stable and coherent individuals possessing an inner and unique selfhood or identity that thinks for itself and is separate from both other people and the world outside it. Loosely speaking, this self is what social and political thought refers to as the individual subject. Classically, this subject has been understood to be an inherently rational source of human agency. This suggests that we are capable of exercising sovereignty over our own affairs and it promotes the idea that we are people fully in control of ourselves. As such, it is a concept closely related to conceptions of the individual, society and politics associated with the Enlightenment project.

Understanding the nature of the human subject has been a central concern for political and social theory, since it is only through a critical examination of ourselves that we can begin to understand the nature of our capacities, thought and behaviour. Only then can we begin to consider how we might live together. Conceptions of the subject usually underpin theories of rationality, power and the sources of social criticism, while work on language, culture and the body has often challenged this primacy. Indeed, the concept of the subject has become a kind of nodal point around which contrasting theoretical perspectives have oriented themselves.

The theory of subjectivity developed by Enlightenment thinkers dominated social and political theory for many centuries. Enlightenment thought suggested that the key to understanding the human subject's capacities, and its relationship to the world, lay in its ability to reason. Rational reflection was viewed as a form of pure thought, uncontaminated by external forces such as the customs and habits of a particular culture or tradition. The philosophers of Enlightenment thought of us as essentially rational subjects capable of producing valid knowledge about ourselves and our society. They viewed our capacity to reason as providing a secure foundation for knowledge that would guide our actions (see Chapter 1).

While it is comforting for us to view ourselves in these terms, the notion that we are disengaged, rational subjects now seems far less tenable than it did in the late eighteenth century. Ever since Marx developed his account of historical materialism (see Chapter 2), many social and political theorists have argued that our ways of thinking and being can be produced by unconscious cultural or social forces. This claim takes its strongest form in the poststructuralist idea that the subject has no essence. The idea of essence comes from Aristotle, who used it to name that which made a thing what it was. The essence was the core, unchangeable component that made a stone a stone or a society a society. For the Enlightenment thinkers, the subject was understood to have some sort of essence that made it what it was, regardless of time and place. But poststructuralists reject essentialist theories of the subject. Our ways of thinking and acting are, they claim, produced by a network of social forces within which we are immersed. Thus, poststructuralism rejects notions of a stable, unitary self and views the subject as a provisional entity that varies across time and cultures. The subject is 'decentred' and so is understood not to be an autonomous self-producing agent but a product of changing cultural and discursive fields. This chapter examines how the Enlightenment concept of the subject as a stable, autonomous and rational being has been challenged, and how this challenge has led to a reformulation of subjectivity as a variable product of discourse and culture.

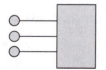

THE BIRTH OF THE SUBJECT

The rationalist philosophy of René Descartes is generally credited with having had an enormous impact on Enlightenment conceptions of subjectivity. Indeed, Descartes is often understood to have first identified the autonomous, rational subject of the Enlightenment. While searching for a solid basis for the justification of scientific and philosophical truths, Descartes assumed a position of radical doubt towards all his beliefs (see Chapter 1). By systematically discounting all sources of knowledge that could be the result of trickery or delusion, and so refusing to trust his senses, Descartes came to the conclusion that, even if he could not be sure of any other belief, he could be certain of his own existence because it was self-verifying: 'I have convinced myself that there is absolutely nothing in the world, no sky, no earth, no minds, no bodies. Does it now follow that I too do not exist? No: If I convinced myself of something then I certainly existed' (Descartes 1984: 16).

This is the source of Descartes's famous claim: 'I think, therefore I am' (*cogito ergo sum*). This idea of an individual consciousness (an 'I') aware of itself before it is aware of anything else has had an enormous impact on the dominant conceptions of the subject in Western thought. The claim did more than simply assert that the subject's existence could be guaranteed through rational reflection. Descartes posited that it is through our consciousness, our innate ability to reason, that we as human subjects become present to ourselves and can know our own defining qualities. The essence of our being, our point of fixity or centre, for Descartes, is the mind. The mind is the centre of the subject because nothing internal or external to it is essential to its existence. Even the body was relegated to a non-essential status as Descartes's notion of immortality convinced him that the conscious dimension of the subject could exist after the death of the body. Consciousness was explained in Cartesian philosophy with reference only to the human mind.

The Cartesian mind facilitated knowledge about the self but also made possible, under certain conditions, knowledge about the external world. In order for this knowledge to be valid, we must, from the perspective of Descartes's philosophy, separate our rational capacity from all other internal and external influences, since these are likely to deceive us. By isolating the mind from the subject's other characteristics and its external world, Descartes presented it as an independent and universal human possession in control of its own processes. In this way, Cartesian philosophy enthroned the subject as sovereign, regarding it as the sole foundation for certain knowledge of truth.

This conception of the subject was not, however, universally embraced. Cartesian rationalism was quickly challenged by the scepticism of empiricism. Philosophers such as David Hume (1978) argued that the only knowledge we can have about the world must be based on sense-perception and on custom or habit. For Hume, the only grounds for our knowledge of cause and effect is our growing accustomed to seeing one particular event following another, such as sulphur burning on combustion with a yellow flame (see Chapter 1). There can be no rationally grounded knowledge of any universal laws of natural necessity. Similarly for empiricists, Descartes's attempt to provide a foundation for knowledge prior to any experience of the world through sense-perception is irredeemably flawed. So philosophers were divided as to whether to view our experience or our reason as the source of knowledge.

The philosophy of Immanuel Kant, especially as developed in the first of his three Critiques – the *Critique of Pure Reason* (1781) – provided the most significant breakthrough in this conflict between rationalists and empiricists. By reconciling some of their basic claims, Kant attempted to overcome the inadequacies of both. This allowed him to provide an alternative grounding for the human subject as the source of knowledge. Kant (1993) argued that the grounds of knowledge could not be rooted solely in experience, as Hume and the empiricists had argued; nor could they be limited to the pure reasoning of a human consciousness or mind, as Descartes and the rationalists had suggested. For Kant, the human capacity to reason about the world had to be explained by examining the complex relationship between experience and understanding. The key was to think about the concepts that are needed by a human subject in order for that subject to have experience of an objective world. So Kant argued that the mind does not simply generate knowledge about the world through experience; rather, the external world that we perceive conforms to certain structures present in the mind. The understanding does not derive its structure from nature but imposes its own structure on to its experience of nature.

Kant suggested that human experience is only possible at all because there are certain concepts that are thought by the understanding prior to experience. If we did not have sense-perception then we would not know anything. But if we did not have any conceptual framework of understanding then we could not make sense of, or put some order on, the experience we have of the world through sense-perception. To make sense of our experience of the world, therefore, we must have a certain kind of knowledge or understanding that is independent of any particular experience. This understanding derives solely from reason, and this *a priori* knowledge, or knowledge prior to experience, takes the form of mental capacities, or categories, that are structured in a way that allows the subject to order its experience of the world. Space and time are primary among these, but Kant proposed a number of other categories of thought that structure our experience.

So, on the one hand, Kant was critical of Descartes's rationalism, since it fails to acknowledge the fact that our becoming self-consciously aware of our own existence must involve some knowledge of an objective world. I could not know that I myself existed if I did not also know that there were objects existing in space outside of me. On the other hand, he was critical of Hume's empiricism, since we can only have knowledge of particular events that we observe through sense-perception if we already have knowledge that an objective world existed. While all knowledge does indeed begin with experience, it is not the case, according to Kant, that all knowledge derives from the senses. Any knowledge that could be derived from experience, or *a posteriori* knowledge, is only possible because of the *a priori* knowledge of the categories, provided by the understanding, that allows us to make sense of our experience.

Kant claimed that these mental structures, or 'categories', are both universal and necessary. They represent the only conceptual framework through which the world can be understood, and they remain the same across time and culture. Kant's concern was with the conditions for the possibility of our experiencing an objective world, or the *a priori* grounds for knowledge. Another way of putting this is to say that he was interested in the transcendental conditions, or the conditions of possibility, of human subjectivity. He was also interested in the experience of the moral subject, or the grounds for knowledge of the moral law, and he provided a test according to which the validity of a moral principle could be tested. This test is known as the categorical imperative: 'Act only on that maxim through which you can at the same time will that it should become a universal law' (Kant 1964: 88). Morality, for Kant, requires us to act according to whatever principles we could wish to stand as the norms everyone would adhere to. If I could not wish everyone else to be free to lie to me, then I have a moral duty not to lie to them. This imperative is categorical, rather than hypothetical, in that it is a necessary and unavoidable test for moral action that all human beings must undertake regardless of the particular goals and aims they wish to pursue in their own lives. It does not depend, in other words, on any prior goal or aim. Furthermore, the categorical imperative does not itself prescribe a specific set of principles; it specifies a general test to which all valid moral principles must conform. So the transcendental features of human subjectivity are the grounds, for Kant, of our knowledge not only of the objective world outside of us but also of the moral law within.

Kant, like Descartes, had an enormous influence on modern conceptions of the subject. Ever since Kant's contribution, the idea that there are certain transcendental features of subjectivity that are essential and fixed has been the foundation of much of the work in the Western tradition of philosophy. The Enlightenment project required a powerful and controlling subject, capable of utilizing its reason so as to realize the dream of human progress (see Chapter 1). This conception of the subject as the rational foundation for scientific and moral knowledge became a powerful political device. It was used to carve out for the individual spaces of economic and social freedom, and this in turn facilitated the rise of political claims that articulated the interests of the bourgeois social class.

The notion that man was by nature essentially rational under-pinned the liberal attack on traditional social hierarchies as outmoded forms of political authority. Liberals argued that deference to authority was both unnecessary for social order and stifling to the individual. Indeed, the prized liberal value of individual liberty was rooted in the belief that the rational mind could guide the action of the subject. These liberals propounded the view that the subject's rational capacity meant that it was the most qualified agent to pursue its own interests. Self-determination and self-government for the individual thus became the liberal ideal. It was, from this perspective, the imposition of ideas by authoritarian forces such as monarchical government or the Church that was the main obstacle preventing individuals from attaining these ideals. These agencies of tradition hindered the rational subject in its efforts to develop its reason so as to calculate its own interests. Thus, liberalism articulated a concept of the subject as an autonomous agent capable, through an independent use of reason, of the successful pursuit of an individual plan of life.

Despite the emancipatory thrust of this formulation, this conception of the subject has been the focus of much forceful criticism in this century. Enlightenment theorists' accounts of the subject imply that we can transcend the effects of social and cultural forces on the way we think. Descartes and Kant both assumed the human mind to have an innate capacity that enables the subject to gain knowledge so as to control itself and the world around it. Contemporary opponents of this view reformulate the notion of the subject as a product of culture, ideology and power. Rather than seeing subjectivity as autonomous and fixed, they view the subject as open, unstable and tenuously held together. From this point of view, in giving birth to the modern subject Descartes was labouring under the misconception that the mind and its external world could be sharply separated. While Kant had moved beyond this sharp separation of reason and experience, he continued to claim that the subject was capable of reasoning in a manner that was free from the forces of tradition.

By neglecting the effect of contextual factors on subjectivity and knowledge, the Enlightenment philosophers, it is claimed, could not fully examine how the subject's social location and experience affects its perspective on the world. Culture, class, tradition, ethnicity and gender may all affect the way the subject views the world and the knowledge that can be generated about it. If one particular worldview is privileged over others, then it operates to exclude and devalue those other perspectives. Any universal notion of the subject or transcendental view of reason is likely to overlook the contextual grounds of knowledge.

In its more recent manifestations, this critique has been given shape by structuralist and poststructuralist theorists. These theorists have attempted to 'decentre' the subject by illustrating how its particular characteristics do not arise through the workings of a rationally disengaged mind, but through the subject's internalization of social and cultural norms and assumptions. To simplify, we may say that these theorists have conceptualized four factors that should be central to any account of the subject. Each of them undermines the Enlightenment conception of an autonomous self-conscious agent. These four factors are the unconscious, language, ideology and power. They have been combined in various theoretical investigations of the nature of human subjectivity and this has led to a number of competing conceptions of the subject (see also the discussions on language in Chapter 3, power in Chapter 4 and ideology and culture in Chapter 7). To this has been added an attention to the specificity of subjects in their particular context. This has highlighted the significance of questions concerning class, race, gender and so forth. We will begin an examination of this decentring of the subject by looking at Freud's claims about the unconscious.

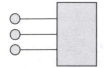

DECENTRING THE SUBJECT

Freud's clinical studies of the symptoms of hysteria and neurosis in his patients, combined with his own extensive self-analysis, made him certain that the human psyche had hidden and unconscious regions. While these were not accessible to the conscious mind, they did, nevertheless, affect human thought and behaviour. Freud (1986: 127–90) argued that within the mind there existed a reservoir of unconscious drives which he termed the 'id'. The id was devoid of logic and reason and consisted of uncontrollable and insatiable drives that were themselves contradictory in nature. Freud believed that the impulses of the id were directed primarily towards pleasure. These drives, he maintained, were potentially destructive for the individual and for society as a whole. Therefore, they had to be controlled.

Freud believed that this control was maintained partly through an agency within the mind called the superego, through which the subject unconsciously incorporated into itself (or introjected) the moral laws and prohibitions of society. According to Freud, both the id and the superego exerted pressure on the subject's behaviour, and it was the function of the third agency, the ego, or rational self, to cope with their conflicting demands. The ego attempted to satisfy the demands of the id in ways that were permissible in terms of the superego. For example, if the sexual demands of the id were insatiable in reality, the ego would attempt to satisfy them through fantasy.

Freud's contention that unconscious forces affect our behaviour challenges the security of the Cartesian *cogito* or the Kantian account of the transcendental conditions of human subjectivity. Freud's arguments suggest that desire rather than reason is the basis of our behaviour. If Freud is correct in his assumption that there are areas of the mind that the subject is unaware of but which affect its conscious action, its perception and its ways of thinking, then the consequences would appear to be potentially quite devastating for Enlightenment accounts of the subject. Given the reality of the unconscious, how could the human subject come to know itself, or its world, with any certainty?

Freud's 'discovery' of the unconscious does not, however, necessarily place him in opposition to Enlightenment thought on subjectivity. There is clearly, on the one hand, an Enlightenment streak in Freud's theorizing about the self, reflected in his much quoted dictum 'where id was there so shall ego be'. This suggests that the ego, the self-possessing 'I', is concerned to tame irrational desires by enabling the subject to act in accordance with reason. The purpose of psychoanalysis might then be conceived as concurring with Enlightenment ideals, in as much as it seeks to restore supremacy to the ego so that the subject may act rationally. Such an approach reflects a common strand in Western thought that regards humans as possessing a dual nature, where a base side of passions and appetites must be controlled by a higher moral and rational side.

On the other hand, an alternative reading of Freud's work reveals it to be much more radical in its implications, even if Freud himself was not fully aware of them. For thinkers of Enlightenment, the essence of the human self was its ability to reason, to know itself and its world. Two aspects of Freud's theory of the human psyche cast doubt on this essentialist assumption. First, even if the ego can control the impulses of the id, Freud suggests that the ego itself is involved in repression and fantasy. Thus, to be rational we must first deceive ourselves. Second, the subject cannot be seen as separate from and in control of its external reality, since Freud argued that historical and social forces constitute a part of the mind, the superego. This suggests that the subject's external reality impacts on its internal mental functioning and its cognition. If this is the case, then how far can individual autonomy be assumed? The relationship between self and society is reformulated in Freud's work such that the two are not clearly separate, but interpenetrate in significant ways. Where liberal theories had argued that the rational self could throw off the shackles of social forces, from a Freudian viewpoint these social forces form an integral part of the self.

Freud's thinking has indelibly marked the twentieth century. Freudian ideas about our psyche have entered mainstream, everyday discourse when we talk about repressed desire, hysteria, the meaning of our dreams and so forth. But of course Freudianism is far from uncontroversial. The reception of his work stretches from fanatical attachment to derisory dismissal. This is not the place to discuss the justifiability of his central claims. We must acknowledge, however, the undeniable fact that Freud's thinking has influenced artists, writers and intellectuals, and so it has also marked social and political theory. In particular, the dissolution of the distinction between the rationally autonomous self and the social world of law, force and ideology has shaped contemporary theory. Of particular relevance in this context is the way Jacques Lacan developed these more radical elements of Freud's theory using the framework of structural linguistics. The formulation of subjectivity that Lacan offers is the antithesis of the Cartesian *cogito* or the Kantian subject of knowledge. It is not only 'decentred', it actually seems to dissolve entirely into language.

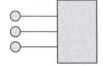

THE SUBJECT AND LANGUAGE

Lacan's work (1977) has been very influential in continental philosophy, as well as in diverse fields such as literary theory, cultural theory and even film studies. But in affecting the way we think about concepts such as identity and subjectivity, Lacanianism has also come to shape parts of contemporary social and political thought. Announcing a 'return to Freud', Lacan extended, within the framework of structural linguistics, what he considered to be Freud's most radical insights. Through a particular interpretation of the Freudian corpus, Lacan explored the external forces that constitute the subject, and in doing so took apart essentialist theories of subjectivity. Lacan turns the Enlightenment account of the self on its head by positing that the most basic and primary feature of the subject is not an essential core but its fundamental lack of any secure core or origin. Lacan's work is one example of the assault on the idea that subjectivity is fixed, centred and in control of itself. This attack focuses on ways in which the subject may be understood to be the product of cultural forces, specifically language and the ways in which language and desire interact. For Lacan, the subject emerges from the interaction of desire with the linguistic and symbolic systems which mediate our intersubjective relations with others. It is by internalizing these external forces that the lack of the subject is filled and a separate 'I', with an identity, capable of comprehending social rules and symbolic logic is formed.

Lacan's theory of the mirror stage gives us an insight into the claims he makes about the status of the subject. In many ways, Descartes's *cogito* resonates with the self as theorized by a branch of psychology that Lacan was keen to attack, ego psychology. Ego psychologists argue that the ego represents a point of fixity for the subject. They claim that the subject can take control of and cope with the demands of the other two psychic agencies identified by Freud if the ego, the rational part of the mind, is strengthened. Lacan views such an endeavour as folly. He rejects these conceptions of the ego, and uses the metaphor of the mirror stage to expose the ego as something that alienates the subject from itself by providing it with a mistaken, or misrecognized, image of itself.

Lacan argues that the ego develops in infants between the age of six and eighteen months. During this period of development, the human infant begins to recognize its own image in a mirror and comes to identify with that image as its self. However, this identification involves a misrecognition of its real self. It regards its image to be more complete and in control of itself than it really is. The mirror presents an ideal image which forms the basis for the subject's future development; this fictional sense of unity hides the split in subjectivity that occurs once the child separates from the mother's body. Just as the infant lacking corporeal completeness misrecognizes itself as complete in the mirror, we as subjects, lacking any stable centre of selfhood, seek out images of completeness and identify with them. Other people in particular represent this completeness for us. This image of completeness is, however, a distortion of the truth of our own and others' condition. By identifying with these images, we fool ourselves and misrecognize our true condition, which is one lacking any intrinsic stable selfhood. Lacan's claim is devastating, for he is suggesting that the ego, our rational centre, is a product of distorted images that cover over the fact that there is no intrinsic core to our self.

For Lacan, this process occurs in what he calls the realm, or register, of the imaginary. This imaginary realm is not, however, sufficient to produce the subject. In order for the subject to take up a social position, it must enter language, or what Lacan calls the symbolic order, and it must submit to its rules, processes, logic and law. Entering the symbolic, and thus becoming a subject, involves a rejection, or a form of repression, that creates an irreducible trauma or lack, a void at the heart of subjectivity. This lack is obscured within the realm of the imaginary by the identification of subjects with something that offers a sense of closure or completion. This identification may be with one of our parents, but it may also be with archetypal images, such as those that predominate in our culture, or with a powerful political leader or a forceful concept, such as nation or class.

Lacan draws on Saussurean linguistics in order to comprehend this production of the subject in language. The subject, as sign, operates as both a representation in language, or signifier, and the meaning that is represented, or signified (see Chapter 3 on Saussure). From the perspective of structural linguistics, there is no intrinsic connection between a representation (signifier) as a differential position in language and the meaning it represents (signified). All signs are arbitrary in nature, and it is the differential position of a signifier within the linguistic system that determines the meaning of the sign. Lacan understood the unconscious to be structured like a language. A subject's meaning can be produced only by its entering into the symbolic order of language. On entering the symbolic realm, the subject takes up a position in language, a signifier, as a separate speaking 'I' with a particular social identity. But the subject is simultaneously barred from access to a stable signified, or a fixed meaning outside the shifting sands of language. The unconscious is structured around this absence, shifting between signifiers and attempting to establish a fixity that, for Lacan, is always illusory and impossible.

Thus, the meaning assigned to the subject, as a distinct and separate 'I', in one sense anchors the subject in language by giving it an identity within the symbolic structure. But this has a high cost, since in another sense the subject has no anchor, given its restless shifting between signifiers in its illusory quest for fixity. In other words, the position the subject takes up as an 'I' is a highly unstable one. The subject 'falls out of view' once it takes up a position in language. This position hides the fact that the subject has no identity or meaning – indeed, it is a non-subject – until the point of entry into language. As Lacan (1977: 86) puts it, 'I identify myself in language, but only by losing myself in it like an object.'

On the basis of this theory of the subject, Lacan reformulates, rather provocatively, the Cartesian dictum 'I think, therefore I am' into 'I think where I am not, therefore I am where I do not think' (cited in Sarup 1992: 40). Lacan's account of subjectivity throws radically into question the subject's capacity to understand or to know either itself or its external environment. The sovereign, rational subject is nothing more than a distortion of symbolic and imaginary networks. What is going on, then, in the reflections of a subject that is fundamentally a distorted reflection of itself?

This assassination of the autonomous and enclosed subject by Lacan causes serious problems for practical politics. He leaves us with a subject unable to find the truth about either itself or its world, and strips it of any agency. We shall return to these issues later. For now, we can note that Lacanian theory suggests a subject that is open and vulnerable to cultural forces. However, in order for this approach to be developed in the direction of social and political theory, it has to be related to a theory of social power and its relationship to the subject. The work of Althusser (1971) offers such a theory and pulls the insights of structural analysis into the realm of political analysis.

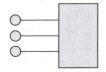

THE SUBJECT AND POWER

At the same time that Lacan was re-reading Freud to undercut the claims of ego psychologists, Althusser was re-reading Marx in an attempt to challenge the humanistic theories of writers such as Sartre that had achieved great popularity in France in the 1960s. Indeed, Althusser felt that he had found a kindred spirit in Lacan, and used his concept of the mirror stage to theorize the subject's constitution in the context of capitalism and in relation to Marxist theories of ideology. Althusser agreed with Lacan that the subject was a contingent entity constituted by symbolic systems, arguing that it was ideology that pulled the subject and its social world together.

This was a radical reconceptualization of the concept of ideology and broke sharply with traditional Marxism, which viewed ideology as simply a system of false ideas deriving from the economic base of society. Ideology, Althusser claimed, was a necessary component of any social formation. All societies need some mechanism for reproducing not only the means of production of social life but also the kinds of people, or subjects, that make up that society; a mechanism for engendering in individuals a disposition that encouraged them to take up their social roles and to occupy social positions. Ideology's function is to represent the 'imaginary relationship' of individuals to their real conditions of existence: 'All ideology represents . . . above all the imaginary relationship of individuals to the relations of production' (Althusser 1971: 155).

Ideology, Althusser claimed, operates through the category of the subject, such that 'all ideology "hails" or "interpellates" concrete individuals as concrete subjects, by the functioning of the category of the subject' (*ibid*. 162). In other words, ideology operates to create categories of subject and to assign people to them. Ideology calls or 'hails' the subject, in the sense that it says 'Hey you, I know who you are.' In answering to this call, the individual is incorporated into ideology in general and given subjectivity. The subject can only be defined within ideology, constituted in the ideological mirrors that surround it. Like the Lacanian infant of the mirror stage, the subject is unaware of the nature of its constitution and misrecognizes itself as autonomous and stable. In capitalism the subject is positioned in political relationships through the engendering of forms of consciousness required for it to take up its role, imagining itself as a free individual rather than as subjected to the domination and exploitation of class society. We do not have an identity but are assigned one by ideology, the mechanism through which the subject is subjected to capitalist exploitation. Althusser, like Lacan, strips the subject of its creativity and agency, and it becomes the product of structures outside itself. It cannot bring about political change of its own volition. Instead, change derives from the complex interaction of political, economic and ideological structures. The individual thus comes to appear as little more than a helpless figure determined by social structures.

This determinism has been a problem for most varieties of structuralism, Althusser's Marxist variant included. Certainly, the structuralist perspective is dogged by all sorts of theoretical problems concerning agency. It is also a disturbing view for all those who would like to think of human beings as active participants in the creation of social life. If social structures determine everything, how is it possible for a theorist such as Althusser to break free and develop a critical perspective on them? Certainly, Althusser tried to establish Marxism as a science free from ideology, but the attempt seemed to compound rather than resolve such problems. In attacking the claim that bourgeois philosophy could provide a rational analysis of society,

Althusser might well appear to be simply substituting the ideology of Marxism as the one tool capable of understanding everything.

Political developments in France led to a number of Marxists turning away from structuralist theories such as Althusser's, although his attempt to theorize subjectivity as the product of social power opened up a rich theoretical terrain. Poststructuralist writers, in varying ways, theorize subjectivity as a social production rather than as a product of some human essence or capacity. It is in the work of the poststructuralist writer Michel Foucault that we find the most vivid illustration of the modern subject's production in networks of power.

In his early work, Foucault (1970, 1972) argued that knowledge did not arise through the great discoveries of key thinkers. For Foucault, thought emerged through discursive structures and processes beyond the consciousness of the individual subject. Modern conceptions of the subject, according to Foucault, arose out of the specific organization of knowledge in the modern period. He thought this formulation of human subjectivity to be in decline as a new configuration of post-humanist knowledge began to emerge. The conception of the subject that arose out of Enlightenment thought, according to Foucault, did not free us from the operations of power, but made possible new and more insidious operations of power in modern societies.

Kant's philosophy represented for Foucault the defining moment of Enlightenment thought on the subject. In Kantian philosophy, he argued, man becomes both the subject who generates knowledge and its object. This conception opened the way for the emergence of the so-called sciences of man, notably disciplines such as medicine and psychiatry that took human beings as their object of study. We usually think of these disciplines as having provided us with valuable knowledge which is of benefit not only to us as individuals but also to society as a whole. Foucault (1977, 1978) sought to shake us out of this assumption by undertaking a Nietzsche-inspired examination of the effects of these knowledges on the subject. In these studies he illustrated how these forms of knowledge had led to an intensification of the control of individuals in modern societies (see also Chapters 2 and 4).

Foucault paid particular attention to the effects of the human sciences and disciplines. He argued that these forms of knowledge are involved in the monitoring and classification of individuals, providing us with new 'truths' about ourselves. The modern subject is generated out of the practices and discourses that derive from these disciplines operating as a form of social power that, in some cases, the individual comes to exercise on itself. Foucault's (1977, 1978) contention was that these discourses constitute our subjectivity, shape our consciousness and regulate our thought and behaviour.

Modern power is, for Foucault, extremely effective, since it operates, in part, by encouraging individuals to monitor their own behaviour. Bentham's panopticon represents, for Foucault (1977), a model of the operation of power on the subject in modern societies. Bentham's design was for a prison where the inmates can potentially be observed at all times. The cells are arranged in a circular form facing into the middle, where there stands a central observation tower. Every cell is visible from this tower, thus enabling the observation of a prisoner's behaviour. Since, however, the prisoner cannot tell whether or not he is being watched by the guard in the tower, he becomes self-surveilling, policing his behaviour at all times. In this way, the prisoner internalizes the gaze of power. The notion of the gaze was a major theme of Foucault's writings at this time. However, power extends beyond the gaze to encompass techniques of regulation, classification and monitoring. Moreover, it produces us as specific kinds of subject, designating what is normal and acceptable, and what is not.

There can appear to be certain similarities between Foucault's earlier works, on the treatment of the insane and criminal, and the research of the American sociologist and social-psychologist Erving Goffman. In the 1950s and 1960s, Goffman studied the development of concepts of self in their social context, and specifically investigated the treatment of the handicapped and those confined to institutions, such as prisoners and mental patients (Goffman 1968a, b). Goffman argued that inmates of what he termed a 'total institution' experience something like the removal of identity, since they are under constant observation, their time and space permanently invaded.

For Goffman, our identity or sense of self derives from the performance or adoption of socially approved roles. He called this approach to the presentation of self 'dramaturgical' in order to emphasize an analogy with acting and the theatrical (Goffman 1959). People are understood to perform in certain socially sanctioned ways, and to do this they use what Goffman suggestively calls 'props', 'routines', 'settings' and so forth, in order to carry off a performance. For Goffman (1968b) there isn't a 'more real' identity underneath such performance (indeed, he described such a conception as 'vulgar'). It is quite possible for actors to be taken in by their own performance. We internalize the social rules of performance, such that it makes 'of every man his own jailer'. Like Foucault, then, Goffman is interested in how our experience of identity or subjectivity may be the result of social forces.

However, the similarities between Goffman and Foucault, while suggestive, can be over-stated. They shared some interests and some conclusions but had fundamentally different approaches and aims. Goffman's work derives from the tradition known as 'symbolic interactionism'. Centred at the University of Chicago in the first part of the twentieth century, this intellectual 'school' was led by figures such as William Thomas, Charles Cooley and especially George Herbert Mead.

Although it derives from American philosophical pragmatism, symbolic interactionism has an affinity with phenomenological and ethnomethodological approaches, in that it emphasizes the meaningful nature of social life and action (see Chapter 3). It also rejects the scientific or positivistic approach to understanding social and political life, accepting that there is a strong degree of cultural specificity to meaning, as well as a degree of conflict and indeterminacy. As Thomas stated, 'if men define situations as real, they are real in their consequences.' A claim such as this is indicative of the fact that symbolic interactionism rejects any simple relationship between the study of society and that of the natural world. It treats social life as the result of sustained, creative and interpretive activity.

For the interactionists, human behaviour is best understood by appreciating that we behave on the basis of the meanings we give to our environment. But these meanings are the result of open-ended processes of interpretation and reflection carried out continuously by individuals in the context of interaction with others. Hence Goffman was interested in small-scale social interactions and the way meaning was conventionalized and maintained through implicitly agreed procedures for social performance. For the interactionists, we are constantly interpreting our own and others' actions, judging what they mean to ourselves and others, and modifying our behaviour accordingly. One can see how such a perspective might come to fit with the pluralism of American society, and there may be connections between this derivation from pragmatism and that of the liberal 'postmodernist' Richard Rorty (see Chapter 1).

The underlying assumptions of interactionism, and hence Goffman, are quite different from those of Foucault. Foucault made a deeper philosophical claim about the very status of the concept of the subject. This he regarded as the result of particular configurations of knowledge/power which could be understood in terms of their place in the history of systems of thought. For Foucault, a sense of self was not simply the product of social conventions. The very idea of a self which had to be worked on and maintained by the individual was, for Foucault, a product of 'regimes of power'. From the start, Enlightenment thought understood the subject in ways that were restrictive. Furthermore, Foucault was not concerned to preserve in his theory any space for individual agency, whereas Goffman was more ambivalent on this point.

Goffman's concepts (like those of interactionism generally) led to small-scale studies of face-to-face interaction that sought to identify the underlying rules of performance in such exchanges. As such, this work tends to be less applicable to a political understanding of society (though Goffman's work on asylums and stigma is certainly motivated by the desire to criticize social practices of institutionalization). But Foucault aimed at the heart of Western thought itself, and sought to lay bare the underlying forces of a whole social order. It is thus more radical in implication and has consequently been more influential on the political aspects of social thought.

Foucault may also appear to share similar ideas with thinkers such as Weber or the writers of the Frankfurt School, for whom modern forms of rationality had a repressive effect by limiting, isolating and confining individuals. For example, Marcuse (1964) argued that modern forms of rationality were creating conformist and one-dimensional subjects (see also Chapter 7). But while Foucault shared with these thinkers a critique of the modern conception of rationality, once again this is aimed at the very concept of rationality and the subject. His claim is not that a narrow conception of rationality leads to a narrow conception of the subject, but that the very notion of the rational subject is a modern development that derives from power/knowledge and produces certain power effects. Where Goffman argued that the institutionalized inmate had his or her identity removed, for Foucault the inmate was produced by a particular kind of subjectivity, and this process was a microcosm of modern society as a whole. We are all inmates in the normalizing 'carceral' and 'disciplinary' society of surveillance.

In *The History of Sexuality* (1978), Foucault gave his clearest illustration of the way that power/knowledge produces subjectivity. We normally think of Victorian times as a period of sexual repression. But Foucault argued that this was not the case, that far from repression there was an 'explosion' of discourses surrounding sex. By examining medical and psychiatric discourses on sexuality at that time, he cast light on the ways in which these discourses actively produced particular 'truths' about sexuality. This led to the categorization of sexual behaviour as being normal or abnormal. Foucault tried to show how these discourses operated on the subject by producing a form of self-knowledge, and were internalized by the subject as a form of self-knowledge. Thus, Foucault illustrated that, rather than silencing talk about sex, Victorian discourses actually generated particular truths about sexuality and our understanding of it. For Foucault there is no true, hidden sexuality: the truth of sex is a product of discourse and forms of power/knowledge.

For example, we may like to think of ourselves as being more sexually liberated than our predecessors. We think that we can and should express ourselves sexually, avoiding any internal repression. To ensure that our sexual practice and pleasure is the best it can possibly be, we can refer to the numerous guides, textbooks, training manuals, statistical analyses and multiple magazine features that offer advice. All this must surely be evidence of our superior understanding of, and open attitude to, sex and sexuality. But if Foucault is right, then we may see this as another form of power/knowledge. The 'discoveries' of sexology become like injunctions to think and to behave in certain ways. As 'knowledge' of sex expands, so new 'discoveries' are made, as if it is only through such research that sex can be 'truly' explored. Sexology creates new problems and devises new practices which we are encouraged to follow in the name of liberation. And despite this obsession, we remind ourselves that all this effort is made to get us in touch with something natural. In this way, we are formed as particular sorts of subject, defined by our sexuality and policing ourselves so that we conform to what we think is the true and right way to be. It is not that our true sexual selves are repressed by such discourse, rather that this form of subjectivity is produced by it. As Foucault claims, 'One has to dispense with the constituent subject, and get rid of the subject itself, that is to say, to arrive at an analysis which can account for the constitution of the subject within an historical framework' (Foucault 1980: 117).

From Foucault's point of view, thinking with essentialist notions of the subject was a historically necessary feature of modern societies. He did, however, question the continuing relevance of such notions, and he argued that they would lead us in the wrong direction not only theoretically but also politically. Political movements need to avoid essentialist notions of the subject that view subjectivity as singular and fixed. Such notions restrict the potential of subjectivity by reifying one sort of subject and making it universally valid. Subjectivity should be thought of as a constant process of becoming, rather than an achievement of a particular sort of being. This formulation of the subject as a thoroughly social construction has been highly controversial. Poststructuralism has been charged with bringing about the death of the subject, stripping it of all its autonomy or capacity for creativity and, in consequence, making politics impossible.

Poststructuralists, despite this criticism, continue to claim that political and social theory can no longer operate with the notion that human beings possess some transcendental rational capacity unaffected by culture. Instead, they believe that we have to recognize the subject's rationality to be constituted by the specific configuration of discourses within which it is embedded. If we recognize this, then we have to rethink our political strategies. If our knowledge and critical capacities are constituted by discourse, then we need to be more careful about setting up political discourses that seek to explain the whole of society and the procedures we should follow in transforming it. Progressive political interventions should aim to show the partial, restraining and constructed nature of our social discourses and the apparent 'truths' that surround us. Poststructuralists also claim that if our subjectivity is inherently unstable, changing as the social and cultural forces which constitute us change, then many different ways of being and thinking are potentially open to us. If we base our politics on rigid notions about the type of human beings we are or should be, then this prevents us from exploring other possible ways of being and thinking.

In his later work, Foucault (1985, 1986, 1988) gives us an idea of how the socially constituted subject can develop a potentially less normalizing and more open subjectivity. He suggests that the subject, although limited by the meaning systems of its culture, can enter into an exploration of itself and its society and develop forms of subjectivity that resist the tendency to normalize and restrict. Much has been made of this idea of an explosion of different subjectivities and the different perspectives that might herald the break-up of ethnic, gender and sexual identities which provide the foundation for oppression and conflict.

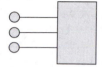

GENDERED SUBJECTS

As we have seen, Enlightenment thinkers viewed rationality as the defining feature of the subject. However, as Victor Seidler puts it, Enlightenment philosophers like Kant drew the 'circle of humanity' tightly (Seidler 1994: 16). Kant, Rousseau, Hegel and various other Enlightenment thinkers viewed women as lacking reason, believing that women's biology made them different kinds of subjects. They suggested that women possessed 'natural', usually maternal or emotional, capacities that made them suited to the domestic rather than the public sphere. When it came to matters of reason, it was suggested that women should seek intellectual guidance from their husbands and fathers. These gendered constructions of subjectivity effectively denied women their autonomy and freedom. We will recall that it was reason that underpinned the subject's capacity to make autonomous decisions and to exercise its agency without interference. As subjects supposedly less well endowed with rational capacities, women needed to be cared for and helped by those who knew better than they.

Liberal feminists (Friedan 1965; Wollstonecraft 1975; Mill and Taylor Mill 1983) responded to this denial of female agency by claiming that women had the same capacity for reason as men. They therefore campaigned for legal and educational reforms which they believed would enable women to develop their rational capacities. It was felt that these reforms would empower women by enabling them to gain intellectual equality with men. Women would then, it was claimed, have the same social and personal freedom as men. According to liberal feminism, male and female subjectivities were essentially the same, men and women were both rational, free and self-forming subjects.

While this formulation of male and female subjectivity as essentially rational and similar appeared to be a much needed corrective to sexist formulations of the subject of reason, other feminists began to question it. Liberal feminists had, like their masculine counterparts, conceptualized the subject as having intrinsic capacities blocked by social factors, and ignored the social forces at work in the construction of subjectivity. As the focus of feminist research shifted away from analysing social, economic, political and legal restraints on women, attention turned to the effects of women's social experiences as mothers, daughters and child-rearers on the construction of their subjectivity. Many feminists began to argue that male and female ways of reasoning were different. Cultural and radical feminists argued that women's biological and social experiences meant that men and women had different ways of thinking about and acting in the world. Feminists such as Rich (1977) and Chodorow (1978) argued that female experiences gave rise to an essentially caring and compassionate subjectivity, concerned about the needs of others. Men, it was claimed, were different types of subjects: instrumentally driven, domineering and controlling. While cultural and radical feminists agreed with Enlightenment philosophers that male and female subjectivity were different, they waged an attack on Enlightenment thought giving rise to the generation of specific female knowledge. These feminists charged that women's knowledge and ways of knowing had been excluded by Enlightenment thought (Harding 1987, 1991; Lloyd 1993). Female traits such as emotion had been removed from the sphere of reason and rejected by Enlightenment discourse as a basis for rational thought. Feminists pointed out that Enlightenment thought had devalued women's knowledge through its exclusion of all characteristics associated with the feminine. We will recall how Descartes and Kant separated reason and the understanding from the emotional and the bodily.

Gilligan's work *In a Different Voice* (1982) illustrates the nature of cultural feminism's critique and rejection of Enlightenment constructions of the masculine subject of reason. Gilligan's research suggested that men and women reasoned differently about moral questions. Her research indicated that men reasoned on the basis of an ethic of justice which involved following abstract moral principles. Women appeared to reason about moral questions on the basis of an ethic of care which involved considering the concrete effects of their decisions on others. Gilligan argued that because men had defined reason in masculine ways anything that deviated from this construction, such as women's moral knowledge, was viewed as flawed. Gilligan tried to illustrate that while women's moral decisions were different from men's, they were just as legitimate (see Larrabee 1993).

Female knowledge and values were used as a foundation for women's agency and politics (Daly 1979, 1984). Women were asked to turn away from masculinist modes of thought characterized as domineering, controlling and competitive, which had given rise to social conflict, wars and inequality. Politically, faith was placed in the formation of a female culture. For example, Rich hoped that female values would 'alter human existence' and predicted that 'sexuality, politics, meanings; thinking itself will be transformed' (Rich 1977: 292). By valorizing femininity, these theorists gave dignity and authority to women often denied them in cultures where ways of thinking characterized as feminine are typically devalued and where women are often represented as sexual objects. They also exposed the fact that the basis of a subject's knowledge is not transcendental but dependent on the subject's social location.

Cultural and radical feminism suggested that the subject's traits, values and knowledge are shaped by its social experiences. However, despite the focus on social factors in the construction of gender and knowledge, radical and cultural feminism posited the notion of a universal and ahistorical womanhood which ignored differences between women. Some women who viewed themselves as attempting to break out of narrow social definitions of femininity as nurturing and caring – for example, women choosing careers rather than motherhood – felt that radical and cultural feminist discourse was pushing them back into a socially moulded and restrictive subjectivity. Black and working-class feminists argued that radical and cultural feminism had ignored the effects of racial and class identities on the construction of subjectivity. Its conceptualization of the female subject's knowledge seemed to its critics not only to be problematic but also to be context-bound and exclusionary (see, for example, Davis 1982; hooks 1984; Lorde 1984).

What made matters worse was that radical and cultural feminists, feeling secure in the validity of their construction of female knowledge and values, began to legislate about the nature of women's political action. Given the negative conceptualization of masculinity, there were calls by some for a separatist politics. Black and working-class feminists protested that their political concerns had been sidelined and excluded. For example, separatists ignored the fact that these other feminists felt that they should be working with men against class and racial inequalities, a feeling that arose from their experiences of multiple oppressions. Critics argued that radical and cultural feminists, and indeed liberal feminists, were imposing their white, middle-class interpretation of the world on other women. The problem of privileging one explanatory perspective was also brought to light by various lesbian feminists. These feminists began constructing, on the basis of their specific viewpoint and experiences as gay women, different interpretations of practices such as pornography, which had been labelled by some radical feminists as inherently bad, masculine practices.

The problem seemed to be that of recognizing differences among women and avoiding the privileging of one interpretation of female subjectivity, knowledge and politics over others. If poststructuralist critiques of Enlightenment-inspired theories of knowledge were, in general, correct then feminism had no way to differentiate between a variety of competing interpretations of gender, all of which might be potentially progressive. Several feminists seeking to avoid the pitfalls of an all-encompassing explanatory framework began to turn to poststructuralism as a way of formulating a non-essentialist and non-foundational feminist politics. Poststructuralist feminists, like their male counterparts, operate with the notion that there is no subjectivity except that which is socially constituted. Subjectivity is a variable and dynamic construct. They contend that, given this fact, there is little to be gained by our setting up rigidly essentialist accounts of subjectivity. Our time would be better spent opening up opportunities for the development of more progressive subjectivities. These feminist writers focus on the forces that construct the subject. They believe that if we can destabilize and change the discourses that produce subjectivity then we might be able to open up a space for the production of new forms of subjectivity that could evade normalization. Like other poststructuralists, they tend to favour a local politics that avoids the dangers involved in advancing large-scale strategies.

French poststructuralist feminists follow Lacan in arguing that the subject is produced within symbolic networks. They see the symbolic as characterized by phallocentric forms of logic and representation. Women, they argue, have no way of defining themselves within this symbolic order except through phallocentric thought, which represents women as being inferior and lacking in relation to men. Kristeva (1986) argues that men and women can find the resources to challenge this kind of thought in a pre-oedipal, pre-symbolic realm, the so-called 'semiotic', that is outside the restricting logic of phallocentrism. This semiotic realm refers back to a time when the bodies of mother and child were one, and it consists of a set of drives and impulses with the potential to disrupt the symbolic. Kristeva believes that tapping into this semiotic realm will enable the analysis of gendered subjectivity and gender politics. One possible criticism of this position is that it draws on an essentialist notion of sexual difference that is biologically based. It might, however, be argued in Kristeva's defence that the semiotic is open to both men and women, and so this suggests a less static definition of subjectivity.

Another poststructuralist feminist arguing for fluid notions of subjectivity is Judith Butler, in her book *Gender Trouble* (1990). Butler, however, is influenced more by Foucault than by Lacan. She attempts to find the resources for resistance to gender discourse within the field of discourse rather than in a realm beyond culture. Butler believes that the exposure of the constructedness of gendered subjectivities and the way they work in suppressing potential alternative ways of conceiving gender and sexual subjectivity could open the way to the critique of such restrictive identities and encourage more free play of our subjective selves. In place of the binary structure of gender with which we work (male versus female), Butler suggests the possibility of a multiplicity of genders (see Chapter 6).

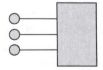

CONCLUSIONS

We have seen in this chapter the ways in which the classical notion of the autonomous, self-contained and rational subject, a notion central to Enlightenment thinking and modern social and political thought, has been challenged by a variety of forms of contemporary theory. Theories of the unconscious, language, ideology, power and discourse have asserted that we are always caught within a complex network of culturally generated presuppositions that define who and what we are. This in turn suggests that subjectivity, or identity, is a deeply social and political phenomenon. While we may like to think of ourselves as having an intrinsic identity which we simply bring to social and political life, poststructuralist theories seem to imply that our identity should instead be thought of as the result of social and political activity. If this is so, then notions of reason, freedom and justice have to be rethought. But is it possible to reconceive politics without reference to rational, enlightened subjects deliberating with one another about their individual and collective choices? If we are the productions of historically rooted cultural systems beyond our immediate grasp, is any challenge to the status quo possible? Certainly questions of identity seem to be the source of much recent political controversy in struggles regarding differences of gender, race, sexuality and ethnicity (see Chapter 8). Should we be trying to transcend these particularities so as to find a universal basis on which to formulate principles of social justice that are rationally acceptable to all, or should we acknowledge an irreducible plurality of potential subjectivities and perspectives? If we take the latter option, on what basis could we adjudicate between competing claims? The challenge posed by such questions is the challenge of contemporary social and political thought.

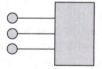

QUESTIONS

1 What has been the political significance for modern societies of the Enlightenment conception of a rational and stable human subject?

2 Does Freud's 'discovery' of the unconscious necessarily require us to abandon the notion that human beings are autonomous agents?

3 To what extent do poststructuralist investigations of human subjectivity open up possibilities for a new form of politics?

4 What implications does the feminist rejection of a rigid opposition between reason and emotion have for conceptions of the subject?

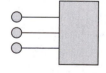

FURTHER READING

Fortunately, there are a number of helpful commentaries on particular authors. Benvenuto and Kennedy, *The Works of Jacques Lacan: An*

Introduction (1987) is probably the most comprehensive introduction to Lacan. Other commentaries include Bowie, *Lacan* (1991) and Macey, *Lacan in Context* (1988). See also Muller, 'Language, psychosis and the subject in Lacan' (1983). An accessible commentary on both Lacanian and Freudian theory is Frosh, *The Politics of Psychoanalysis: An Introduction to Freudian and Post-Freudian Theory* (1987). Grosz in her *Jacques Lacan: a Feminist Introduction* (1990b) examines both Lacanian and Freudian theory from a feminist perspective, and it is also worth looking at Flax, *Thinking Fragments: Psychoanalysis, Feminism and Postmodernism in the Contemporary West* (1990). Flax rejects Lacanianism as a theoretical framework for feminism, and suggests instead an appropriation of Freud.

For commentaries on Althusser, see Benton, *The Rise and Fall of Structural Marxism* (1984) and Elliot, *Althusser: The Detour of Theory* (1987). For a poststructuralist account of Althusser, see Laclau and Mouffe, *Hegemony and Socialist Strategy* (1985). A good introduction to Foucault is Sheridan, *The Will to Truth* (1980). For critical assessments, see Hoy (ed.), *Foucault: A Critical Reader* (1986) and McNay, *Foucault and Feminism* (1992).

For a critique of radical and cultural feminism, see Jaggar, *Feminist Politics and Human Nature* (1983). For different feminist approaches to subjectivity, compare Benhabib, *Situating the Self: Gender, Community and Postmodernism in Contemporary Ethics* (1992) and Butler, *Gender Trouble: Feminism and the Subversion of Identity* (1990). Further explications of debates around feminism and poststructuralism can be found in Nicholson (ed.), *Feminism/Postmodernism* (1990) and Benhabib *et al.*, *Feminist Contentions* (1994).

Rose, *Sexuality in the Field of Vision* (1986) offers an overview of theoretical shifts in Kristeva's work, and see also Kristeva's 'Women's time' and 'Woman can never be defined', both in *The Kristeva Reader* (1986). Another French feminist thinker who proposes an original and significant poststructuralist position is Irigaray, *The Sex which Is not One* (1985). For an evaluation, see Fraser and Bartky (eds), *Re-evaluating French Feminism: Critical Essays on Difference, Agency and Culture* (1992).

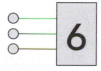

6 THE BODY
Moya Lloyd

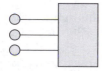

INTRODUCTION

When we walk into a room, the kind of body that we have both defines us in certain ways and helps to shape our interactions with others. Whether our body is black or white, female or male, disabled or not, ill or healthy, tall or short, fat or thin can affect how others view us and how we conceive of ourselves. Indeed, many of us spend considerable time and effort working on our bodies through the use of make-up or diet, in the gym or on the football field, through cosmetic surgery, body-piercing or tattooing and in the choice of clothes we wear to hide, or expose, parts of our body. There is something very personal and intimate at stake in defining and moulding the body. Our bodies are not only intrinsic to our personal identities and social encounters, they are also political, subject to all kinds of power and control. The law, for example, circumscribes specific kinds of bodily act (under-age sex, paedophilia, rape and even interracial sexual relations); it regulates the availability of certain medical procedures (abortion, contraception, the use of amniocentesis); and it controls access to certain representations of the body (pornography). Similarly, the media portray certain idealized images of female and male beauty that many of us desperately attempt to live up to. We are offered images of 'alternative' embodied lifestyles and particular representations of racial and ethnic identities centred on bodies that are valued or coded in different ways, from the stiff upper lip to the Gallic shrug. The body has become the very stuff of contemporary cultural politics. This is demonstrated in the increasing interest within academic circles about particular practices of the body and the ways in which they are underwritten by certain relations of power. Over the past fifteen years or so there has been a veritable explosion of interest in the body, covering such subjects as aerobics (Markula 1995; Lloyd 1996), male and female body-building (Wacquant 1995a; Aoki 1996; St Martin and Gavey 1996), cosmetic surgery (Davis 1991, 1995; Morgan 1991), male and female boxers (Wacquant 1995b; Hargreaves 1997) and music and dance (Jordan 1995; DeNora 1997), to name but a few. What explains this shift and how does it figure within social and political thought?

Unlike disciplines such as philosophy, social anthropology or psychoanalysis, social and political thought has paid scant attention to the body, deeming it to be outside its theoretical concerns. Where the body was discussed it was either as a metaphor for something else, as in Hobbes's famous depiction of the state as the King's body (the literal body politic), or as a physical limitation to the operations of political rationality, as in Rousseau's claim that man needed to quell his passions in order to function as a citizen. In neither case was the body theorized as a political or social concept in its own right. The one exception perhaps was Nietzsche, for whom it was 'essential to start from the *body* and employ it as guide' (Nietzsche 1968: 289, emphasis in the original text).

This tendency to neglect the body, however, has changed in recent times, partly because of the move to take Nietzsche seriously as a social and political thinker. As a result of a number of factors, the body has become understood as socially and politically significant. Perhaps the most important factor has been the so-called 'crisis' of the project of Enlightenment (see Chapter 1). The apparent failure of the Enlightenment ideal has led theorists to rethink the nature of rationality, and this has entailed a reassessment of the way in which we think about the body.

· Critics of Enlightenment conceptions of reason have highlighted the 'binary' structure of Western thought, arguing that it is structured around a series of prejudicial dualisms, such as: reason/emotion, mind/body, culture/nature, public/private and man/woman. The terms contained in these dualisms are held to be opposites and logically contradictory (one cannot be both at once). But they also contain an implicit value judgement, where the first term is more highly valued than the second. Thus, the body is thought to be in opposition to mind and inferior to it. For mind to function (that is, to reason), the body must be repudiated. Critics point out, however, that to see people purely as rational beings centred in the mind is to ignore, even deny, their corporeality and to fail to inquire as to how this bodily existence affects knowledge of the world. Discussion of the body, in this context, not only represents a challenge to dualistic thinking by stressing the significance of the body *as such*, but also acts as an important corrective to the tendency to view subjects in abstract terms. It opens the way to other modes of theorizing.

The second major factor influencing debate on the body was the women's movement. It prompted a glut of feminist writing on the body, as well as spawning a plethora of political campaigns centred specifically on issues affecting *women's* bodies: reproductive rights, abortion, conceptive technologies, beauty, rape, domestic violence and pornography. In developing their analysis of the politics of the body, some feminists initially drew on the liberal notion of the 'possessive individual' (Macpherson 1963). This idea derived largely from Locke's (1988) claim that in the state of nature every man was the owner of his body, his labour and thus of whatever was produced by that body. Far from being a theory of the body, this was essentially a theory of property rights. In the hands of feminists, however, the emphasis changed to a theory concerning who was legitimately entitled to control the bodies of women. If women are also possessive individuals entitled to determine how their bodies are used, then, it was asserted, they alone should determine when, and if, they wanted to have children, or when, and if, they wanted an abortion and so on (Petchesky 1986). Although the body is more thoroughly centred in this account than in Locke's initial formulation, it remains principally a theory of rights about who is entitled to use, abuse and control a particular piece of property – the body. The impact of feminism, however, lay in raising awareness of the ways in which the body is directly implicated in relations of power and domination. From being regarded as a phenomenon outside of politics and society, the body came to be viewed as the locus of complex social and political interaction. This awareness permeated other areas, including the effects of race, nation, disability and disease on our understanding of, and on the politics of, the body.

The aim of this chapter is to explore some of the ways in which the body has been theorized in recent social and political thought. As such, little attention is paid to representations of the body or to the body as it is treated in popular culture. We begin with the idea of the natural body. This view is important, because it presents the sexed body as both natural and unproblematic and has been responsible for an over-concentration on sex difference in theories of the body.

THE NATURAL BODY

Perhaps the obvious starting point for debates about the body is to look at what have been called 'naturalist' theories. Naturalist theories presuppose a number of things. First, the body in question is the biological body and should be understood in anatomical, physiological or genetic terms. Second, this body exists prior to and independent of society. In other words, biological bodies existed and functioned before humans lived together in societies. As such, the body derives its meanings from its functions rather than from culture. It is the way that humans eat, sleep and reproduce that determines the evolution of society and not society that determines the ways our bodies behave. Third, naturalist theories of the body regard differences between the sexes as both natural and innate. A fourth presupposition is that these purportedly fundamental differences affect the way in which society is organized. Thus, for instance, the fact that women give birth to children and that men do not has been used to explain the sexual division of labour between the home (the site of woman, the nurturer) and the outside world (the site of man, the hunter/gatherer). One of the basic premises of this kind of theory is that 'biology is destiny', and that we do what our bodies allow us to do. These kinds of assertion can be described as biological determinism. One of the effects of this kind of thinking is to focus attention on the sexed body to the almost total exclusion of other kinds of politically and socially pertinent bodies, such as those that are disabled, aged, racialized or diseased.

Naturalist theories are found in a number of quarters, particularly in sociobiology, but also within certain strands of feminism. There are, however, significant substantive differences between them. Sociobiological theories tend to regard social inequalities as natural and somehow evolutionarily inevitable. The inequalities between the sexes are regarded by sociobiology as the result of natural differences between the sexes. However, as critics have pointed out, the reasoning used to arrive at these conclusions is often circular. The existence of sexual inequality is taken to have a biological origin; therefore, biology must determine the existence of sexual inequality (Sayers 1982: 76). What, in fact, happens is that certain historical ideas about appropriate roles for the sexes are used *as if* they were ahistorical; as if, that is, they were neutral biological terms. Critics argue, however, that these biological explanations of women's inferiority versus men's superiority are not biological at all, but social and historical explanations. Arguments grounded in biological differences between the sexes, deployed to justify keeping women at home, or to exclude them from certain jobs or from education, are really historically and culturally rooted. Similarly, so-called evidence of biological differences between the races has been used to prove and explain differences in ability, claiming, for example, that 'white men can't jump' or black bodies are naturally more rhythmic. Critics of naturalism and biological determinism see such claims as the effects of imperialist and capitalist discourses rather than scientific facts.

Feminists, by contrast, have tended to use biological arguments to different ends, most usually to criticize patriarchal control over women's reproductive processes. Here they differ quite substantially in their underlying view of biology. For some, such as Firestone (1976), women's biology is seen as a limit to their opportunities. She argues that only through the use of technology (abortion, birth control, contraception and ultimately *ex utero* gestation open to both men and women) can sexed difference be overcome. Others have been much more critical of the use and abuse of contraceptive, fertility or reproductive technologies on women's bodies (see Corea 1985; Chadwick 1987; Arditti *et al.* 1989; Klein 1989). Still others have argued for a revaluation of women's biological role that would accord them their rightful status in society. It is to one of these accounts that we now turn, for accepting the existence of sexed differences opens the way to what might be termed embodied theory. What is potentially radical about this kind of thinking is that it suggests the possibility of specifically feminine modes of thinking, creating and being that are intimately connected with physicality. As we shall see, such views are far from unproblematic.

Women, Adrienne Rich argues, are endowed through their biology with an essential feminine nature that is encapsulated in the experience of motherhood. This feminine nature is alienated in contemporary male-dominated society because of the ways in which motherhood is institutionalized. It is subject to all kinds of interference – legal, medical, political, and psychoanalytic – that turn it from an experience of joy and creativity into one of (primarily, if not exclusively) pain and suffering. Only the overthrow of the patriarchal institution of motherhood would enable women to experience the fullness of female power associated with mothering in its natural state. What is crucial to Rich's account is her sense that women's physiology enables them to see the world in different ways to men. Women's bodies endow them with a different epistemological position, a 'gynocentric' position:

In arguing that we have by no means yet explored or understood our biological grounding, the miracle and paradox of the female body and its spiritual and political meanings, I am really asking whether women cannot begin, at last, to *think through the body*, to connect what has been so cruelly disorganized – our great mental capacities, hardly used; our highly developed tactile sense; our genius for close observation; our complicated, pain enduring, multi-pleasured physicality.

(Rich 1977: 290)

Where men are associated traditionally with rationality and abstract thinking, women have been treated as if they are purely body. Moreover, this corporeality is, within binary thinking, less valued than mind or reason. To remedy this, women should be allowed to think through their bodies, to which their consciousness is intrinsically connected. Such corporeal thinking, Rich claims, is at least equal to masculine epistemologies. However, her argument is subject to the same sorts of criticism as reductionist sociobiology. Women's bodies are held to reveal their essential natures, and this claim, like biological essentialism, assumes that women's fundamental natures are given or determined by their biology.

Naturalist theories of the body, although appealing to common sense at one level, have been criticized for reducing all social difference exclusively to biological difference. They have been condemned, in other words, for being 'biologistic' or biologically reductionist. What this means is that consideration is not given to historical, social-structural or cultural factors in determining how we think of the body or, indeed, of what the body can do. The whole idea of what precisely is natural about any body is left unexplored, with the result that theories of the body, in general, often become theories of the sexed body, in particular. This problem about what counts as 'natural' has been compounded by the development of various kinds of technology that can be used to transform the body: cosmetic surgery, heart implants, operations designed to reassign sex (transsexualism), even such activities as diet and exercise. These so-called advances raise questions about our ability to talk at all about the natural body. What is 'natural' about a cosmetically altered or about a transsexual body? Here recent work on cyborg bodies is especially pertinent, for it focuses attention on the ways in which human and machine increasingly blend together to form hybrid creatures (Haraway 1991; *Body and Society* 1995; Balsamo 1996). As bodies come to be worked on more and more by technology and as machine parts replace body parts (pacemakers, or hip replacements), the possibility of purely natural bodies wanes. Instead, a cybernetic future looms before us, where science and technology can continually refashion corporeality.

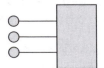

THE CONSTITUTED BODY

Like theorists interested in cyborgs, many social and political theorists are highly sceptical of naturalism, rejecting it in favour of constructionist accounts of the body. Constructionists reject the assumption that the body produces meaning. In its place, they argue that the body is the effect of meanings that are ascribed to it. It is moulded, even constituted, by societal factors. Phenomena such as sex and race are revealed as social constructs. Such accounts, while sharing the view that the body is a social/political product, differ in their explanations of how bodies are constituted. Thus, Foucault, for example, regards discourse and power as pivotal, Goffman focuses on social interaction and Butler offers a theory based on the notion of performativity. We will examine these three approaches in turn.

In the first volume of *The History of Sexuality*, Foucault described his work as: 'a "history of bodies" and the manner in which what is most material and most vital in them has been invested' (Foucault 1978: 152). Contrary to naturalist claims that the body remains constant throughout history, a mere biological mechanism that is born, eats, sleeps, has sex and dies, Foucault (1984) contended, following Nietzsche, that the body is an entity thoroughly saturated, or invested, with historically specific meaning and moulded by the forces of history and power (see Chapters 2 and 4). In this respect, for Foucault, the body is unstable; it is a pliable entity, constructed in different ways at different times. This implies that the body does not give rise to meaning but becomes meaningful through discourse (see Chapters 3 and 5).

Let us take the example of sexuality. Sexuality only comes into existence, Foucault asserts, when it is named as such within discourse. Discourses of sexuality regulate and order not only statements, but the kinds of sexual desires that bodies can be said to experience. Discourses thus divide and classify forms of sexuality. They produce, moreover, the effect of sexuality upon the bodies that they generate. These bodies are then experienced and understood as particular kinds of sexualized body. There is nothing natural about sexuality. Crucially, for Foucault (1978), the kinds of discourse operative at any one time will vary. This suggests that our comprehension of the body is itself contingent, or historically specific. It is not only how we understand the body that is at issue, but also how the body is made to function in certain ways. Here the focus is on the practices that generate the bodies that discourse regulates. A quick examination of one of Foucault's works will illustrate what this means.

At the start of *Discipline and Punish*, Foucault juxtaposes two descriptions: one of the bloody, gory torture and execution of Damiens the regicide in 1757; the other of the timetable regulating the lives of the young prisoners of a Paris jail some eighty years later (Foucault 1977: 3–7). The purpose of this comparison is to map the connections between power and the body at different historical periods. In the case of torture, the power of the state works on the body of the criminal, tearing it to pieces. Here, the operations of power are transparent: Damiens, who attempted to kill the King, is himself shown the extent of kingly power through the excessive and spectacular nature of his punishment. In the instance of the timetable, however, Foucault contends that power works to produce *disciplined* bodies that are made docile and useful. But what does it mean to talk about a body that is disciplined? To understand this, we need to turn briefly to Foucault's account of modern power, for it is this that produces the bodies in question (see also Chapter 4).

Modern power, Foucault surmises, has a number of features. It is productive rather than repressive; it is exercised rather than possessed; it is strategic in operation rather than being the 'privilege' of a particular class (Foucault 1977: 26). In relation to the body, this has a number of consequences. First, it means that:

> the body is . . . directly involved in a political field; power relations have an immediate hold upon it; they invest it, mark it, train it, torture it, force it to carry out tasks, to perform ceremonies, to emit signs . . . the body becomes a useful force only if it is both a productive body and a subjected body.
>
> (Foucault 1977: 25–6)

When a soldier performs drill in the parade ground, the movements that are made with the gun (presenting arms, lowering arms, etc.) are movements that are learned through training. No matter how natural or spontaneous these movements become over time, they are nevertheless the effect of a set of regularized techniques. Disciplinary power works here to produce a martial body that is altogether more productive than it was formerly:

> By the late eighteenth century, the soldier has become something that *can be made*; out of formless clay, an inapt body, the machine required can be constructed; posture is gradually corrected; a calculated constraint runs slowly through each part of the body, mastering it, making it pliable, ready at all times, turning into the automatism of habit; in short, one has 'got rid of the peasant' and given him 'the air of a soldier'.
>
> (Foucault 1977: 135, emphasis added)

Power, therefore, inscribes itself on the body. It constitutes the very operations of the body and renders it more manipulable and useful. Likewise, when we sit at a table and hold our cutlery in a specific way, or when we perform a pirouette in ballet or an overhead kick in football, we too are exhibiting instances of bodily discipline. The military body, the body exhibiting appropriate table etiquette, the balletic body or the footballing body share, for Foucault, a quality of docility. 'A body is docile', he charges, if it can be 'subjected, used, transformed and improved' (*ibid.*: 136). The docile body is the effect of power. Specifically, it is the effect of the 'procedures of power that characterised the *disciplines*' (Foucault 1978: 139).

Despite its impact, however, reactions to Foucault's work have been varied. Some feminist critics have taken Foucault to task for failing to differentiate adequately between technologies of power that affect all bodies similarly and those that affect male and female bodies differently (Bartky 1988; Grosz 1990; Braidotti 1991). Others, by contrast, have drawn on Foucault precisely for a feminist account of

embodiment (de Lauretis 1987; Butler 1990, 1991, 1993). Other commentators have drawn attention to the fact that Foucault fails to
address the materiality of the body, in so far as he has no satisfactory
account of the body outside of discourse. His attention to the historical meanings that attach to the body obscures the physical matter
that makes up the body. As we shall see, this problem of the relation
between discourse and materiality is endemic to much work on the
body.

In contrast to Foucault's emphasis on discipline and power, Erving
Goffman's earlier sociological version of constructionism concentrates on the types of conduct that constitute modern social life. In
particular, he is interested in the ways in which the self is presented in
everyday encounters and the forms of interaction this facilitates or
disallows. As an interactionist, he places a high priority on relations
between, and communication among, individuals. So what is meant
by presentation of the self? What is the role of the body in this
process?

In *The Presentation of the Self in Everyday Life* (1959), Goffman offers
an analysis of the ways in which social encounters are structured.
Drawing on the idea of a theatrical performance, he explores how the
individual in ordinary situations presents 'himself and his activity to
others, the ways in which he guides and controls the impression they
form of him, and the kinds of things he may and may not do while
sustaining his performance before them' (Preface). The body, for him,
is a medium that allows people to intervene in everyday social activities. All kinds of physical gesture impact upon our meetings with
others: a firm handshake, sustained eye contact, our physical proxim-
ity to another. Furthermore, interacting with others requires us to
adopt specific roles at specific times. When I stand before a class to lec-
ture, I become a lecturer in manner, tone of voice, gesture and movement. When I leave work and go home, I become variously an irritated
driver, a concerned patient, a customer. Each of these requires from
me a different kind of performance.

One of the most trenchant criticisms levelled at Foucault concerned
the relation between power and the body. He was attacked for presenting the body as merely passive, unable to resist the effects of
power and apparently permanently available for the application of
discourse to it (McNay 1992, 1994). This suggests that the body is
simply a cipher over which the subject has no control, and implies a
lack of autonomy or agency on the part of Foucault's embodied subject (see also Chapter 5). By comparison, Goffman contends that the
individual has agency in relation to her or his body in so far as she or
he can use that body to (attempt to) produce different effects in the
course of social interaction. Thus, for instance, an individual may
adopt a particular walk in order to generate a particular impression.
Alternatively, the way people sit, eat or stand can be manipulated by
them to some degree so as to convey different impressions in different

contexts. The body is, therefore, a resource at the disposal of individuals that may be used to influence the dynamics of social interaction. That said, Goffman is aware that subjects cannot do just anything with their bodies in a social encounter for the reason that there exist 'shared vocabularies of body idiom' (Goffman 1963: 35). This means that certain kinds of behaviour, specifically non-verbal kinds (gesture, dress, posture, movement, 'facial decorations, and broad emotional expressions') operate according to social conventions (*ibid*.: 33). These conventions are, as it were, the norms that determine what is appropriate conduct in a specific context. The advice given in women's magazines as to how one should act in an interview is a typical example. Detailed information is provided on how to sit, what to wear, what gestures to use or to avoid and so forth. The purpose of this advice is to make known the body conventions (the 'vocabulary') appropriate for an interview. The body for Goffman is, thus, a social phenomenon in the sense that the meanings ascribed to it are socially determined. Although the individual has some room for corporeal manoeuvre, their body is always already imbricated in a web of social meanings. Furthermore, these meanings determine how successfully an individual embodies a particular social role. For a performance to be a success, it must accord with socially approved standards or codes of behaviour, and it must be acknowledged as such by those who are witness to it (Goffman 1972). In this respect, it is not so much the performance itself that matters but how it is interpreted by others. Take the following example cited by Goffman:

> The skilled waitress tackles the customer with confidence and without hesitation. For example, she may find that a new customer has seated himself before she could clear off the dirty dishes and change the cloth. He is now leaning on the table studying the menu. She greets him, says, 'May I change the cover, please?' and, without waiting for an answer, takes his menu away from him so that he moves back from the table, and she goes about her work. The relationship is handled politely but firmly, and there is never any question as to who is in charge.
>
> (Goffman 1959: 23)

To stamp her authority on the situation, the waitress takes control of the situation both verbally (asking to change the cover) and non-verbally (taking the menu). She engineers the interaction and, thereby, secures her social role. Had her customer grabbed the menu back off her or had he told her not to change the cover until he'd made his choice of meal, then the waitress would have failed to establish her social role. She might, as a consequence, have blushed, got flustered or felt embarrassed (Goffman 1968a: 12). In future, therefore, she may have attempted to manipulate her body further in order to generate the 'right' impression of herself.

Goffman gives greater place to agency in his account of the body than does Foucault, viewing it as a material entity that is pliable and controllable. What is unclear from his work, however, is the exact relation between his account of interactionism and the wider social order. Where do the meanings that attach to particular bodily idioms come from? Is it from a set of pre-existing norms or conventions? Or is it from repeated performances? Although his analysis offers insight in terms of well established practices, it is not able to tell us how those practices came to be established in the first place. Compared to Foucault, there is no real sense of history here. Like Foucault, however, Goffman provides little information about the body *per se*. The body is meaningful only in so far as it is embedded within systems of social signification. Goffman, while drawing attention to the place of the body in the construction of a social identity or self, never develops a particular theory of embodiment (Turner 1991: 11).

Judith Butler has been mistakenly credited with following Goffman in the development of a theory of gender as performance (Benhabib 1992). In actuality, Butler's work is much closer to that of Foucault (and Derrida) than to that of Goffman. Following Foucault, Butler (1990) asserts that there is no such thing as a natural sexed body. Every sexed body bears the traces of discursive inscription, and in particular of gendered inscription. In making this claim, Butler rejects not only the idea common to feminism that sex is natural and gender cultural, contending instead that both are the effects of discourse, but also the idea that sex somehow gives rise to gender (such that men inevitably become masculine and women feminine). Gender itself, for Butler, is a form of bodily signification. Discourses of gender inscribe sex on to bodies. It is in her account of how the process of engendering operates that she appears close to Goffman:

> Gender is the repeated stylization of the body, a set of repeated acts within a highly rigid, regulatory frame that congeal over time to produce the appearance of a substance, of a natural sort of being.
>
> (Butler 1990: 33)

And, she adds, gender is a *'corporeal style, an "act" as it were'* (*ibid.*: 139). It seems as if she is suggesting that gender is a performance in the theatrical sense implied by Goffman. This is, however, a mistake. For Butler, gender is 'performative'. The idea of performativity comes from linguistic theory where it is most associated with Austin and Derrida (see Chapter 3). A linguistic performative is a 'speech-act' that produces what it names. The standard example is the marriage ceremony, where saying 'I do' is the act that marries the individuals concerned. There is no difference here between saying and doing (getting married).

Similarly, gender, Butler avers, relies upon producing that which it names. This works through the body. Thus, to comprehend gender we have to understand the body. In particular, we have to understand that it is stylized repetition of acts, gestures and movements that generate the impression of sex and gender in the first place; or, put differently, that *doing* gender creates the illusion of *being* a particular gender. Although this appears to be like Goffman's claim that the body is used in performances of the self in order to create specific impressions, the difference between the two is that for Butler these acts are not voluntary. We have, that is, no choice about performing our gender. It is compulsory in the societies in which we live, and we make no sense without it. As such, it is not something that we can evade at will; from the day we are born we are gendered beings.

Given her affinities with Foucault, it should not be surprising that she too has been criticized for apparently presenting the body as infinitely malleable. Her claim that one way of disrupting dominant norms of gender and of heterosexuality is to parody them (through acts such as, but not limited to, drag) suggests that the material body is irrelevant to the gender that can be performed. Critics, however, have contended that it is not that simple: the biological body presents limitations to the ways in which gender can be troubled (Bordo 1990, 1993, 1997; Hughes and Witz 1997). Again like Foucault, the problem seems to be that Butler fails to acknowledge the materiality of the body; in her case both the sexed body (Moore 1994) and the racialized body (hooks 1992). Indeed, she goes as far as to say that the gendered body has no 'ontological status apart from the various acts which constitute its reality' (Butler 1990: 136). There is no gendered body without the performance of certain gestures, styles, movements. To her credit, Butler attempts to resolve this deficiency in *Bodies that Matter* (1993). Here she offers an account of what she terms 'materialization'. Her point is that there is no ontological or natural body, only a discursive process of '*materialization that stabilizes over time to produce the effect of boundary, fixity, and surface we call matter*' (*ibid.*: 9). What we take as intrinsic to the body, for example, where its boundaries are drawn (that is, at the surface of the skin), are, Butler contends, always themselves the effects of the regulatory norms of discourse (see Haraway 1991). It is hegemonic discourse that constitutes, through its repetition, the bodies that matter (and those that do not). Butler, thus, continues resolutely to pursue a constructionist explanation even for the matter of bodies by refusing to see matter as either a substance or a set of attributes accruing to bodies independent of discourse. While this is an interesting, albeit difficult, attempt to theorize the matter of bodies, it is not entirely clear that it does, in fact, release Butler from the charge of ignoring the materiality of the body, since it refuses to recognize that what we call bodies do things irrespective of discourse.

As we have seen, naturalist accounts of the body have been criticized for their failure to deal with historical and socio-cultural factors affecting both the literal body and our understandings of what counts as a natural body. By contrast, constructionist accounts have been challenged for over-stating the influence of power and discourse, and thus for their inability to recognize the actual materiality of the body. One theory that attempts to resolve this dilemma is that offered by Thomas Laqueur. His aim is to maintain a distinction between the body as flesh and the body understood as historical, between as it were what is 'real' and its representations. His focus is the sexed body. His aim is to refute the idea that sex is natural.

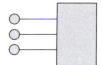

THE HISTORICAL BODY

Freud in an essay on 'femininity' wrote that 'When you meet a human being, the first distinction you make is "male or female?" and you are accustomed to make the distinction with unhesitating certainty' (Freud 1986: 413). We believe that we know the sex of a body from certain attributes. We are so accustomed to distinguishing between male and female bodies, as the only two kinds of body that exist, that the idea of mistaking the sex (assuming the person was neither in convincing drag nor a transsexual) seems absurd. But for how long has this seemingly unproblematic model of biological sex held sway over us? What, for instance, are we to make of the following tale?

> The servant Germain was a well-built young man with a thick red beard who, until the age of fifteen . . . had lived and dressed as a girl [named Marie], showing 'no mark of masculinity'. Then once, in the heat of puberty, the girl jumped across a ditch while chasing pigs through a wheatfield: 'at that very moment the genitalia and the male rod came to be developed in him, having ruptured the ligaments by which they had been held enclosed'. Marie, soon to be Marie no longer, hastened home to her/his mother, who consulted physicians and surgeons, all of whom assured the somewhat shaken woman that *her daughter had become her son*.
> (Laqueur 1990: 127, citing Montaigne, emphasis added)

How are we to understand the proposition that sex, far from being unequivocally determined at birth, can change as a consequence of jumping across a ditch? What does it mean for a conception of the body?

In *Making Sex*, Thomas Laqueur examines the ways in which our understanding of our bodies, sex and anatomy has changed over time. Far from the objective certainties offered by naturalist accounts of the body, Laqueur's historical account demonstrates the malleability of dominant ideas about the body. The focus of Laqueur's book is the transition from the one-sex model of the body to the two-sex model that is current today. According to the former view (illustrated in the tale of Marie/Germain), there existed only one sex but two genders; here 'woman was understood as man inverted: the uterus was a female scrotum, the ovaries were testes, the vulva was a foreskin, and *the vagina was a penis*' (Laqueur 1990: 236, emphasis in the original text). Men and women, it seemed, shared the same basic anatomy. The difference was that in the male the reproductive organs had dropped, while in the female they remained inside. These organs, however, were identical: ovaries were testes and not a distinct biological phenomenon in their own right. Implicit in this one-sex model, however, was a notion of hierarchy: man was superior to woman, more perfect than she. It might be surmised, therefore, that woman was at best a *potential* man; at worst, a *failed* man. The idea that there was only one sex did not mean, however, that the categories of male and female did not exist. They did. Male and female were categories not of sex but of gender. As Laqueur (1990: 8) explains:

> To be a man or a woman was to hold a social rank, a place in society, to assume a cultural role, not to *be* organically one or the other of two incommensurable sexes. Sex before the seventeenth century, in other words, was still a sociological and not an onto-logical category.

> (Emphasis in the original text)

It was not until relatively recently that male and female bodies were construed as incommensurable. Not only that, but the relation between sex and gender also altered. We are accustomed to regarding gender as the set of social and cultural characteristics that accrue to persons of a particular sex. Put differently, sex comes first, followed by gender; being a man or a woman precedes being masculine or feminine. Laqueur's interpretation of the one-sex model reveals that to talk about men and women at all is always already social or cultural, not biological or sex-based. Men and women did not exist as distinct anatomical bodies but only as cultural entities. In this respect, gender in the one-sex model was more 'real' than sex (the reverse of contemporary understanding of the body).

What, then, explains the transition from the one-sex to the two-sex model? The most obvious explanation would be advances in science that debunked the mistaken myths underpinning the one-sex model. This view is, Laqueur surmises, inaccurate. First, both models of sex coexisted, although one dominated for a considerable length of time before being displaced by another. Second, many of the scientific developments that seem to confirm the incommensurability of the sexes came long after the ideological shift to the two-sex model occurred. So how could the dominance of one view over the other be explained? For Laqueur, it can be explained principally as a part of changing political circumstances. As the foundations of the old social order came under threat, so the body was remade and two opposite sexes were created. The sexed body is 'situational': 'it is explicable only within the context of battles over gender and power' (Laqueur 1990: 11). What is crucial for understanding Laqueur's theory is to appreciate that he contends that how the body is understood or represented at a given time does *not* depend at all on historically given 'facts' about the body. In other words, there is no causal connection between the 'facts' known about sex at any one time and our understanding of sex difference; whatever links exist are entirely contingent and arbitrary, effects of politics and epistemological categories. The cultural politics of representation, and not evidence of the actual functioning of the body, determine our understanding of anatomy (see also the discussion of science in Chapter 1). That is, our understanding of the natural body is itself culturally determined. Where Laqueur differs from constructionist authors is in arguing that the body is real; that irrespective of discourse or history, it exists, it breathes, it bleeds. We may not be able to talk about it without entering into a historicized dialogue, but it is there nevertheless. That Laqueur makes little attempt to theorize the 'real' body is evidence of the difficulty of talking about it outside of culture and history.

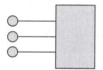

THE BODY AND PHYSICAL CAPITAL

Hitherto, none of the accounts of the body that we have examined explains why it is that the body has become such an important consideration in contemporary society, nor why people spend so much time, money and/or effort investing in their bodies. In recent times we have seen a growth in what might be termed body 'projects', including such things as body-piercing, tattooing, exercise, cosmetic surgery, diet and the use of make-up, all of which are designed to improve, beautify or remodel the flesh. But why are these things so popular now? What has happened to propel people into such projects? One partial explanation is offered by Pierre Bourdieu through his account of how the body as project has become a kind of cultural or physical capital (Bourdieu 1977, 1978, 1984).

Bourdieu contends that in today's consumption-oriented society the ability to determine taste is a power held by the dominant class and used to perpetuate that domination. He explores the processes by which the body becomes commodified and how certain kinds of body come to be seen as valuable, while others are regarded as less so, or not at all. Although he does not try to develop a theory of embodiment *per se*, Bourdieu does offer several insights into the effects of capitalism on the body.

Bourdieu understands the body as always 'in-process', not static or fixed but developing and always being made and remade. He examines how this body operates as a bearer of symbolic value; that is, how the body conveys to its possessor status, power or the ability to accrue certain benefits (financial, cultural or social). The body, in this way, is said to be a sort of capital. For instance, a successful, lucrative, modelling career is dependent upon the possession of a particular kind of physique. Likewise, fame and success in sport rely upon having particular physical skills or abilities. Clearly, however, there are differences between these two cases and the multitude of other instances in which the body works as physical capital. One of the most important forms of difference that exists is that of social class. According to Bourdieu, dominant groups are those that are able to ensure that the attributes and qualities they possess are those society recognizes as having value. This proposition is based on the idea that social reproduction depends upon three class-related factors, all of which have a direct bearing on corporeal development. The first factor is the material conditions in which people live on a daily basis. The second is their 'habitus', or how class members internalize a certain worldview (that includes tastes) as being natural to their class. Importantly, habitus impinges immediately on how classes treat their bodies including how people walk, talk and eat (Bourdieu 1984). Finally, the third factor is people's taste. Bourdieu declares that 'the body is the most indisputable materialization of class taste' (*ibid.*: 190). Different classes have different tastes, largely as a product of the different kinds of things available to them. Thus, one finds a correlation between class position and differences in taste, be it for food, fashion or music.

Taken together, these three elements determine how competing corporeal forms are generated, the value that is assigned to them and the functions that each can perform. Moreover, these factors combine to generate and to naturalize class differences. The dominant classes, with time and resources to devote to their body, may concentrate on the generation and maintenance of a healthy body. Their body project is multidimensional and relatively time-consuming. The prevailing attitude among this class is that their bodies represent 'an *end in itself* that signals mastery and control to others (Bourdieu 1978: 838, original emphasis). By comparison, the working class view the body in 'instrumental' terms. It exists as a means to achieve certain ends and is treated as such. Men engaged in manual labour tend not to have the inclination for the kinds of health-oriented activities of the dominant class (running, tennis, golf), preferring, instead, the physical hurly-burly of a game of football; that is, a game that requires 'a considerable investment of effort, sometimes of pain and suffering' (*ibid.*: 838). Likewise, working-class women may deprive themselves of food, not in the interests of dieting (as their bourgeois sisters might), but in order to ensure that partner and children are fed first. Their bodies merely enable them to do so. For the working classes, therefore, the body is a project in a narrowly circumscribed way: it is a mechanism that requires the occasional service to keep it operational. (Within these classes there are, of course, many variants, including those affected by gender and race.) Each of these styles has some symbolic value, although that of the dominant class will be more significant than that of the working class. We may think, for example, of body posture. The British bourgeoisie trains its children not to slouch, to stand upright, to shake hands firmly and to look people in the eye, but not to stare. This way of holding one's self signifies status and confidence. The British working-class is not usually so trained and may even regard such posture as somewhat alien. This is indicative of the way the body is shaped according to class culture, and of how physical capital accrues differentially to each class.

Bourdieu is not concerned only with how physical capital is produced but also with how it is converted into other forms of capital. Although certain opportunities do exist here for the working class, the advantage lies with the elite. Where some members of the former class may turn physical prowess into an economically rewarding career, the elite tend to have more physical resources already at hand: for instance, their speech and accent may convey an impression of intelligence, while their bearing may be interpreted as refined and polished, both of which are assets in the job market. Furthermore, the kinds of social activity in which the dominant class engage (say polo or equestrian activities) may operate indirectly as a form of capital, in as much as these venues open up chances for work, for appropriate marriages and so on. The types of conversion of physical into other forms of capital differ between classes. For workers, economic conversion is usually vital. For the elite it may be enough that it converts to social capital: contacts or significant friendships.

While the dominant classes determine, in effect, the differential valuation of class capital, it should be noted that this process is fluid. The symbolic value of specific forms of capital can change as struggles occur to fix their relative worth over time, and the value of certain modes of physical capital may vary depending on context: what is important in sport is not important in business. Age too can have an effect. Since physical capital is essentially personal, it often diminishes with age, and certainly disappears with death. Since it is also individual, there is no assurance that what someone develops as physical capital will actually be recognized as such. The central point, however, is that the elite endeavour to ensure that they are the embodiments, quite literally, of class and taste, and that they secure distinction for what they do. It is this that ensures the reproduction of class cultures and social inequalities.

Bourdieu's sociological theory is important for the way that it links the body to the imperatives of capitalist social reproduction. This, in turn, has an effect on its adequacy as a theory of the body in general. For although Bourdieu has insightful things to say about race and gender, these two categories remain subservient to class. As such, the specificities of patriarchal and racist structures on the gendered and racialized body, respectively, are left underdeveloped. They are subsumed within a class analysis. In addition, Bourdieu focuses on contemporary capitalist society and as a consequence his theory has no adequate analysis of the historical development of this mode of relating to the body and thus no real explanation for broader structural changes. This impinges directly on the question of agency since his conception of the production and maintenance of physical capital (through the concepts of habitus, social location and taste) suggests that individuals and groups have little room for manoeuvre. How do tastes appear that seemingly do not have a pre-existing class correspondence? Indeed, can they actually appear (Shilling 1993: 146)?

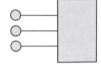

CONCLUSIONS

What do these recent developments within political and social theory tell us about the body? One of the most persistent tensions in writing on the body has concerned the best way to negotiate the divide between the body as a material entity in its own right and the body as it is embedded within historical and cultural discourses about it. Writers have tended, generally but not exclusively, to line up on either side of this divide. They argue either in favour of the biological body or in favour of the body-in-discourse. This mode of thinking operates by setting up the two interpretations of the body as binary opposites: either natural or constructed. This suggests that an accommodation between the two is impossible to reach. Recent critics have begun to disagree, however, contending instead that the challenge that is faced by theorists of the body is how to reconcile these two sets of claims. To do so, it is necessary to modify the terms of the debate somewhat. It would be impossible to hold on to the naturalist idea of the body as having a set of irreducible characteristics that determine once and for all how it operates alongside the constructionist claim that the body is entirely malleable, a product of interaction or of discursive constitution. It is not impossible, however, to argue that the thing we call the 'body' has certain forces or does certain kinds of things (gives birth, eats, sleeps, dies), but that the only way that we can talk or write about the body is through social constructs. The 'body', as such, can never be directly known. Any knowledge that we have of it is always mediated by other factors (discourse, language, interaction). It may seem futile to bother with the material body if it can never be thought of outside of social constructs; if, that is, our understanding of it is always already social or cultural. The point in acknowledging its materiality, however, is to accept that the 'body' is more than merely a construct; that it exceeds the meanings that are attached to it. It may also mean that we argue for a theory of the body that allows space for some recognition that the 'body' can itself inspire certain non-discursive effects.

The second issue raised in relation to the accounts that we have covered is the persistent charge that they fail (with the possible exception of feminist accounts) to accommodate the meanings that individuals themselves ascribe to their bodies, actions and behaviours (Dews 1987, 1988; Turner 1992). Here social and political theory could learn from the philosophical tradition of phenomenology associated with Merleau-Ponty (Crossley 1995). The problem with some of the accounts that we have considered is that they see the body primarily as inscribed or made by certain external factors, cultural codes, discourses and so on. In contrast, the phenomenological idea of the 'lived body' emphasizes the body as it is lived by subjects. The body is the basis for human subjectivity and thus all subjectivity is inherently embodied. Every experience that we have is an embodied experience. We are our bodies. It is with or as our bodies that we interact with others. Some sense of our actual experiences as embodied subjects (not necessarily phenomenological) is needed to counter the weight that is given to those theories that stress what is done to the body by outside forces. We need also to think about what our bodies enable us to do.

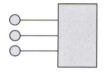

QUESTIONS

1 Given the amount of time and effort that many of us spend in body modification (e.g. diet, exercise), does it make any sense to talk of the 'natural' body?

2 What is meant by the politics of the body? How does it operate in current social and political movements?

3 How might the theories discussed in this chapter be applied to an analysis of either the body and disability or the body and 'race'?

4 In what ways does class affect the kinds of body that we have?

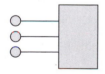

FURTHER READING

A good introduction to work on the body in social, political and cultural thought is Woodward (ed.), *Identity and Difference* (1997), which covers various theories of the body alongside issues of sexuality, bodily practices and identity. For reviews of the body in sociological thinking, dealing with many of the ideas addressed in this chapter, see Shilling, *The Body and Social Theory* (1993) and Turner, *The Body and Society* (1984). A more general collection of political and social theoretical writings is Featherstone *et al.*, *The Body: Social Process and Cultural Theory* (1991), which has pieces on Foucault, Nietzsche and others. Given the centrality of feminism to debates about the body, there are several texts of note. These include O'Brien, *The Politics of*

Reproduction (1981), a critique of traditional political thought from the perspective of male and female experiences of biological reproduction; Bordo, *Unbearable Weight: Feminism, Western Culture, and the Body* (1993), a largely Foucauldian influenced account of the female body in relation to food and slenderness (including analyses of anorexia and bulimia); and Grosz, *Volatile Bodies: Toward a Corporeal Feminism* (1994), an engagement with philosophical and psychoanalytic theories of the body covering thinkers such as Freud, Nietzsche, Foucault, Merleau-Ponty and Lacan. For some slightly more radical writings, see Kroker and Kroker (eds), *Body Invaders: Panic Sex in America* (1987), which explores the body in postmodernity, and their *The Last Sex: Feminism and Outlaw Bodies* (1993), dealing with the body in the context of gender politics. These last two texts include analyses from social and political theory as well as work from cultural studies, literature and the visual arts.

7 CULTURE
Alan Finlayson

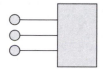

INTRODUCTION

The twentieth century has seen a revolution in the production of culture and the means of communication. The modern mass media create new experiences, new sensations and new social constituencies, while transforming old ones. But how can social and political theory engage with these phenomena? Under the impact of such cultural transformations, some central features of this tradition of thought must be reassessed or, at the very least, expanded. Can we really consider the nature of public discourse or debate, the conduct of social affairs, without taking into account the means by which such debate is shaped and disseminated? As Marshall McLuhan (1974) famously pointed out, the printing press revolutionized the world. The 'typographic explosion' enabled words and ideas to live beyond the lifespan of their articulators. The capacity of printing to make texts available on a mass scale gave greater numbers of people than ever before access to information previously the privilege of a Latin-speaking clerical elite. The ability to store such information made possible new concepts of time and history (and 'history' is, in part, knowledge of the records of the past).

The forms of culture that printing made possible – novels, newspapers and so forth – extended the human reach and enlarged our communities. As Benedict Anderson makes plain, the advent of these forms 'provided the technical means for "re-presenting" the kind of imagined community that is the nation' (Anderson 1992: 25). Print capitalism 'made it possible for rapidly growing numbers of people to think about themselves, and to relate themselves to others, in profoundly new ways' (*ibid.*: 36). The nation, a core feature of modern society and politics, is intimately related to the forms of culture we produce and the communication systems we use. What is a community if it is not, at the very least, a group of people communicating with each other over a sustained period of time, sharing and recognizing a common 'culture'? And would the modern state be possible without the means of storing and disseminating the information that is the blood of bureaucracy? Contemporary forms of communication dominate both the production of communities and the members' understanding of them. At a moment when such systems of culture and communication are set to smother the globe, what more important focus is there for those interested in the critical analysis of politics and society?

This chapter introduces a variety of different approaches to the conceptualization of culture in social and political theory. We will understand the concept in the context of mass society and of what some have regarded as the 'problem' of the masses. This will involve us with the work of the English nineteenth-century critic Matthew Arnold, the links between culture and power in the work of Bourdieu, Marxist-influenced cultural analysis (where we contrast the approach of the Frankfurt School with that which derives from the work of Antonio Gramsci) and the approaches to cultural theory associated with semiotics, structuralism and postmodernism. The conclusion restates the significance of theories of culture for contemporary social and political analysis.

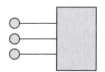

CULTURE AND THE MASS

The term culture is notoriously difficult to define. As Raymond Williams (1988) famously pointed out, it is one of the two or three most difficult words in the English language. Its meaning derives from farming, from the cultivation or development of crops: hence the word agriculture, and the use of the term in biology to refer to bacteria. The use of culture to mean cultivation has persisted in the context of defining culture as something developed, something (or someone) refined or a particular quality. Yet culture can sometimes refer generally to the 'artefacts' of a society, its paintings, music, writing, films and so forth. Or it can refer, in an anthropological sense, to the 'whole way of life' of a people: language, values, customs, economic and social organization, religion and artefacts, an entire history and tradition.

'Culture' is indeed all these things. The concept occupies the intersection of a dense range of issues, questions and phenomena – and never more so than now. In contemporary Western capitalist societies, culture (taken as 'a way of life') is bound up with the way in which we communicate through our enormous capacity to produce culture (as 'artefacts') on a vast scale. This in turn is bound up with the economic system of capitalism that commodifies 'culture' in order to reproduce and market it. The hierarchies of this system are in turn legitimated by the kind of culture it produces and by the divisions within society that are manifested and reproduced by the differentiated acquisition of culture. We may assert, in a limited recognition of the 'postmodern', that today everything is cultural.

To seize on a moment when the 'problem' of culture clearly intrudes into the social and political let us turn to Matthew Arnold. The eighteenth and nineteenth centuries, the period of rapid industrialization and consequent social change that shaped modernity, saw an increasing concern with culture. New ways of living moved people from the country into concentrated urban units to form a 'mass', a concentration of people quite different from that found in predominantly rural or agricultural societies.

Matthew Arnold, a former head of Rugby School, professor of poetry at Oxford University, inspector of schools and member of government bodies inquiring into educational policy and practice, was truly a man of 'culture'. He was concerned about the rapid changes he was witnessing in nineteenth-century Britain. He was particularly interested in those changes in industrialized society that affected the patterns of cultural development. Defining culture as 'the best that has been thought and said in the world', Arnold argued that without such an understanding, social standards and respect for authority would decline (Arnold 1961). He believed it was the role of the cultured class to maintain authority through an appreciation of the 'best' and the spreading of its virtues. For Arnold, the pursuit of culture is an inward one through which a person gets 'free play of the best thoughts upon his stock notions and habits' (*ibid.*: 7). It stimulates the mind to reflection and inculcates within it the 'best' thoughts. Culture is by definition perfection, 'sweetness and light'.

As Arnold wrote, new forms of working-class activism were challenging the rules of politics. Workers were beginning to demand equal political rights as well as adequate parliamentary representation. But for him, cultured people rise above this level of conflict and wish simply to inspire in others higher aspirations and better standards of cultivation. Industrialization has given people, especially working people, the sense that they should be able to do what they like, an anarchic sentiment of which only culture can disabuse them. The masses will never really grasp the essentials of true culture, they

> will never have any ardent zeal for seeing things as they are; very
> inadequate ideas will always satisfy them . . . whoever sets him-
> self to see things as they are will find himself one of a very small
> circle; but it is only by this small circle resolutely doing its own
> work that adequate ideas will ever get current at all.
>
> (Arnold, in Storey 1994: 4)

For Arnold, it is the social function of culture and the cultured elite to
restrain the anarchic tendencies of the mass, spreading 'sweetness and
light', ensuring that the mass recognizes the necessity for it to be def-
erent to true culture. Culture teaches us to value stability, to value the
state and to wish to make it part of the process by which reason may
develop. To be cultured is to have a conservative respect for the ven-
erability of social and political institutions, and an appreciation of the
need for their maintenance.

It is important to highlight one of the reasons why Arnold is moved
to express such concerns. Culture only becomes an issue, something
that is explicitly thought about, because certainties about our way of
life have been called into question. We would not think about our way
of life as such unless the presence of someone else's way of life had
caused us to ask questions. The Arnoldian perspective still exists, and
it can be found regularly disseminated through the means of mass cultural communication. This perspective expresses an anxiety that contemporary mass culture has brought about a decline in standards and
respect for authority. To put this another way, the presence of new
voices in the public arena puts into question things that were once
taken for granted. This is an important argument, since it highlights,
with great clarity, the connection between culture and power.

The wide dissemination of culture raises important issues. It is not
adequate to answer the question 'what is culture?' by defining it as
'the best'. This simply raises further queries. Who decides what 'the
best' is? Who has access to 'the best'? To put it another way, who is
to count as cultured? This is a question of power and democracy.
Arnold's conception of culture is inseparable from the development of
mass society. His is a reaction to an increase in social scale, or, more
precisely, an increase in the number and types of people who would
wish to count themselves as being members of a culture or society.
Thus, culture is related to notions of the public.

Classical Greek political thought made a firm distinction between
the *polis*, the public realm of free citizens, and the *oikos*, the private
realm of the individual. The citizens of the *polis* were free to go about
their business of politics freed from labour by a slave economy. Slaves
belonged only in the *oikos*, but the free citizen had access to the public
sphere, where political activity occurred (see Arendt 1956). In
medieval society, the public did not exist. Power was exercised by
absolutist monarchs with an authority that derived from God. Matters
of general concern were decided upon by the monarchical authority.

The Renaissance revival of Greek notions, symptomatic of the demands of a rising mercantile class, challenged this state of affairs and reinstated a public sphere for the political participation of citizens. Increasingly, throughout the modern age, the court became a privatized sphere and the governmental functions of military and bureaucracy were separated from the monarch and became public institutions. The definition of the public expanded, though this expansion was limited.

The new traders demanded that they should count as citizens, although they did not make the same demand on behalf of those on whose labour the merchants' businesses depended. Yet it is the logic of capitalism to disrupt traditional arrangements. As trade networks increased, more people had to be drawn into their operations. Towns, nations, even continents, became tied together by systems of economic exchange and their necessary corollary: formalized networks for the transmission of information and the spread of culture. Capitalism does not only disseminate goods, or even a system of production and exchange. It exports a way of life, a system of values, a culture. In doing so, capitalism has no respect for traditions or standards.

In many respects, although he may not have realized it, it was the corrosive effects of capitalist industrialization that Arnold was reacting against. But his vision was a conservative one, that of a reactionary hanging on to a dying culture. His views inspired an elitist desire to protect culture and civilization from new cultural forms by finding in art, and especially literature, a haven from modernity. This was to become the impetus behind the passionate, yet conservative, literary criticism of F. R. Leavis (a major influence on the study of literature in England) and the more left-wing writing of Richard Hoggart (regarded as a founder of cultural studies). Both these writers reacted against the mass culture manufactured by capitalism, and sought to defend something from its effects: the standards of the past and the romantic spirit, in Leavis's case; and the venerable traditions of the Northern English working class in Hoggart's. For both writers, modern mass culture destroys something in social life and cultural expression by replacing the authentic and the unique with the standardized and the formulaic (see extracts from their work in Storey 1994).

What is made clear by Arnold's exposition is that definitions of culture (and the circulation of artefacts that are defined as 'culture') are, as has been suggested already, intimately related to forms of power and structures of hierarchy. Pierre Bourdieu has undertaken detailed study of the way in which culture, and the status that is attached to it, allows groups in society to differentiate themselves from others so as to maintain hierarchical social relations (Bourdieu 1984). He shows that a cultural hierarchy of taste is an integral part of maintaining class division in society. Bourdieu speaks of a 'cultural economy' and of 'cultural capital'. We can think of culture, and knowledge of how to understand it, as an unevenly distributed resource on which people draw in converting it into status and consequent rewards. To know about classical culture and fine art is to have a resource that is, in Western cultures, a marker of social status and power.

Bourdieu brings back into the sociology of culture (in its anthropological sense) the study of culture in its normative, qualitative sense, and he attempts to analyse judgements of taste in the context of wider questions about social power. Cultural needs and tastes are the product of upbringing and education, the inculcation of a 'competence' in understanding art that in turn reflects and reproduces social hierarchy. To understand and appreciate opera we have to know how opera works, its history and development, its stylistic features. Art is thus understood formally, as part of an autonomous artistic tradition. It is to be experienced in a 'disinterested' manner. This detachment is the reverse of the popular aesthetic that seeks 'vulgar' enjoyment from art. Bourgeois aesthetics detaches art from the social; indeed, it denies the social world. Popular taste, by contrast, 'applies the schemes of the ethos, which pertain in the ordinary circumstances of life, to legitimate works of art, and so performs a systematic reduction of the things of art to the things of life' (Bourdieu, in Storey 1994: 447). Works are judged not by their formal characteristics and style but by their capacity to induce pleasures and by their function and relationship to norms of morality or taste. This different attitude is manifested not only in art appreciation but in a wide range of cultural practices: the consumption of food, for example. The bourgeois and working-class attitudes to food are distinguished by the 'antithesis between quantity and quality, substance and form, correspond[ing] to the opposition between the taste of necessity, which favours the most "filling" and most economical foods, and the taste of liberty – or luxury – which shifts the emphasis to the manner (of presenting, serving, eating, and so on) and tends to use stylised forms to deny function' (Bourdieu, in Storey 1994: 448). Think of the way that in more expensive restaurants eating is transformed into an abstract aesthetic experience. There is less food but it is carefully presented and the surroundings and ambience are as much a part of the experience as the need for nutrition. This reference to food draws attention to the way forms of culture are related to apparently natural phenomena such as the body. Social class determines certain tastes and cultural habits, which in turn inscribe themselves on the body, making that body suited to particular, class-defined, tasks, and thus reproducing the distinction between social classes (see also Chapter 6).

Such 'distinctions' are a product of the different positions social classes occupy, the different 'systems of disposition' from which they come, what Bourdieu refers to as 'habitus' (see also Chapter 3). These social differences are themselves legitimated and fulfilled by this distinction between art and cultural consumption. The aesthete is set apart by an apparent power of understanding that appears to be found in particular people but is in truth the product of possessing a certain 'cultural capital'. The limited access to this resource and its distinction from a mere 'common' aesthetic perpetuates class hierarchy and functions, as we saw in Arnold, to block the claims to culture made by the mass. Again questions of culture bring us back to the point of entry of the 'mass' into society.

The presence of the 'mass' transforms the nature and function of art. This was recognized in the 1930s by German critic and theorist Walter Benjamin in his analysis of the effects of mechanical reproduction on art. While art has always, in theory, been reproducible, modern techniques such as printing, photography and film are capable of manufacturing mass reproductions of otherwise unique works and disseminating them widely. This reproducibility undermines the uniqueness of a single work, removing it from a singular place in space and time, denying it authority. The unique work of art had authenticity and what Benjamin calls 'aura'. Once the work of art, because of its singularity and aura, had an air of magic or ritual about it. For Benjamin, this is the origin of art. But as it is increasingly separated from its ritualistic function, art responds, with the doctrine of 'art for art's sake' establishing an autonomous realm for its purity, for an art with no social function. This freeing of art from any 'parasitic' relation to ritual leads to the politicization of the aesthetic (as manifested in movements such as surrealism, dada and futurism). A continuing focus on uniqueness, however, on the history, provenance and authenticity of specific works, helps to form restrictive notions of tradition and authority that maintain a distance between art and society. It is the advent of mass reproduction that destroys this for good.

With reproduction, art becomes more accessible. The viewer or listener no longer has to go to the art but can meet it 'half way', placing the work in situations inconceivable for the unique production. One can hear a symphony at home, view a print of a painting in any number of situations. Thus art is severed from its traditions. Plurality is substituted for uniqueness, and the meaning of the object is reactivated by the diverse circumstances in which it may be found. This, for Benjamin, corresponds to the irruption of the masses into society and culture. Things are brought 'closer, spatially and humanly'. Magazines and newsreels replace uniqueness and permanence with reproducibility and transience. In short, things are equalized. Art's ritualistic function is finally destroyed and a new capacity unleashed: 'the instant the criterion of authenticity ceases to be applicable to artistic production, the total function of art is reversed. Instead of being based on ritual, it begins to be based on another practice – politics' (Benjamin 1973: 226).

Mechanical reproduction changes the nature and experience of art. Singular forms of art such as painting cannot be viewed collectively, and there tends to be a process of mediation between viewer and viewed (think of the assumption that if one is to understand a painting one has to be trained and experienced in art). But for Benjamin, when art began to be exhibited to mass audiences, when it was removed from the homes of wealthy patrons and placed in public galleries and beyond, it became harder to organize the response of the masses. Indeed, while galleries do impose a disciplined, and intimidating, regime on the viewer (Bourdieu and Darbel 1992), these days one might also see a classic painting on a postcard, on television, even on a T-shirt. In such circumstances, the capacity for regulating the encounter with art is severely curtailed.

Contemporary philosophers of aesthetics sometimes manifest a fear of how the masses might respond to or interpret art. Roger Scruton has bemoaned the reproducibility of classic paintings and, although he does not put it like this, the destruction of their aura. Scruton, a particularly conservative philosopher, is moved to advocate the view that the reproduction of paintings should be banned and the works themselves returned to private owners who can prevent most people from seeing them. What Scruton wants is the return to art of a sense of the magical and rare, something that inspires reverence and authority and halts the equalization of all things. This is current in much aesthetic theory since the Enlightenment. As Frith (1996) shows, some philosophers of music would prefer that it never actually be heard, the better to contemplate the abstract beauty of its form. The value of a composition is held to reside in its formal, aesthetic structure, and this must be rigidly separated from any emotional response on the part of listeners. But this is no longer possible once the mass enters society.

Benjamin is also somewhat regretful of the loss of aura, but he regards the process as irreversible. Instead, he explores new forms of art, such as photography and film, which arguably transform our whole way of seeing things. Both these media offer to us completely new experiences and visions. In the close-up, for example, we can see the bodies and faces of strangers in ways in which we might otherwise see only our intimate loved ones. We can scrutinize the lines of expression in the face and we can gaze into the eyes. As Benjamin points out, this combines artistic with scientific vision, allowing us to see and dwell on fascinating detail. Subsequent theorists of film have drawn attention to the power of the gaze as embodied by the movie camera. They have drawn on psychoanalytic theory in advancing the thesis that these contemporary forms of artistic technology have transformed the way we look and have made manifest our voyeuristic desires (Metz 1982; Mulvey 1989).

The crucial point in Benjamin is the possible political effects of the new forms of art. Film, he argued, could produce 'shock' effects, reordering perception of the world. In turn, art could mobilize the mass. It is not the case, as is sometimes thought, that Benjamin advocates an aestheticization of politics (he is quite explicit that this, as in the case of the Italian futurists, can only lead to violence and war). Instead, he advocates a politicization of aesthetics. Film provides new opportunities for collective experiences. The film is inseparable from its nature as a mass art form. Classical painting is consumed by a con-centrating and absorbed spectator seeking to bridge the distance between artist and viewer. Film collapses this distance – we are absorbed emotionally and physically as well as intellectually, and there is here the potential for a revolutionary response.

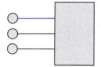

MARXISM AND CULTURE: THE FRANKFURT SCHOOL AND GRAMSCIANISM

In contrast to Benjamin, his one-time colleague from the Frankfurt Institute of Social Research, Theodor Adorno, did not take an opti-mistic view. Marxist theorists have been quick to point out how mass culture is related to the reproduction of capitalism, and few have done so with such coruscating insight as Adorno. For him, the 'culture industry' is one of the primary agents that produces (and reproduces) the characteristics of the pliant subject of a repressive social system. Cultural products are produced like any other commodity – in bulk and all the same. The industry does not respond to our needs but cre-ates them, manipulating our desires, offering us mindless distraction.

For example, Adorno argues that popular music is 'standardized' and comes 'pre-digested'. The imperative of the industry is profit, and to be profitable it will rework the formulas that have proven success-ful before, imitating them until they become 'frozen'. Thus, popular music is characterized by standardization and 'pseudo-individualiza-tion':

> By pseudo-individualisation we mean endowing cultural mass production with the halo of free-choice or open market on the basis of standardisation itself. Standardisation of song hits keeps the customers in line by doing their listening for them, as it were. Pseudo-individualisation for its part, keeps them in line by making them forget that what they listen to is already listened to for them, or 'pre-digested'.

> (Adorno, in Storey 1994: 208)

The culture industry appears to be a sphere where individualism and free choice persist, where the consumer who works all day in a boring, repetitive job can express his own choice in the form of personal taste. But this is part of the process – the industry offers the illusion of free choice through the invention of apparent differences, while all the time we are buying the same pre-packaged and standardized stuff. 'Pseudo-individualization' is the false appearance of uniqueness. Different bands and song styles are marked off from each other by their production and style to give the appearance of a great variety when offering only an illusion or 'halo' of free choice. The worker, fearful of unemployment, exhausted and stupefied by dull work, seeks some kind of relief from boredom and tension, yet is unable to put any effort into relaxation or reflection. The culture industry provides distraction without demanding effort: 'relief from both boredom and effort simultaneously' (Adorno, in Storey 1994: 210). With a pitiful irony, the escape from work follows exactly the same underlying pattern as work: routinized, standardized and dully repetitious. According to Adorno, this reproduces the irrational and repressive character of modern societies.

Good music could present opportunities for rethinking the world, it could present discrete elements bound together into a totality greater than the sum of its parts, while those parts would still have value and autonomy. Mass culture presents only subordination to a repressive totality. It is a 'social cement' that adjusts us to life in the current social system. The incessant and insistent rhythm of popular dance music engenders an attitude of obedience and conformity in the listener, of subordination to a mechanized and authoritarian society. Sentimental romantic music evokes a response of emotion, producing a space where listeners can experience loss and unhappiness in a way that reconciles them to it, pacifying them into acceptance (Adorno in Storey 1994: 213).

This bleak view of culture in capitalist society has struck a chord with many. In the 1960s, however, we saw an apparent revolt against this conformity when students railed against 'the system', denouncing consumerism and mass culture even as they produced it themselves. Adorno's colleague, Herbert Marcuse, became something of a guru for the student movement, advancing the thesis that under modern conditions of consumerism, culture industry and capitalist labour, human beings were reduced in scope, depth and autonomy such that we were seeing the formation of 'one-dimensional man' (Marcuse 1964). The routinization of work and social life, the domination of thought and emotion, were destroying humanity, reducing us to alienated and dependent automatons.

Adorno's work manifests a similarly reactive tendency to the one we encountered in Arnold, and at times he appears to criticize popular culture in order to reinstate classical avant-garde art forms (although it would be a foolish and hideous misrepresentation to regard Adorno and Arnold as comparable). While it is true that Adorno at times championed the difficult 'high art' of composers such as Schoenberg, it is not true that he was merely a cultural elitist. He did, however, tend to assume the passivity of the audience and to read off effects of cultural forms without researching what audiences actually do when they consume popular culture. Contemporary research into popular culture suggests, at the very least, that audiences are not passive in any simple sense.

It is important to remember that Adorno wrote before the advent of current popular music styles and also that he wrote partly with the intention to provoke. The proliferation of forms that characterizes the commercial world of music today may have engendered a markedly different situation. But then, of course, this may just be 'pseudo-individualization'. Certainly it is not possible to separate the 'art' of popular music from its commercial function and imperatives. One might suggest that this commercialism is precisely part of the artistry of pop (Frith 1996). The reproducibility and ubiquity of popular music are important features of the form, and the technology has its virtues. The very possibility of hearing the same song over and over, even of dwelling on parts of it, is in a way the pleasure of popular music. Perhaps we should remember that contemporary forms of expression are simply not comparable to their classical forebears.

This caveat aside, the writers of the Frankfurt School are important for their recognition that culture could not be treated as something separate from a social totality. Culture is intimately related to, and a part of, the very organization of mass society, and it encompasses art, ideas, norms and values. This is not to say that culture can be reduced to a product of social organization (and certainly not as a simple reflection of class interests). The research tradition inaugurated by the Frankfurt School has maintained a strongly critical attitude to forms of mass or popular culture. This perspective has been matched by work in the Anglo-American school of media studies that has tended to utilize models of behavioural sociology to investigate the process of communication represented by modern media (see Gitlin 1978). This approach often focuses on questions of effect.

We find a departure from this focus in a body of work carried out under the influence of the early twentieth-century Italian communist and Marxist theorist Antonio Gramsci (1971). Gramsci's ideas on culture, politics and ideology were revived in the 1970s as a way of theorizing the intersection of contemporary culture and social formations. In this context, the crucial concept developed by Gramsci is that of hegemony. This term derives from the Greek for leadership or domination, but Gramsci used it to refer specifically to what he termed 'intellectual and moral leadership'. Gramsci argued that the capitalist class did not rule by means of coercion, but that it maintained hegemony through dominating ideas in such a way that capitalist society came to be regarded as entirely fair and just. Because people's values were apparently well expressed within the social system, capitalism was able to dominate through the willing consent of those it ruled.

Gramsci argued that in any social order there exists a 'common sense'. These are the kinds of 'everyday', perhaps unsophisticated, views that we hold about society; popular myths, superstitions, proverbs and clichés. You might think of 'common-sense' attitudes such as 'a woman's place is in the home', 'you've got to have law and order' or 'society must be built on respect and the family'. Such observations appear to be straightforward, but they contain quite complicated assumptions about the way the world is and what people are like. These apparently simple notions come to seem obvious and beyond dispute; they become unquestioned 'norms'.

The process of producing such ideas does not involve a passive population that simply accepts the truths offered it by a ruling class. Rather, they are active in accepting these ideas because such ideas help to make sense of a complex world. This is not a one-off event but a continual process, where a dominant class has to keep on persuading people that its way of seeing the world is the natural and obvious one, despite whatever contradictions may appear. Thus, the hegemonic ideas of a ruling class are not stable but adaptive, and they may involve concessions to subordinate groups in an ongoing process of incorporating or assimilating people to the views of the ruling class. The activity of producing hegemony occurs on two levels. The first of these is the level of 'civil society', those areas of social life commonly thought of as 'private', as being beyond the concern of public or political life. We might think of civil society as entailing, on the one hand, economic life, private enterprise, the press and so forth, and, on the other hand, social institutions such as the family, the church and all other forms of collective activity not directly regulated by the state – our social/cultural life as carried out in sporting organizations, voluntary societies and so forth.

The second level at which the production of hegemony operates is that of the state. Included here are the specifically political activities people engage in, as well as the coercive practices of the army, judiciary and police force. Gramsci argues that we should conceptualize the state as being made up of a combination of the properly political and coercive elements of government, as well as the elements of civil society which are part of the process by which a dominant class maintains hegemony. The state may be understood to have an 'educative function' to the extent that it is through public institutions, such as schools, as well as 'private' civil organizations, that it tries to bring people up to a certain cultural or moral level. This is the level that corresponds to the needs and interests of the dominant group. It thus manufactures (at both the cultural and coercive levels) consent, a 'common-sense' ideology that justifies certain social interests but is never stable or easily fixed. Other groups in society will also always be trying to construct counter-hegemonic programmes in seeking to supplant a dominant group. What Gramsci is saying is that with the entry of the masses into society and politics, the modern state takes on the role of regulating and controlling that mass. One of the main sites for this regulation (and one that becomes a battleground) is culture.

For cultural theorists in the 1970s, Gramsci appeared to have developed a way of understanding social values and their production within everyday social experiences. Gramsci recognized that this is a complex and uneven process of production, and that it must involve the active consent of people (even if that consent is partly the result of force). This raises the possibility that everyday engagements with culture can be understood to be the sharp end of the process of generating consent and producing social values. This can then be theorized in such a way as to steer between an economically deterministic

analysis and an empty subjectivism that explains culture by reference
to individual 'taste'. The theory of hegemony helped to explain
popular culture as a dynamic process intimately related to a broader
context of social power relations. Popular culture came to be conceptualized as an arena in which images and ideas helped to construct
a conception of the world. This conception tended to be one that
favoured the status quo, but popular culture was also recognized as
having the potential to produce counter-hegemonic perspectives or
alternative worldviews.

In Britain, the 'turn to Gramsci' was spearheaded by researchers at
both the Open University and the Birmingham Centre for Contemporary Cultural Studies (CCCS) led by Stuart Hall. Developing highly
influential, groundbreaking research into popular culture and the
media, members of the centre put Gramscianism to work. An example
of this work is *Policing the Crisis*, published in 1978. The 1970s were
marked by an increasing 'crisis of legitimacy' within the United King-
dom. State structures were under attack in Northern Ireland, the economy was faltering as a result of both the oil crisis of 1973 and the
sterling collapse. Unemployment was rising, and with it social unrest.
Trade unions became increasingly militant and the 'consensus' politics of post-war Britain was collapsing.

The CCCS argued that this sense of crisis was reflected and represented within popular culture and news media through a number of
seemingly unrelated themes, such as race, deviant youth and football
hooliganism. These converged on the issue of crime and disorder.
Television and newspapers tended to demonize certain social groups,
especially young people and blacks. These groups were presented as a
disruptive presence within the social order, as antithetical to the supposedly natural adherence of British citizens to law and order. News
media presented themselves as above all this, as neutral observers, and
their reporting was thought to be authoritative and accurate. This
tended to create a certain unified vision of crisis which drew on the
'common-sense' notion of respect for law and order without asking
'whose law?' and 'whose order?' Tension in society was portrayed as
the result of a 'threat' from deviant groups. Media coverage drew
attention to this threat and amplified it. One striking example of this
is the so-called 'mugging panic'. No doubt people have been attacked
and robbed on city streets for some time, but in the 1970s this crime
received the specific label 'mugging'. The CCCS argued that the way
this crime was reported created the impression that mugging was a
crime committed by young black men, who attacked elderly white
women. They went so far as to suggest that this perception became so
great that robberies by other people were often not reported, or even
officially recorded not as muggings but as other sorts of assault or
robbery. This increased the impression that mugging was something done only by young black men. At the same time, new types of
television drama, such as *The Professionals* or *The Sweeney*, focused on

crime, law and order. All these things combined to put across one view of the state as the only body that could protect the public. At the same time, they portrayed the state's failure to deliver this protection as being caused simply by the activities of a few deviant groups.

What is striking about *Policing the Crisis* now is its argument that all these processes were part of a redefinition of the nature of state and politics in Britain. The consensus politics of the post-war was, it was argued, being rewritten, with an emphasis on a strong state committed to both a firm law and order policy and a scaled down social welfare programme. In effect, the CCCS predicted the development of a new authoritarian and populist hegemony. One year after the publication of the book, Margaret Thatcher's first government was elected, and proceeded to develop just such an approach.

By means of the theory of hegemony, analysts could relate culture to wider ideological and political struggles. They came to see the media not simply to be distorting or obscuring reality, but to be actively constructing that reality by producing more or less unified visions of how the world worked; visions that related to intellectual, political and economic developments and struggles. This perspective on the 'construction' of reality in popular culture and the media has been developed in a variety of ways. In some cases, the approach develops beyond the parameters of a theory of ideology. Researchers stress the active engagement of audiences when interpreting or using popular culture, and seek out dissident readings. For example, Janice Radway (1984) has found in popular romantic fiction a potentially feminist subtext, John Fiske (1991) finds Madonna to be an empowering role-model for teenage girls and Henry Jenkins (1992) sees *Star Trek* as a complex text involving its audience in, among other things, debates over sexual politics. Such researchers are careful to stress the contradictory nature of such texts (they are neither definitively progressive nor reactionary), but there is a tension in the assessment of these cultural forms. Do 'resistant' readings inspire people to oppose a social system that limits their autonomy, or do they merely provide them with a means of reconciling themselves to it?

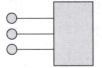

SEMIOTICS, STRUCTURALISM AND CULTURAL THEORY

Many of those working from a Gramscian perspective have felt the need to focus on issues that might be thought to represent aesthetic concerns: the form of culture understood as texts whose meaning must be decoded. In part, this has led to the development of a variety of techniques for analysing or reading the texts of contemporary culture, or, indeed, reading contemporary culture as a text. Under the influence of the linguistic theories of Saussure (see Chapter 3), some investigators have used language as a useful paradigm for conceptualizing and analysing social or cultural formations. The linguistic model draws attention to cultures as systems of meaning, to the way people in a culture are embedded in frameworks of knowledge and perception that shape the way they see the world and act in it. Actions are in turn thought to reproduce the structures of meaning. Such work has developed in part from the structuralist anthropology of Lévi-Strauss and the structuralist Marxism of Althusser.

Structuralism argues that society and culture are not made up simply of the actions of individuals. Culture forms, or is, whatever makes such actions possible and meaningful. For Lévi-Strauss (1963), social relations are structured by a series of conceptual binary oppositions that shape the way we view the world. These include oppositions such as culture/nature, human/animal, man/woman and rational/irrational. Analysing culture in terms of these oppositions could, for Lévi-Strauss, provide a way of understanding the unconscious foundations of culture. Myths and stories from across cultures could be shown to revolve around these oppositions, with the same basic structures always apparent. Lévi-Strauss was an anthropologist and wanted structuralism to enable us to appreciate the mythic 'poetic wisdom' of non-Western cultures. He was firmly opposed to what he saw as the ethnocentrism and sense of superiority of European social science.

The Althusserian form of structuralism emphasized the ideological basis of structured cultural systems and their relationship to the economic and class basis of capitalist society. The formulations of both Lévi-Strauss and Althusser emphasized structure over agency in understanding social formations and they focused on the way in which identity or subjectivity can be understood as something produced by cultural systems of meaning or signification (see Chapter 5). The structure makes possible a set of meaningful subject-positions and then both invites and forces us to occupy one. Not to occupy such a position is to be a non-subject. In social theory this has been an influential, if problematic, way of understanding the cultural and ideological basis of social identity. In literary and cultural theory, structuralism has been used as a tool for the analysis of cultural texts. It allows theorists to seek out the binary oppositions that structure stories, novels, films and so forth, and to relate them to the larger cultural system of which they are a part (see, for example, Will Wright on Westerns, in Storey 1994: 117–32). In these studies structuralism is often linked with semiotics.

Semiotics refers to the study of signs, where the term 'signs' refers to images or symbols that carry some sort of meaning (see also the discussion of Saussure in Chapter 3). As C. S. Pierce put it, 'a sign is something which stands to somebody for something else, in some respect or capacity' (quoted in Eco 1976). Road signs, such as those for danger or sharp bend, are sign-images that carry a particular meaning, that stand for something. In a similar way, we might say that flags are signs, as are logos; they are things that stand for something else, such as a country or a company. Semiotics is all about investigating how this 'signing' works. Understanding how certain images take on and transmit certain sorts of meaning will be of immense help in understanding cultural products.

Semiotics studies the way signs communicate and the rules on which this usage is based. Where we often ask of things what their meaning is, semiotics asks how that meaning comes to be (Seiter 1992: 31). Semiotics and structuralism have been powerful tools for the analysis of a range of cultural phenomena. In the field of popular culture, pioneering semiotic/structuralist analyses have been made of film (Metz 1982) and fashion (Barthes 1983), as well as literature. Judith Williamson (1978) uses semiotics and structuralism to analyse the meanings of particular advertisements, or rather how advertisements produce particular sorts of meaning. She relates the system of meaning in advertisements to a cultural system beyond that of advertising. Williamson argues that adverts do not sell products just by referring to their specific and 'innate' qualities and attributes (such as 'value for money' or durability), but by making these attributes mean something to us. For example, a car that does many miles to the gallon can be associated with thrift to such a degree that a connection can be established between the car, thrift and the 'clever' or 'sensible' person who uses that particular car. Conversely, a car that does fewer miles to the gallon can be associated with a 'devil-may-care' attitude that rises above the pettiness of 'value-for-money' in affirming the value of excitement and enjoyment (Williamson 1978: 12). These adverts take a fairly simple 'factual' statement about miles per gallon and make it mean something else, something more. The phrase 'low mileage per gallon' comes to mean 'sensible, efficient, cleverly economical'.

The distinction to be drawn here is that between denotation and connotation. To understand this, let us consider the example of fashion (Barthes 1983). Clothes are cultural signs as well as providers of warmth and protectors of modesty. Clothes can signify formality (the suit and tie or the evening dress). They can signify elegance or casualness, even 'a long, romantic, autumn walk in the wood'. Thus clothes can be 'read', like language, as signifiers (the clothes themselves) and signifieds (the meaning they have). We are working here with two levels of meaning. The first is that of denotation, the merely descriptive level at which clothes mean 'trousers' or 'jeans'. But there is a second level, that of connotation, at which the clothes signify a more complex cultural meaning, such as formality or casualness. At this level, the clothes are linked into wider assumptions and systems of meaning within a culture. This second level of connotation is of particular interest, since it is here that signs connect up with ideology.

In the essay 'Myth today', Barthes (1972) offers a now famous example. Reading a copy of *Paris-Match* in the barbers, he sees that the cover is of a young black man in soldier's uniform, 'saluting with his eyes uplifted probably fixed on the fold of the tricolour'. This is the denotative meaning of the picture, but at the connotative level 'I see very well what it signifies to me: that France is a great Empire, that all her sons, without any discrimination, faithfully serve under her flag, and that there is no better answer to the detractors of an alleged colonialism than the zeal shown by this Negro in serving his so-called oppressors' (Barthes 1972: 116). Thus, the form of signification here is slightly more complicated than that in Saussure. All the images in the picture, the soldier, the flag and so on, are understood in the form of signifiers which signify the simple message of black soldier saluting the flag. This forms a sign in the Saussurean sense. But this sign then forms part of a larger chain of meaning, a more elaborate and ideologically charged level of connotation which Barthes refers to as myth.

This is an important and useful concept, not just for understanding cultural artefacts (films, books, television programmes), but also for the analysis of a wider cultural or 'signifying system'. Thinking back to the work of the CCCS, we could conceptualize the racist discourse of Thatcherism in these mythic terms. The figure of the black mugger comes to be a signifier for much more than simply mugging. He comes to embody the notion of 'threat', of a challenge to the English 'way of life' – the mysterious and frightening outsider, the dark force of 'otherness'. Perhaps, then, one could study a whole cultural system just as Saussure set out to study a linguistic one. We could 'read' various forms of material culture as forms of *parole*, seeking to uncover the deep structure or *langue* from which they derive. This was part of the project of the anthropologist Lévi-Strauss. Such a project, however, runs the risk, as with Saussurean linguistics, of stressing the rigidity and determinism of a social system and of being unable to think through the nature of contestation and cultural change. It is important to remember that meanings are always contestable and that a cultural system is always dynamic and politicized.

Semiotics and structuralism can provide illuminating, sometimes startling, analyses of many forms of culture. However, the readings and interpretations which semioticians offer can sometimes seem like little more than imaginative, and sometimes clever, speculative work. Semioticians are often accused of simply finding what they expect to find. They expect to find coded messages and images that reflect a dominant ideology of some sort, and they do just that. But the extent to which this is simply creativity on the part of the investigator is unclear. While semiotics does provide a way of thinking about images, we should not overestimate the power and importance of the text narrowly defined. We must pay attention to factors of production and audience reception. Semiotics can downgrade the significance of the audience and it has little interest in researching how an audience makes sense of the signs and codes with which it is confronted. It is better to avoid methodological purity in favour of drawing on whatever method is most useful in a given context; semiotics and

Bourdieu's sociology, for example, need not be mutually exclusive. Above all we should recall that culture becomes a contested region when fragmented and discontinuous agricultural societies become mass societies, and that this process, in turn, is inextricably related to the way contemporary culture and the technologies that produce it enable mass culture to exist. There is conflict between the developmental tendencies of mass society and the 'traditional' culture it supplants, as well as conflict between competing conceptions of mass society itself. To be blunt, we might say that culture comes to be of social, political and theoretical significance because it emerges at a moment and site of contradiction, which serves to assist us in negotiating and clarifying that contradiction.

This brings us to the importance of representation and its modes. We are now totally surrounded by representations. As meaning-creating creatures we employ concepts – thoughts about what the world is 'really' like – and we express those thoughts in representative form, primarily through language. Representation thus mediates between our thought and reality. We would like to think that there is clarity to representation, so that there is no gap between thought and reality but a perfect correspondence. But representation suggests the re-presenting of something, looking at aspects of the world and then re-presenting them to us in a different way. This implies that a representation is one version of the world, not a real or simple reflection of reality. We might even say that representation could have a determining effect on our thought.

If representation is the medium by which we grasp and affect our social world, then control of the means of producing and disseminating such representations is of immense political importance. Representation might not matter much if we are scattered and isolated. In this situation, we could perhaps just go about thinking the world in idiosyncratic ways, needing only to express ourselves in limited communities. But in contemporary mass society we do not and cannot live like this. We are surrounded by representations emanating from the mass electronic media, while pictures and paintings are reproduced in mass form on postcards, in newspapers and on T-shirts. It is as if the imaginative representations of millions of people had been taken over and given objective form.

The meanings and potential dangers of such a situation are the object of analysis of the broad school of thought labelled 'postmodernism'. Postmodern conceptions of contemporary culture emphasize the power of representation in an overwhelmingly electronic world of media and mass reproduction. Analysts draw attention to the increasing domination of such images and with it the breakdown of old distinctions, such as that between high and low culture. They point to the way in which different forms of culture now draw extensively on each other (films refer to other films and make use of pop music, while pop videos refer to movies and fine art imitates advertising at the same time that advertising imitates fine art). In short, postmodernism entails a proliferation of cross cutting and interlinking styles, perhaps the domination of surface style over depth or substance. Even the once certain boundaries of local culture can melt away in a globalized and eclectic culture where 'one listens to reggae, watches a western, eats McDonald's food for lunch and local cuisine for dinner, wears Paris perfume in Tokyo and "retro" clothes in Hong Kong' (Lyotard 1984: 76). This blurring of boundaries leads, it is claimed, to the undermining of any certain distinction between representation and reality, a general condition of 'slackening' and a sense of fragmentation. Where once there was perceived unity, now there is confusing plurality.

Coherently defining the reference of the term postmodernism is an appropriately difficult exercise. It has been used to describe changes in philosophy, economics, politics, art and architecture, to mention just a few realms where its influence has been felt. There is not necessarily a clear connection between ideas of the postmodern in these differing contexts, but they do tend to share a sense that boundaries and distinctions are blurring, and refer to a fragmented and discontinuous experience of reality that may be an opening for the expression of hitherto marginalized perspectives. It may also allow the crushing of alternatives in a world now closed in on its consumer-oriented and capitalist self.

Thus, Umberto Eco writes of Disneyland as a quintessential experience of the postmodern. It is a 'city of robots', of the 'hyperreal' and the 'total fake'. Disneyland supplants reality: 'When in the space of twenty-four hours, you go (as I did deliberately) from the fake New Orleans of Disneyland to the real one, and from the wild river of Adventureland to a trip on the Mississippi, where the captain says it is possible to see alligators on the banks of the river, and then you don't see any, you risk feeling homesick for Disneyland, where the wild animals don't have to be coaxed. Disneyland tells us that technology can give us more reality than nature can' (Eco 1993: 203). For Eco, Disneyland is the 'quintessence of consumer ideology', it is an 'allegory of the consumer society, a place of absolute iconism . . . a place of total passivity. Its visitors must agree to behave like robots' (*ibid.*: 205).

Jameson regards postmodernism as indicative of a distinctive stage in the development of consumer capitalism. Indeed, it is the dominant cultural form under this 'logic of late capitalism'. From his perspective as a Marxist, postmodernism represents for Jameson the destruction of 'old fashioned ideological critique, the indignant moral denunciation of the other' (Jameson 1991: 85). He does not aim to dismiss or embrace the postmodern, but to understand it in the context of global and electronic capitalism. Jameson argues that culture in contemporary capitalist societies now has a new function as a level or instance of the social. This is to be understood in terms of 'a prodigious explosion of culture throughout the social realm to the point that everything in our social life – from economic value and state power to practices and to the very structure of the psyche itself – can be said to have become "cultural" ' (*ibid*.: 86). In this condition, we live in a society 'of the image or simulacrum', where the 'real' is transformed into 'so many pseudo-events'. This situation demands something of a rethink of traditional political practices that have sought to criticize and transform society by taking up a position outside of it. For Jameson, under current conditions the space for critical distance has been compressed (see Chapter 2).

Perhaps the key thinker of the postmodern is Jean Baudrillard, who is sometimes spoken of as its leading enthusiast. But Baudrillard, while one of the most assiduous chroniclers of a certain aspect of postmodernism, is certainly not enamoured with it. His work is an insistent polemic against the excesses of contemporary culture. Indeed, Baudrillard often sounds most like Adorno. Where Adorno and Horkheimer wrote in 1944, 'The whole world is made to pass through the filter of the culture industry . . . today the illusion [prevails] that the outside world is the straightforward continuation of that presented on screen . . . Real life is becoming indistinguishable from the movies' (Horkheimer and Adorno 1973: 126), Baudrillard wrote in 1987 that 'For us the medium, the image medium, has imposed itself between the real and the imaginary, upsetting the balance between the two, with a kind of fatality which has its own logic . . . The fatality lies in the endless enwrapping of images (literally: images without end, without destination) which leaves images no other destiny than images . . . images become more real than the real; cinema itself becomes more cinema than cinema in a kind of vertigo in which . . . it does no more than resemble itself and escape in its own logic, in the very perfection of its own model' (Baudrillard 1993: 195).

Representation and the image have become detached from any 'reality'. Images do not merely mask reality or distort its reflection. They utterly cut us off from it. We are immersed in an environment of images that refer only to themselves. If we chase down that to which an image refers, we will find only other images, which, if also chased down, lead only to other images in an endless circuit from which reality is excluded. We live in a world of simulated realities. There is no truth to be unmasked behind the images, only the endless proliferations of signs without referents and the recycling of what has gone before, such that, as Baudrillard famously put it, 'When the real is no longer what it used to be, nostalgia assumes its full meaning' (*ibid*.: 197). This is the condition of a culture which, in expanding to absorb a new 'mass', has come to focus inwardly with such narcissism that, in Baudrillard's terms, it 'implodes' upon itself. Is this the contemporary world? What is certain is that contemporary social and political theory cannot refuse to take full account of the culture of which they are part.

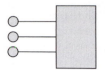

CONCLUSIONS: POLITICAL THEORY, SOCIAL THEORY AND THE STUDY OF CULTURE

We began this chapter by looking at Arnold's hierarchical defence of elite culture as a representative response to the entry of the masses into society. We then turned to Benjamin's optimistic outlook on the new mass arts. It should be clear that, at heart, questions about culture are questions about democracy. Who is to count? Who is to be counted? Raymond Williams, a pioneer of cultural theory, saw this more clearly than many. While writers such as Arnold dwelt on what has been lost in mass culture, Williams recognized how much was yet to be achieved. Williams understood culture as 'ordinary', as encompassing ordinary behaviour as well as the products of intellectual and artistic endeavour. For him, the analysis of culture had to focus on all these aspects or levels, including art, writing, social and political institutions (and trade, cooperative or credit unions) and the history or traditions of a people (see Williams, in Storey 1994: 56). To build a common and worthy civic culture that can battle against the crudity and crassness of latter day individualism we do not need an Arnoldian intelligentsia defending the 'best', but the construction of a culture of political democracy. A decent shared tradition is not something we once had that we have since lost. It is something we must strive to build as a realization of democracy.

Williams argued for a distinctive sociology of culture capable of assessing cultural forms and works of art in themselves. At the same time, he related these forms to the social factors from which they emerge and of which they are part. This sociology would be more:

> a distinctive mode of entry into general sociological questions than a reserved or specialised area. At the same time, while it is a kind of sociology which places its emphasis on all signifying systems, it is necessarily and centrally concerned with manifest cultural practices and production. Its whole approach requires . . . new kinds of social analysis of specifically cultural institutions and formations, and the exploration of actual relations between these and, on the one hand, the material means of cultural production and, on the other hand, actual cultural forms. What brings these together is distinctively a sociology but . . . a sociology of a new kind.
>
> (Williams 1981: 14)

We cannot understand an artistic project without understanding the social formation of which it is a part. We must recognize that the project is no mere illustration of that formation, just as the formation is not merely the background to the project. We must be concerned with both, with 'a refusal to give priority to either the project or the formation – or, in older terms, the art or the society' (Williams 1989: 152). This is a founding principle for a sociological or political understanding of culture.

Often we casually speak of culture as if it were 'out there' somewhere, external to what we are doing or being. We speak of television or popular music as an external force that enters into a society to corrupt it or to invigorate it, and we think of reintroducing values into a culture as if values were formed magically in the ether and were simply waiting to be put to work. But the study of culture reveals that this is not how it is at all. Culture is the terrain on which we live or, perhaps a better metaphor, it is the very air we breathe. It is our complicated, contested, historic cultures that make us the kind of people we are, just as we make the culture we inhabit. If we don't like the sexism or violence of movies and newspapers then we cannot simply blame these products. We must ask how our culture came to produce them. Our values, our sense of self and community, are part of that culture. As Luke Gibbons helpfully expresses it:

> Cultural identity does not pre-exist its representations or material expressions but is in fact generated and transformed by them – whether they take the form of the mass media, literary genres such as the novel and drama, visual representations or other cultural or symbolic practices.

> (Gibbons 1996: 10)

Culture is the production of identities and values and 'the mass media are not just neutral observers but are major participants in politics in their own right, locked into competition with other powerful ideological agencies such as the churches, educational institutions and the family' (*ibid.*: 11). Popular music, television, fashion, film and so forth are part of a culture and part of the ongoing political argument of a society as it questions its own identity and goals, just as schools, churches, trade unions and political parties would also do.

The ancient Greeks, Vikings, Saxons and Celts produced epic stories of battles between gods, the deeds of brave heroes, great battles and odysseys of discovery. These stories affirmed the community, delivered messages about moral problems and answered questions about the nature of existence. They were a way of thinking about things. Such 'myths are not always delusions . . . they can represent ways of making sense of universal matters, like sexual identity and family relations . . . they enjoy a more vigorous life than we perhaps acknowledge, and exert more of an inspiration and influence than we think' (Warner 1994: xiii). Contemporary culture also produces stories and experiences that communicate ways of envisioning our society. Fears, hopes, aspirations and social concerns are explored and communicated in our mass popular culture in a way analogous to the telling of tales around a campfire (and as families sit around television sets their faces are lit by the reflected glow and flicker).

Of course, it would be naive to think that contemporary mass culture is exactly the same as old-style folk tales. What happens to us if the stories we tell each other about ourselves come to be told by a major industry? Perhaps in previous eras folk tales were passed on by word of mouth, and at each retelling adapted and changed according to circumstance and need. But now these tales are set down on video tape, or recorded and replayed on laser-read compact discs. Huge corporations influence what will and will not be told, and there is no guarantee that their interests, their 'stories', are the best for society as a whole. But at the same time this means the story teller loses control of the audience. We can hear the story at whatever speed or volume we choose, we can rewind over dull bits and watch the good bits over and over. The story teller no longer has quite the authority he or she might once have had. 'Consumers', to some degree, take and retell these stories in different ways, thus making the interpretation of culture an active and conflictual process as well as a vibrant and contradictory resource. This resource gives people a means by which they can continue to construct stories and myths for our time. These stories may have no precise political meaning, but are part of the very process of social debate and development. In a 'culture' that includes an uneven distribution of power, this will be the process of hegemony, whereby different groups within society are engaged in complex 'intellectual and moral' competition. This is a process that never ends.

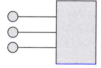

QUESTIONS

1 When you think about your social world, how it works, what values are important or what expectations you can have of others, to what extent are your thoughts shaped by the cultural influences around you?

2 What are the main differences in approach between the ideas of Adorno and those of Gramsci?

3 Do you think there is now such a weight of electronic mass culture that 'postmodern' society is collapsing under it?

4 In the contemporary world, we can meet many people from very different cultures. How do you think this affects our worldview?

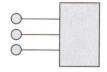

FURTHER READING

I have deliberately taken a large number of the quotations and references used in this chapter from Storey (ed.), *Cultural Theory and*

Popular Culture: A Reader (1994). Here you will find extracts from Arnold, Leavis, Hoggart, Williams, Barthes, Althusser, Adorno, Gramsci and Bourdieu. The volume also contains helpful extracts on semiotics and structuralism, feminist approaches to culture and the general Gramscian turn (see, for example, the readings by Weedon, Bennett, Radway and Schiach). Also useful is Thomas Docherty's *Postmodernism: A Reader* (1993), from which I have also deliberately quoted. See in particular the extracts from Baudrillard, Eco and Jameson, but also relevant extracts by Bauman, Rorty and Laclau. Another helpful reader is During (ed.), *The Cultural Studies Reader* (1993).

Good introductions to this area of study include Storey, *An Introductory Guide to Cultural Theory and Popular Culture* (1993) and Strinati, *An Introduction to Theories of Popular Culture* (1995). To set the conceptualization of culture in a broader framework, linking it with the idea of modernity and other themes covered in other chapters of this book, you could consult the highly accessible volume edited by Hall and Gieben, *Formations of Modernity* (1991), especially Bocock's chapter entitled 'The cultural formations of modern society'. The basis of current cultural trends in consumer capitalism is perhaps not stressed enough in this chapter, so this theme could be explored in Featherstone, *Consumer Culture and Postmodernism* (1991).

Raymond Williams's little book *Culture* (1981) is certainly worth a look, but for more fashionable approaches to studying popular culture in social context see Fiske, *Understanding Popular Culture* (1989) and *Reading the Popular* (1991). Fiske is very keen on celebrating popular culture, so for balance see McGuigan's critique, *Cultural Populism* (1992). A good introduction to Cultural Studies is Turner, *British Cultural Studies: An Introduction* (1990). On the relevance of culture to the analysis of politics, an article aimed at students is Finlayson and Martin, 'Political studies and cultural studies' (1997), while the book *Politics and Popular Culture* (1997) by Street is definitely worth a look. Readers and introductions cannot stand in for the real thing, so do consider having a go at some of the original texts of the main theorists discussed here.

THE SOCIAL AND THE POLITICAL

James Martin

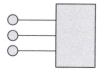

INTRODUCTION

The way we understand the 'political' is intimately and unavoidably bound up with the way we understand 'the social'. Our assumptions and beliefs about the nature of society cannot but inform our concept of what politics is for and what it is about. If we think that society is like a delicate organism, fragile to the touch, we will probably think of politics as the art of gently protecting and maintaining the balance. Alternatively, we might think that society is a volatile collection of competing individual egos, and politics the name for their power struggle. Other visions of society will entail other conceptions of politics. Indeed, it might be that politics is the process of formulating and deciding between different conceptions of what society is. Trends in contemporary social and political thought, and society generally, have suggested to some that it is of vital importance to address just what we think 'the social' and 'the political' are. So it is to the relation between these two concepts that this final chapter turns.

The term 'politics' derives originally from classical Greece, where it denoted the activity of the *polis*, or 'city-state', in which common affairs were deliberated upon and collectively binding decisions made. Thus, as Agnes Heller (1991) points out, the 'political' denotes a domain, or sphere, in which deliberation occurs, and it signifies a quality shared by those objects that enter into that domain ('citizens', 'policies' and so on). The term 'politics', on the other hand, is commonly employed to describe the activities undertaken within that sphere. Thus, discussions of the 'political', rather than 'politics', refer us to the wider *dimensions* within which the practice of politics can occur. The scope and limits of these dimensions are addressed in questions such as 'What are the limits of political power?', 'Who has a right to exercise it?', 'Which issues are significant?' These sorts of question demand that we specify the 'boundary conditions' of politics. How we formulate those boundaries, however, will be heavily influenced by the theories and concepts of society that we hold.

Under the impact of immense social, economic and cultural transformations, the modern age brought a concern to establish social order on the basis of a rational 'foundation' or 'ground' which specified universally agreed assumptions about society. The domain of the political came to be conceived as a distinct and separate sphere, concerned primarily with the maintenance of order. However, with the expansion of democracy in the nineteenth and twentieth centuries, the division of politics from society has become increasingly difficult to maintain. New and previously excluded social constituencies, organized around issues such as sexuality or race, have put in question supposedly 'universal' assumptions about society. Consequently, the boundaries of the political appear to be expanding into spheres of social life that once were deemed to be beyond public dispute. The challenge for contemporary theory is to redefine the political in a way that adequately incorporates new constituencies and diverse experiences.

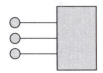

MODERNITY AND THE POLITICAL

Within the historical epoch known as 'modernity', the political came to be defined as a distinct realm located exclusively in the institution of the state and concerned primarily with the maintenance of social order. For many, this is still the received view of politics: it is a practice distant from our everyday lives, revealing itself only to enlist our support or take our money. This view differs markedly from the classical Greek notion of politics, where it was regarded as an inclusive activity in which all citizens participated so as to share in the pursuit of justice and the cultivation of the good life. Political activity involved collective deliberation upon shared norms and was co-extensive with a wide range of concerns. Human beings, according to Aristotle, were naturally political animals (*zoon politikon*), and their participation in the deliberations and decision-making processes of their community was considered an integral dimension of social life. Politics was an ethical activity, concerning itself with questions of how we should live.

However, the classical conception of politics was born in communities small enough in population to permit collective participation and homogeneous enough to avoid extreme ethical disagreements over what exactly justice required or what the good life entailed. It was also premised, notoriously, on the exclusion of women and slaves from citizenship, and hence from participation in political debate. The classical conception of politics, in which the political was broadly co-extensive with the social, all but disappeared from Europe for over a thousand years. And when questions over the dimensions of the political returned with modernity, social conditions were such that the 'natural' overlapping of society and politics could not be presupposed.

The term 'modernity' refers to the socio-economic and cultural changes that originated in Western Europe in the seventeenth and eighteenth centuries (although some of its features can be dated much earlier). These can be summarized in terms of the emergence of Enlightenment rationalism (see Chapter 1), the rise of capitalist economies and the formation of the modern democratic state (Navari 1981). Together, these phenomena instigated new ways of thinking about and organizing society. Dispensing with the image of social life as one element of a fixed and divinely constituted cosmological order, the forces of modernity began to see society as 'self-instituting'. That is, society was governed by its own intrinsic rules, which could be known to man, and not those of a distant, unknowable God.

For instance, in placing emphasis on the capacity of human reason to doubt and to question received wisdom, the Enlightenment distinguished itself from 'traditional' modes of understanding whose point of reference was not reason but scripture, not critical enquiry but accordance with established truths. Above all, the Enlightenment introduced a concept of human agency as rational and essentially free to consider, judge and determine the conditions of its own existence (see Chapters 1 and 5).

Coupled with the emergence of industrial capitalism, which disrupted traditional patterns of social life founded on traditions of kinship and hierarchy, the rational individual came to be held as the primary unit of society and social order. Social relations based on the exchange of commodities, and mediated by money, generated a sense of reciprocal equivalence among social groups once deemed to be innately superior or inferior to each other. The accumulation of wealth and knowledge made possible by increased trade and commerce encouraged the channelling of scientific inquiry into technical innovations for the production of material goods. This in turn put pressure on traditional forms of political governance to recognize and adapt to the increasing dynamism of societies by allowing the free flow of goods and wealth.

Both these processes encouraged the eradication of fixed hierarchies. Hitherto hindered by custom and convention, it was felt that society could be freed from the stale and inward-looking forms of the past and governed in accordance with reason. The formation of the modern state was a crucial step in this new way of thinking. During the sixteenth and seventeenth centuries, as capitalist markets expanded, civil authorities had begun to centralize their structures of authority in order to regulate an expanding population and an increasingly complex set of economic transactions. Throughout Europe, monarchs created a number of mechanisms to ensure their absolute power. These often included a central bureaucracy, a systematic regime of taxation, a formal diplomatic service and a standing army (Pierson 1996: 46). These features of what is called the 'absolutist state' prefigured its modern form, defining authority as a singular, sovereign institution with almost unlimited juridical powers over an agreed territorial boundary.

Under these conditions, the political came to be regarded as distinct from, rather than integral to, the wider society. Politics was conceived as the 'art' of governing; that is, a specific technique of administering power and maintaining social order. A centralized authority had to govern its borders and ensure its laws were obeyed. While classical theories of politics had been revived in thirteenth-century Italy in the form of 'civic republicanism' (see Skinner 1979), by the seventeenth century politics was defined quite separately from ethics, as the doctrine of *raison d'état* or reason of state. Politics was increasingly conceived as an amoral activity, exempt from biblical strictures, with the exclusive purpose of protecting the power of rulers and their territories from aggressors (see Habermas 1974; Viroli 1992). This view was expounded by Machiavelli in the sixteenth century in *The Prince*, and it was later developed by Jean Bodin and Thomas Hobbes in the seventeenth century.

While the institutional centralization of authority marks out one of the most distinctive dimensions of the political in modernity, the state was given a truly modern character with the substitution of absolutism for the notion of 'popular sovereignty'. During the middle ages, kings and princes had claimed legitimacy in the divine order, and they arrogated to themselves the right to determine, alongside the Church, the legal and moral life of their subjects. With the declining validity of such sources of legitimacy, and the increased exertion of power by the absolutist state over subject populations, demands arose among sectors of the emergent propertied classes for secular principles of legitimacy. These extended further the conception of society as self-instituting by making citizens, rather than God, the rational origin of political authority. The grounding of authority in the 'consent' of the governed emptied political power of its 'other-worldly' implications, making it answerable to society alone. For Claude Lefort (1986: Chapter 9), the French and American 'democratic revolutions' of the eighteenth century instituted a radical indeterminacy in the modern conception of the political. The physical body of the sovereign no longer symbolized a divinely granted will to which society had automatically to submit. Political power came to be seen as an 'empty space', an office to be filled by an indeterminate will authorized by society itself. But if society was essentially rational and the sovereign was constrained to act in accordance with its will, how was this will to be manifested in practice? How could this thing called society express itself, if indeed it should? This question has been the major preoccupation of modern political theory.

Broadly speaking, we have inherited from modernity two different conceptions of the relation between the social and the political: one which can be traced from Hobbes and Locke through to Kant and Mill; and another which links such diverse thinkers as Rousseau, Hegel and Marx. The former gives primacy to the rights of the individual and has strongly inspired the tradition of liberal political thought. The latter stresses the collective good that is to be found in the ethical unity that is constitutive of citizens' shared identity. While elements of this kind of collectivist thinking have featured in traditional conservatism, in its modern form its influence has been greatest in shaping the socialist perspective. We will examine, in turn, the individualist and collectivist conceptions.

Liberal political thought is premised on the idea that rationality inheres within individuals understood as essentially private agents. The interests of rational individuals converge on only a minimal set of shared principles, which the state, in so far as it reflects this rationality, is entrusted to uphold. These principles include our 'rights' to civil and political liberties. Political institutions have an essentially 'coordinating' function, ensuring that individuals' private desires do not result in disruptive social conflict. Beyond this, it is up to individuals themselves to organize their own lives and to make their own choices. Hobbes (1991) was not a liberal as such, but he did share an 'atomistic' view of society as based on isolated subjects. For him, the threat of 'perpetual warre' between egoistic individuals demanded that the state take on an authoritarian character. Rule by an absolute sovereign would prevent continuing conflict by imposing order (see Chapter 4). For later liberals, however, such a drastic solution was unnecessary if individuals could be trusted to think less egoistically about their relations with others.

Locke (1988), for instance, claimed that civil government is legitimately established by a contract designed to protect the individual's natural rights to life, liberty and private property from the interference of any potential threat. It is rational, he argued, for us to consent to the power of the state and to take on the obligations of citizenship, so that we can enjoy the benefits of our natural rights in our private lives. Public obligations are legitimate, for Locke, if they protect private interests. There is, therefore, no need for an authoritarian state. Kant's moral and political philosophy (1964) also supported such a conclusion. He sought to show how all rational individuals could affirm the same universal principles which would teach them to respect each other as 'ends in themselves'. Likewise, in the nineteenth century, John Stuart Mill (1972) promoted a vision of a liberal society structured around principles of mutual toleration on the basis of rationally defensible principles.

The liberal tradition of political thought saw the rationality of society in essentially individualistic terms. Typically, liberals have steered away from granting extensive powers to political institutions so that a natural harmony of compatible differences among individuals could flourish. Their suspicion has been that if the state is conceived as anything more than a guarantor of individual rights, tyranny in the name of some 'higher' principle is bound to ensue. A restricted political sphere, constrained by an agreed 'contract' between sovereign and people, is more likely to result in the extension of human freedom.

The second conception of the relation between the social and the political, deriving from Rousseau, Hegel and Marx, has resisted the individualism of the first. For this tradition, rationality does not inhere exclusively in individuals, but in the social collectivities of which individuals are only a part. The political domain was not conceived as a convenient 'mechanism' for coordinating different needs, but as an *expression* of substantive collective needs that transcend the individual. Jean-Jacques Rousseau (1968), for instance, argued that sovereignty was inalienable; it could not be 'transferred' from the people to the state. Rather, the state was to be regarded as an expression of the 'general will', something more than the sum of converging individual interests.

This 'holistic' view was taken up later by Hegel in his critique of Kant. For Hegel (1991), it was insufficient to justify the state in terms of abstract moral principles grounded in the reflections of an isolated rational individual. Moral principles are embedded not in the individual consciousness, but in the ethical substance of particular historical communities. The state can only be justified, then, in a historical context as part of a rational order with a significance greater than that of the individual. In Hegel's view, the state had to be conceived of as the final culmination of human society's historical development through different forms of community. This historical view of the rationality of society was extended further by Karl Marx in his critique of Hegel. For Marx (1996), rationality inhered within the structures of economic production, to whose logic, broadly speaking, political institutions were subject. Thus, under capitalism, the state's claim to be 'above' particular interests served to justify the freeing of the economic market and hence the accumulation of profits by capitalists. Far from being the culmination of human history, as Hegel grandiosely suggested, the modern state supported certain interests in a quite particular stage of social development.

Although they do not constitute a distinctive tradition like liberalism, the thinkers who subscribe to this second conception are united in their suspicion of the claim that political authority stems only from the legitimacy granted by individuals. In advocating holistic theories of social and political order, they have given more attention to the way in which rights are bound up with the wider social conditions that sustain individuals. This view underpins the Marxist approach to social criticism (see Chapter 2).

These two conceptions of the relation between the social and the political differ in crucial respects, but they share one similarity. Both seek to overcome the separation of politics from society by arguing that the one is grounded in the rationality of the other. The tradition deriving from Hobbes, Locke, Kant and Mill regards the political as founded on the interaction of rational individuals who choose to form a society. Politics occurs when these individuals meet to decide the direction of the social. For the tradition deriving from Rousseau, Hegel and Marx, the social collective and its institutions contain a rationality that goes beyond that of any one individual. Politics is the process of attuning individuals to the rationality of the social. Thus, the two traditions differ in their conceptions of the rational grounding of society and politics; whether it is the case that individual reason determines the boundaries of the political or, alternatively, that the individual is subject to a more social form of rationality. These two traditions also inform our thinking on the nature of the social. On the one hand, there is the view that social problems are the result of individuals failing to recognize their roles and responsibilities as rational participants in society. At its extreme, this view advocated social improvement by removing or improving such individuals. On the other hand, there is the view that social problems derive from something faulty at the collective level, leading to advocacy of social change and, at an extreme, social engineering, in order to produce individuals who participate fully in society.

Political theory in the twentieth century has inherited these different approaches in the form of the ideologies of liberalism and socialism. These have sought to incorporate their differing conceptions of society into a modern conception of citizenship. Liberalism has inherited the seventeenth-century conception of the individual as a rational calculator of self-interest. By consequence, it is argued that political participation should be fairly limited, with the state functioning to ensure an adequate legal framework to allow for the individual pursuit of private interests. Socialism, on the other hand, has inherited Rousseau's emphasis on government as a reflection of the people's rational will. Socialists have, accordingly, promoted the expansion of citizenship so as to allow greater numbers to participate at an equal level. In its more successful 'reformist' variety, this has typically involved the creation of egalitarian 'social rights' to health care, social insurance and so on, funded through state taxation (see Marshall 1992). To a great extent, the liberal democracies of the twentieth century have tended to sway between these two poles, between, that is, demands for individual rights and the demand for state-allocated provision (see Taylor 1985: Chapter 10).

It is clear, however, that, citizenship in the modern democratic state has never approximated the highly active version of the classical Greek *polis*. In Greece, to be a citizen meant being directly involved in discussion and debate over common needs, and being prepared physically to defend the *polis*. Citizenship was the primary identity of the members of a political community. As Michael Walzer (1989b) points out, modern citizenship is largely passive, denoting certain entitlements from the state, such as security or welfare, but not involving high levels of active participation. This is because modern citizenship has evolved on the basis of conceptions of human agency that posit a 'pre-political' identity. Politics therefore has importance only in so far as it guarantees something rational that pre-exists it in society, such as the demand for individual liberty or social cooperation. To the extent that these ends are achieved, politics is not itself of any intrinsic value. Indeed, in their more radical variants, both liberalism and socialism offer up visions of social order that entail a severely restricted sense of politics and the political. Free-market liberals, such as Friedrich Hayek (1963) for instance, look to the unhindered pursuit of self-interest in the capitalist economy to ensure the optimal satisfaction of human needs, while the state merely functions to oversee the 'rules of the game'. Marxists, on the other hand, have traditionally held as one of their cardinal principles the future 'withering away of the state' and the self-governance of society by a community of producers (see Pierson 1986). Although these visions are ideologically opposed, for both society contains within it the resources for rational organization and by consequence politics is reduced to the relatively banal task of administration.

These, then, are fundamental perspectives that have informed theories of the political and the social in the period of modernity. However, do the conditions of modernity still define our collective environment? Some have argued that conditions have changed so much in the twentieth century that we must now speak of a 'postmodern' world. Accordingly, they argue that we need to rethink both the social and the political.

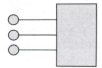

POSTMODERNITY AND THE POLITICAL

The precision of the term 'postmodernity' in describing contemporary social change has been hotly debated. Here I shall use 'postmodernity' to refer loosely to changes in the conditions of modernity rather than a whole new epoch altogether. Some of these changes include: transformations in capitalism from mass industrial production to service industries based on new forms of information technology; the 'globalization' of the economy that these transformations bring; the decline of 'class politics'; the rise of 'new social movements' and ethno-nationalism; a growing disenchantment with 'grand narratives' of 'history' or 'reason' (see Chapter 1); the reduced power of the nation state to regulate national economic behaviour and social conflict. These changes are believed to have set in motion a dramatic fragmentation of societies and a consequent redrawing of the dimensions of the political. The separation of politics from society, one of the principal characteristics of modernity, is being replaced by a growing politicization of social and cultural norms. As a consequence, the political has come to be regarded less as a separate realm outside of society and more as an integral feature of social life in general.

Of primary significance in considerations of politics in postmodernity is the emergence of new social movements that articulate demands over issues such as the environment, nuclear power, feminism, lesbian and gay rights and so forth. It is widely held that new social movements are indicative of two loosely connected phenomena: the increasingly apparent limitations of modern political institutions in aggregating popular demands; and the need for a new kind of politics that challenges the cultural preconceptions of modernity. Let us look at these two issues in turn.

First, we will consider the increasing perception of the failure of modern political institutions. Politics in liberal capitalist democracies has been premised on a conception of the individual as the primary unit of moral and political significance. Consequently, rights and freedoms are defined overwhelmingly in individual terms. As we have seen, these rights have prioritized the private interests of individuals over their public identity, on the assumption that, when left to their own devices, individuals' needs can effectively be coordinated without much interference from the state. However, as democracies have enlarged and citizenship has expanded, the liberal model of individual citizenship has been criticized as being fundamentally limited. This view was first aired in the nineteenth century by critics such as Marx, who pointed to the way modern citizenship works largely in favour of those who can afford to enjoy the life of a private individual, the bourgeois class. In the twentieth century, the modern state has adapted to this limitation by the extension of 'social rights' to health, welfare and insurance. Paradoxically, in order to extend rights the state has had to intervene in the economy and society to an unprecedented degree. The regulation of such areas as abortion, equal pay, health care and so forth has brought political institutions further into society, and this has generated new antagonisms over previously unquestioned areas of social life. The liberal conception of citizenship, because it is limited to questions of the individual, cannot always resolve these antagonisms adequately. New social movements, because they articulate collective demands, have been effective in resisting the narrow confines of modern political institutions.

The women's movement, for example, has challenged the division of politics from society in the form of the dichotomy between 'private' and 'public'. Politics is often regarded by liberals as a sphere in which individuals relinquish their particular interests and meet as citizens to engage in rational debate about the public good. Feminists have argued that liberal politics is in fact highly gendered, because it is premised on the labour of women in the private sphere of the home and the family (see Pateman 1988). The ingrained belief that women are 'naturally' housewives and child-carers has enabled men to treat family and home, and the violence and exploitation that it may at times involve, to be outside the realm of public debate. Relegated to the 'private' sphere, women's experiences and abilities, and the subjection of some women to violence, have been either suppressed or disregarded. The women's movements that arose in the 1960s and 1970s sought to challenge this exclusion by bringing women's experiences into the public realm. The radical feminist claim that the 'personal is political' accurately captures this effort to challenge the public/private division.

The spectacular rise of environmental and ecological movements in recent years has also challenged the boundaries of the political as defined in modernity. Modern capitalist societies have wilfully exploited the natural environment for purposes of industrial production. Natural resources have thus been regarded as a necessary component in the stimulation of economic growth and the creation of wealth, and individual freedom, in industrial societies. Ecologism, in its various guises, has criticized this exploitation of the natural environment for its massively destructive effects, visible, for example, in the depletion of the ozone layer, the eradication of plant and animal life (such as in the rain forests) and the progressive diminution of countryside through the creation of roads and urban centres. Further, ecologism has questioned the value of economic growth in itself. If human needs can be catered for by less destructive and wasteful means, then perhaps the logic of permanent expansion in capitalism should be replaced by more eco-friendly and cooperative forms of subsistence. Like feminism, this argument rejects the very terms in which human needs and interests have conventionally been defined. In ecological destruction, we are all losing out on a common resource in nature.

The examples of feminism and ecologism point us to the way con-temporary political arrangements have been perceived to be inade-quate to certain issues and concerns. As such, they expose the inherent *exclusivity* of liberal democracies; that is, the way the politi-cal has been defined around a narrow range of issues that exclude deliberation upon others. By relegating questions of gender relations to the private realm or treating the environment as a matter of resources, modern politics reveals itself to be founded upon certain apparently accepted values and assumptions, such as the need for economic growth or the natural condition of women as housewives. By questioning these assumptions, new social movements reveal such views to be contestable and specific to particular socio-cultural for-mations, even ideologies.

The second claim about new social movements is that they point to the need for, indeed they represent, a new way of doing politics. This claim is based on a number of features common to many such move-ments. New social movements have been characterized by a strong participatory ethic, which encourages members to be involved in activities such as discussion groups, protests, demonstrations, infor-mation dispensing and so on. This contrasts with the heavily bureau-cratic and elite-based politics in parliament, organized parties and trade unions. It is precisely because of the exclusion or intimidation of ordinary people from official politics that new social movements have become popular. Attached to this participatory element is also an emphasis on *expression* rather than pure utility. People are encouraged to register a protest, to express their own points of view, and not to act from pure self-interest. Participation is often combined with an aware-ness of the local efficacy of political action. The environmentalist sug-gestion to 'think globally' but 'act locally' encapsulates this view. In this way, the results of participation can be measured more immedi-ately. Finally, attention to the particular and the local has swayed social movements away from espousing 'totalizing' ideologies. Instead of competing with traditional political parties, new social movements have looked to single issues rather than grand ideological programmes on which to focus their attention, although they also invoke univer-salist principles that extend beyond the nation state, such as global human rights.

The 'new' politics of social movements points to a widespread dis-satisfaction with the established boundaries of citizenship in modern society. For observers such as Ronald Inglehart (1977), they are evidence of the emergence of 'post-material' values. Whereas nine-teenth- and early twentieth-century industrial societies were broadly founded on movements organized around material (i.e. economic) interests, contemporary 'post-industrial' societies are beginning to see new social constituencies develop. These constituencies have greater economic and physical security than earlier generations, and wider access to education. By consequence, they are less focused on the immediate pressures of material subsistence and more concerned with questions of identity, autonomy and the freedom to define their own life projects. These post-materialist values constitute a 'silent revolution', in Inglehart's view, which is gradually questioning the taken-for-granted expectations and values of earlier generations. Evidence of this view can also be found in the steady decline of mass party politics and the widely noted sense of 'blurring' between traditional ideological divisions of 'right' and 'left' (see Giddens 1994; Bobbio 1996).

However, there are a number of problems with an exclusive association of social movements with post-materialism. First, it crudely lumps together a number of quite different organizations and aspirations, many of which predate the 1960s. Versions of feminism, ecologism and anti-racism existed prior to the twentieth century. Second, to define these movements as a product of changes in 'values' tends to neutralize their impact as radical demands. It suggests that what is at issue is a new set of individual lifestyle preferences brought about by new forms of capitalism (Scott 1990).

Recently, it has been argued that some new social movements express a politics of 'identity', and not simply one based on different individual choices (Young 1990). To talk of identity is to challenge the concept of the pre-existing rational subject (the chooser of preferences), and this changes the status of certain demands. If certain groups and movements represent new identities, there is something non-negotiable in their demands, something that is deeply bound up with who they are. Unlike simple preferences, this cannot be easily 'traded off' against other demands.

The notion of 'identity politics' as opposed to the 'politics of new social movements' also ties in to broader transformations. While social movement theory deals largely with 'progressive' left libertarian movements and demands, identity politics points to a wider field of social transformation. The late twentieth century has not only been defined by demands for greater rights for excluded sectors of society, it has also witnessed the emergence and growth of neo-fascist and racist movements, ethno-nationalism, separatist movements and religious fundamentalisms of different varieties. These movements are similar to each other in so far as they seek to *prevent* the expansion of rights and inclusivity so as to protect something perceived to be under threat. Their demands are based on the claim to represent a particular identity (ethnic, regionalist, national, racial) challenged by the sorts of social groups that make up new social movements (Ignazi 1997).

The changing social bases of postmodernity have undermined the separation of politics from society. New demands for both inclusion and exclusion have brought to attention the increasingly diverse and antagonistic social foundations of liberal capitalist democracies. Contemporary developments in social and political theory often acknowledge the necessity to theorize the political in the light of these changing social structures and constituencies. Postmodernity challenges the constraints of common political structures, requiring them to remain sensitive to the particular needs of distinct groups. Of central importance, then, is the way in which social identities and differences are thought to bear on the concept of the political. The next two sections will consider two kinds of response to this situation, one focused on the political as a sphere of justice, and one focused on the consideration of 'otherness'.

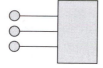

JUSTICE AND THE POLITICAL

Modernity, as we noted earlier, was premised on a conception of the rational subject, who, along with other such subjects, could come to agree common ethical standards. In both individualist and collectivist versions, this idea of the rational subject has functioned as the primary foundation on which concepts of a common political identity have been built. Rationalism involved the belief that there were universally intelligible standards according to which subjects might agree the scope and limits of the political. Yet the proliferation of social identities and differences, among other things, has undermined the appeal to 'universals' on which to found a common political identity. Thus, one of the central problems facing theorists today concerns the need to rethink the 'metaphysical foundations' of political association.

For many liberal theorists and philosophers, what is ultimately at stake here is the guarantee of political justice. Liberals have typically prioritized the 'right' over the 'good'; that is, they accept that all individuals have their own conception of the good life and, in order to respect this moral diversity, political deliberation must be restricted to upholding individual rights, rather than promoting a particular conception of the common good (Sandel 1992: 13–14). Such a view requires that individuals are capable of setting aside their own particular wants and desires in order to establish a framework for regulating fairly the basic structure of society. This was one of the major aims of John Rawls's *A Theory of Justice* (1972). Rawls proposed a 'thought experiment' in which we abstract from our personal needs and consider what kind of arrangements we would prefer to live under if we did not yet know the advantages or disadvantages we would encounter in our lives. In that way, Rawls believed, we would rationally endorse a society that redistributed resources to those who are unfortunate in being disadvantaged by birth in terms of either natural good fortune (intelligence and so on) or social circumstance (such as the socio-economic conditions of our family background). At the same time, we would grant equal basic liberties to everyone.

Rawls faced criticism from other liberal philosophers who were less inclined to agree to such redistributive measures (Nozick 1974).

However, the more devastating critique came in the 1980s from thinkers who rejected the metaphysical foundations of liberalism altogether. For so-called 'communitarians', such as Charles Taylor (1985), Alasdair MacIntyre (1988) or Michael Sandel (1982), liberalism's appeal to the rational individual undermines the necessary foundations of political community from the very start. By conceiving of justice in terms of the priority of individual rights over the good, liberalism makes common bonds a secondary feature of human association. For communitarians, however, the individual cannot exist prior to society, but comes to be an individual only in a society that provides individuals with a context in which to thrive.

What is at stake here is a conflict over different conceptions of human freedom. Liberalism's promotion of the individual has prioritized a 'negative' conception of liberty based on the principle that freedom exists only when the individual is left to do as he or she chooses. Communitarians, on the other hand, advance a 'positive' conception of freedom, which asserts that we are free only when we are able to achieve certain determinate ends which allow us to be fully ourselves (see Berlin 1969). The liberal view is based on an abstract conception of the individual as a rational calculator of self-interest, while the communitarian view sees rationality as dependent upon a moral horizon set by a quite specific community or social context. In offering a critique of the liberal tradition, communitarians condemn any appeal to an abstract rationality in which the individual self is set apart from the cultural values and collective traditions which provide moral horizons for human agency. Liberalism, it is argued, is a self-contradictory and unworkable doctrine because its individualism is unable to support the social conditions that sustain it in the first place.

The communitarian critique of liberalism has tried to shift the focus of political philosophy away from individual rights and towards a consideration of the 'common good'. However, in some instances this has been a rather conservative enterprise, in so far as it endorses models of 'community' based around traditionalist concepts of the family or religion. Both Sandel and MacIntyre have been accused of this form of conservatism. Yet the current diversity of cultural identities and moral values threatens the supposed unity of any such communal traditions, and communitarianism has little to offer a conception of justice for societies in which common traditions are widely contested. This has been recognized by some communitarian thinkers, such as Walzer (1983) and Taylor (1992), who are more inclined to support liberal aspirations to a tolerant form of pluralism. If cultural pluralism is to be respected, they argue, then a theory of justice must at least be more sensitive to the limitations of rationality, its embeddedness in specific social and historical contexts and its capacity to exclude those who do not or cannot conform to its standards.

Of particular note here has been the return of a 'republican' style of political theory. Republicanism is distinguished from liberalism in so far as it prioritizes the common good over the particular interests of the individual. For republicans, politics is not a purely instrumental process in which individuals or groups seek to gain rewards. On the contrary, it is where the group constitutes itself as a community and establishes a shared ethical life. Although in its Aristotelian version republicanism excluded women and slaves from citizenship, a modified form could be applied to contemporary conditions. Quentin Skinner (1990), for example, has argued that the classical republican conception of politics developed by the later Machiavelli allows for a balance between individual rights and the common good, with the emphasis firmly on the latter. Skinner points out that the choice facing political theory today need not be between negative liberty and individual rights on one side, with positive liberty and the common good on the other. The great merit of classical republicanism, he argues, was to 'link the idea of personal liberty with that of virtuous public service' (Skinner 1990: 306). The former was premised on the latter in so far as personal liberty was sustained by the wider freedom of the state from tyranny. Thus, classical republicanism serves as a reminder 'that if we wish to enjoy as much freedom as we can hope to attain within political society, there is good reason for us to act in the first instance as virtuous citizens, placing the common good above the pursuit of any individual or factional ends' (Skinner 1990: 304).

Skinner does not explain precisely how the aspirations for both individual rights and a sense of common obligations should be balanced, but his attempt to build a bridge between the two has clear echoes in other developments in contemporary political philosophy, which do point to a possible answer. Jürgen Habermas, in particular, although rejecting the republican emphasis on ethical unity, has offered a conception of the political which tries to reconcile individual rights and the political autonomy of citizens acting collectively. His most comprehensive effort at such a reconciliation is in his recently elaborated discourse theory of law and democracy (Habermas 1996). For Habermas, the achievement of consensus is not possible unless the obstacles to free communication between subjects are removed. These obstacles come in the form of assumed 'truths' about the world, which are not open to question. Institutions such as the media or forms of technology have come to dominate our lives and determine our range of choices. By drawing on a 'deliberative' model of politics, Habermas argues for an institutionalization of 'intersubjective' dialogue throughout society. Only when truths and norms are open to contestation, and their 'universal' validity is called into question, is it possible to reach a valid consensus on shared values. Habermas believes that such a consensus can only be achieved if we create institutions that facilitate forms of dialogue that are free from coercion.

For Habermas, whenever we argue about social and political arrangements, we implicitly invoke normative validity claims. These claims can be made explicit through open interrogation and deliberation. Anything which hinders the uncoerced participation of all those potentially affected by the implementation of the norm in question is a source of distortion. When we engage in a communicatively rational use of language in an effort to deal with our differences, we necessarily engage in a process of idealization. If we are trying to convince other participants of the validity of our view, then we must assume that they will be motivated to accept this for good reasons and not because they are forced in any way to accept it. This is to presuppose that our free exchange of views takes place in an 'ideal speech situation'. This ideal is not achievable in the concrete, but since it reconstructs the presuppositions of a communicative use of language, the impulse to minimize distortion is a demand of rationality (see also Chapters 1 and 2 on Habermas). The potential for undistorted communication in society will be enhanced if we overcome the dangers caused by the economic, cultural and political constraints that impinge on our efforts to reach consensus through free and open dialogue. Any consensus we can achieve on the basis of some such dialogue will offer us valid and legitimate grounds for political action. The intersubjective features of this approach facilitate pluralism by allowing for the pursuit of justice through a fair exchange of views on competing conceptions of the good.

Habermas's theory of communicative action and discourse implies a 'dialogical' conception of politics that has the potential to overcome the limited liberal democratic model of political citizenship. It reintroduces the possibility of collective ethical deliberation, without specifying in advance what kind of issue is or is not a suitable subject for public debate. The 'universal' quality of any moral norm derives from its active endorsement by a body of citizens, and is not limited to the agenda set, for example, by the structures of capitalism or patriarchy. In a 'post-traditional' world, he argues, justice can only be achieved if we are to adopt a dialogical test that interrogates our assumptions and prejudices.

Habermas has only recently begun to consider the application of his discourse theory to the functioning of law and political institutions (Habermas 1996). However, his theory has been given more concrete application by Jean Cohen and Andrew Arato (1992) in their work on the concept of 'civil society'. For them, discourse ethics can serve as a principle of 'democratic legitimacy' by which universal norms are deliberated upon and agreed to democratically. Cohen and Arato argue that Habermas's discourse theories are most applicable within the sphere of civil society. Sociologically speaking, civil society comprises the network of voluntary organizations and agencies 'between' the formal structures of the state and the economy. The relatively unregulated nature of this sphere permits a wide degree of freedom for individuals to define their own life projects. In recent years, civil society has been identified in both Eastern Europe and the West as a potential site of resistance against forms of state oppression and cultural marginalization (see Keane 1988; Seligman 1992; Fine and Rai 1997). Following Habermas, Cohen and Arato identify the kinds of collective mobilization exemplified by new social movements as a force for a rational form of consensus. It is the public space generated within civil society, rather than in the state alone, they argue, that is the most appropriate site for the form of practical deliberation proffered by the theory of communicative action. Norms that are rationally agreed upon in civil society can act as a check on the 'instrumental' reasoning common to institutional structures such as the state and the economy.

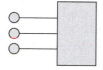

'OTHERNESS' AND THE POLITICAL

If theories of justice approach the political as an arena for the regulation of common concerns in the face of a diversity of conceptions of the good, an alternative strand of thinking has tended to focus on the exclusionary nature of modern politics. Here the concern is with the way in which conceptions of the political exclude and include particular types of person and forms of reasoning. This concern has typically come from those groups whose distinct experiences are systematically excluded from political debate, making them seem marginal, deviant and 'other'. This might include groups such as women, ethnic minorities or lesbians and gays. While the questioning of universal rationality has provoked normative theorists to reconsider the terms of political justice, it has also opened the way to rethinking the role of power in constituting us as subjects (see Chapters 4 and 5). This kind of approach yields a concept of the political that is oriented less to the formation of universal standards than to highlighting the unavoidable particularity and partiality of such standards.

Of primary importance in the consideration of otherness have been the theories of poststructuralist thinkers such as Michel Foucault and Jacques Derrida (see Chapters 2, 4, 5 and 6 on Foucault and Chapter 3 on Derrida). Their innovation has been to dispense with the notion of the subject as a disembodied social agent capable of reason. In this respect, they share with communitarians a scepticism regarding the foundations of politics ushered in by the Enlightenment. Yet unlike the communitarian critics of liberalism, they do not look to a specific community's 'moral horizon', against which the self is constructed, but to language and discourse (see Chapter 3). Whereas thinkers like Habermas view language as a medium of communication and 'discourse' as a mode of deliberation, poststructuralists have tended to conceive of language as being *productive of subjectivity*. 'Discourse', therefore, is not a form of intentional dialogue but the patterning of meanings that define us as particular types of subject with intentions (see White 1991: 23–8).

Foucault's analyses of punishment (1977) and sexuality (1978), for example, have directed attention to the way the subject is constructed through discourses of power/knowledge that operate throughout social institutions (see Chapters 2 and 4). Far from being a universal feature of human life, the rational subject is 'disciplined' and shaped by techniques of bodily control (see Chapters 5 and 6). Broadly speaking, the political implication of Foucault's analyses is to direct attention away from state power and towards the multiple discourses operating throughout social institutions. It highlights the struggles of resistance to power of those 'others' who are marginalized by 'universal' discourses: prisoners, sexual 'deviants' and so forth. Foucault's attention to otherness and the disciplinary and bodily processes through which subjects are constituted has been of considerable interest to certain feminist theorists who share a similar concern with otherness and the construction of gender (Butler 1990). We have already noted how feminists in general have been attuned to the exclusionary nature of modern political institutions. The critique of the universal subject has permitted some to argue for a more female-centred approach to the political, one in which sexual difference is valorized rather than treated as an unfortunate obstacle.

'Liberal' feminists have tended to argue for the greater political inclusion of women despite their 'contingent' bodily differences from men, yet this accepts the assumption that citizenship is gender-neutral. For other feminists, the gender-neutrality of liberal politics is simply illusory. To disregard bodily differences and to promote a universal subject who can reason abstractly is merely to universalize a specifically male set of physiological propensities (Young 1990). As such, women can be seen as equals only in so far as they renounce their own bodies. Feminists who see gender-neutrality as a denigration of female difference have argued for a recognition of the distinctiveness of female subjectivity and modes of reasoning. Carol Gilligan (1982), for instance, believes that women hold to different kinds of morality from men. In what might be called a form of 'feminist communitarianism', she has argued that women are typically oriented to an 'ethic of care' rather than the 'ethic of rights' preferred by men. An ethic of rights prioritizes impartiality and the application of abstract rules, while an ethic of care looks to understand and empathize with the specific differences and needs of the other. This implies a conception of justice that does not abstract from social differences but, on the contrary, is in the first instance motivated to recognize them.

However, as Anne Phillips (1993) points out, empathy is not necessarily superior to impartiality. In her view, an ethic of care is best seen as a complement rather than an alternative to abstract theories of justice. Without some kind of standard that abstracts from particular needs, politics would never get beyond the registering of differences. She goes on to suggest: 'feminism cannot afford to situate itself *for* difference and *against* universality, for the impulse that takes us beyond our immediate and specific difference is a vital necessity in any radical transformation' (Phillips 1993: 71).

Phillips's point is of particular significance when we look more broadly at the variety of differences (of sex, ethnicity, sexuality, class and so forth) that characterize contemporary societies. Unless *some* kind of unitary standard is sought, against which differences can be evaluated, there is no guarantee that an empathy with otherness will not privilege some groups over others (such as those we most empathize with). Yet the inclination of many who seek to import a concern for otherness into a conception of the political is to reject the appeal to universal conceptions of justice, the individual, reason and so on. If these concepts have no validity outside of specific discourses that invoke them, and those discourses are inherently partial and power-laden, then what hope is there for theorizing the political at all?

One approach to this dilemma has been to incorporate into a concept of the political an awareness of its intrinsic contingency and partiality. This view has been promoted by Ernesto Laclau and Chantal Mouffe in a number of their writings (see Laclau and Mouffe 1985; Mouffe 1993; Laclau 1996). Laclau and Mouffe base their arguments on a philosophical 'anti-essentialism' which denies that any social and political identity has an 'essence' that constitutes its unchangeable core. In their view, all identities are 'relational'; that is, they are constructed through symbolic relations of difference and equivalence, or 'discourse'. Their anti-essentialism is directed against the view that there is a universal 'ground' (such as God, reason or history) on which the social is founded. Yet they are just as critical of particularism as they are of universalism (see Laclau 1996: 20–35). To have an identity at all, in their view, is to differentiate oneself from others and, at the same time, to affirm equivalence with others. From a discursive point of view, all identity is constituted through 'antagonism', through a necessary reference to an otherness that limits and threatens to undermine the fullness or fixity of that identity. Such antagonisms abound, be they 'foreigners' against nationals, workers against capitalists, 'hard working folk' against welfare 'scroungers' or whatever. Our identity depends on the difference we see in others, particularly those we perceive to be a threat to us.

In Mouffe's (1993) view, the political must be seen not simply as the moment in which a common good is justly negotiated. Such negotiation must also involve defining what is *not* part of the good. Critically developing the work of Carl Schmitt (1996), she argues that all identities are constituted through a political antagonism that distinguishes between 'us' and 'them', friends and enemies. She argues that,

'As a consequence, the political cannot be restricted to a certain type of institution, or envisaged as constituting a specific sphere or level of society. It must be conceived as a dimension that is inherent to every human society and that determines our very ontological condition' (Mouffe 1993: 3). It follows, she goes on to suggest, that we must 'accept the necessity of the political and the impossibility of a world without antagonism' (*ibid.*: 4).

For both Laclau and Mouffe, the critique of Enlightenment rationalism does not necessarily imply that all universal standards are to be automatically dispensed with. That would mean the abandonment of all forms of politics. If the philosophical foundations of modernity are no longer feasible, its political objectives (democracy, freedom and equality) nevertheless remain crucial as organizing principles. Yet for Laclau and Mouffe, these principles can never be settled or defined once and for all. That, they suggest, was the problem with modern philosophy. It sought 'objective' boundaries to the political by invoking universal concepts, such as consensus, nationality or class solidarity. These were assumed to function as a stable horizon against which common needs could be clearly established. Giving up the search for objective foundations, however, means opening up the political to a variety of horizons and being prepared to accept different kinds of equality, alternative and coexistent forms of democracy and definitions of freedom. Thus Mouffe (1993: 13) points out: 'Universalism is not rejected but particularised; what is needed is a new kind of articulation between the universal and the particular.'

Laclau and Mouffe declare themselves in favour of a 'radical pluralist' and 'agonistic' democracy. Democracy is conceived as 'agonistic' in as much as its parameters can never be fully and finally established. Even the most liberal of political arrangements will exclude certain kinds of options, and thereby create others who feel dissatisfied with it. At best, such arrangements can provide for the expression of social difference by expanding democracy to various aspects of society. In this respect, their objectives are similar to those of Habermas, Cohen and Arato and others, who also envisage an expansion of democracy as the necessary precondition for a form of politics that will be congruent with, and adequate to, the conditions of contemporary society.

However, it is clear that there are also sharp differences between the two sets of views. Whereas the Habermasian view sets store by the willingness of individuals and groups to communicate freely and rationally, Laclau and Mouffe reject the whole notion of rationality as a feasible starting point for deliberation. In their view, to look for a stable universal ground on which to found the political community is a lost and possibly dangerous cause. What is 'political' cannot be grasped by a mode of moral reasoning (such as discourse ethics) and located within the confines of a singular space (such as civil society). Politics, as the formulation of 'friends' and 'enemies', occurs everywhere in multiple ways throughout society. Indeed, this is what society *is*. The political is understood by Laclau and Mouffe as the ontological condition of the 'social', its ungroundable, ever contested, moment of institution.

Thus, to democratize the political in a radical way is not to institute *a* public sphere but to allow for *a variety* of spaces, each with its own terms of deliberation. Whereas, for Habermas, the poststructuralist rejection of universal reason leads to a conservative withdrawal from public life, for Laclau and Mouffe, it represents a huge opportunity to expand democracy in a variety of directions and to open up the political to the 'others' that are its inevitable precondition.

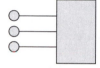

CONCLUSIONS

The social theories and concepts which have oriented political theory and behaviour since modernity are increasingly open to question as society itself changes. Exactly how we should conceive ourselves as subjects, our relations with each other and our common needs is now more than ever a matter of open dispute. This has led to a concern to rethink the political in the face of expanding social differences. While many contemporary theorists have come to support similar projects for the extension of democracy to new areas of society in order to deal with differences, there is nevertheless a wide divergence of views on the nature of the political and its relation to the social. For some, it is simply madness to abandon the hope that reason might still serve as an organizing principle for political justice. For others, that aspect of modernity is dead and neither needs nor deserves to be revived. Whichever argument seems more persuasive, and both have much to commend them, it is certain that today all of us are obliged to face up to the challenge of increasing social difference. How we meet this challenge, in both theory and practice, will determine the quality of our shared existence in the future.

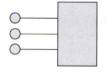

QUESTIONS

1 How has modernity shaped our conception of politics and the political?

2 What have been the consequences of 'postmodern' social and economic conditions for ideas about and participation in politics?

3 What difficulties arise in contemporary society for those who want to support a liberal conception of justice?

4 In order to view positively the current proliferation of social

differences, must we rethink the relationship between the social
and the political?

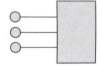

FURTHER READING

The concept of 'the political' is rarely treated as a topic in itself. This
reflects the widespread assumption that the modern state is the political institution *par excellence*. However, see Schmitt, *The Concept of the
Political* (1996), Mouffe, *The Return of the Political* (1993) and Heller,
'The concept of the political revisited' (1991) for more considered
views.

The evolution and characteristics of the modern state are discussed
in Held, *Political Theory and the Modern State* (1989) and Pierson, *The
Modern State* (1996). Skinner's *The Foundations of Modern Political
Thought* (1979) traces the development of political thought from the
thirteenth century until the seventeenth. Jumping ahead, Gamble's
An Introduction to Modern Social and Political Thought (1981) covers the
major political ideologies of modernity, namely liberalism and socialism, and their concerns with the role of the state. The significance of
new social movements is usefully discussed in Scott, *Ideology and the
New Social Movements* (1990). The influence of feminism on theorizing
the political is examined in Butler and Scott (eds), *Feminists Theorize
the Political* (1992) and the contributions of 'green' ideas are considered by Dobson in *Green Political Thought* (1995).

On the various conditions of 'postmodernity' and its implications
for thinking about society and politics, see Harvey, *The Condition of
Postmodernity* (1990), Lash and Urry, *The End of Organized Capitalism*
(1987) and Kumar, *From Post-industrial to Post-modern Society* (1995).
The work of Zygmunt Bauman is important for a broad sociological
perspective on modernity and postmodernity: see his *Intimations of
Post-modernity* (1992) and *Postmodernity and Its Discontents* (1997).
Giddens's work is also illuminating: *Modernity and Self-identity: Self and
Society in the Late Modern Age* (1991).

For recent developments in liberal political theory, see Bellamy,
Liberalism and Modern Society (1992) and, on the liberal–communitarian debate, Mulhall and Swift, *Liberals and Communitarians* (1996).
On the need to rethink justice in dialogical terms, see O'Neill, *Impartiality in Context* (1997). The 'further reading' recommended in
Chapter 2 provides for studies on Habermas's political thought. Poststructuralist and other 'non-foundationalist' approaches to political
theory are relatively recent, and perhaps the best place to start might
be Mouffe (ed.), *Deconstruction and Pragmatism* (1996), especially the
introductory essay. Alternatively, Mouffe's *The Return of the Political*
(1993) gives a clear statement of her own position in relation to debates
in liberal political thought. Connolly's heavy-going *Identity/Difference*

(1991) and Young's *Justice and the Politics of Identity* (1990) deal directly with the issue of 'difference' in politics. A middle way between the Habermasian and the 'non-foundationalist' approaches is offered by White, *Political Theory and Postmodernism* (1991).

Finally, the fortunes and current dilemmas of democratic theory are usefully examined in Held (ed.), *Prospects for Democracy* (1993) and Dunn (ed.), *Democracy: The Unfinished Journey* (1992).

GLOSSARY

Here we have selected a number of terms that are mentioned in the above chapters but not defined, or repeatedly employed and may deserve general clarification. The list is far from exhaustive, and where there are terms that are not defined you are advised to consult one of the many subject dictionaries or reference books available.

Behaviourism A methodological approach derived from psychology that concentrates on the observable behaviour of individuals and groups. In so doing, it privileges objective features of action over the subjective or meaningful dimension.

Communitarianism A term used for a rather loosely connected group of political theorists. What they seem to share in common is a rejection of the individualistic philosophical assumptions that are associated with much of the currently influential theoretical versions of liberalism. These theorists argue that modern societies need a stronger sense of community than would be possible if the state were to adopt a neutral stance towards competing conceptions of the good life, as liberals tend to suggest. Communitarians encourage us to articulate the shared ideas of the good that can act as a source of solidarity and a framework for justice in our own particular cultural context. This involves a rejection of the abstract, rationalist forms of moral universalism that are associated with political outlooks inspired by the Enlightenment. While these thinkers affirm a similar body of ideas, they adopt varied political views, from the conservative (Alasdair MacIntyre and Michael Sandel) to the socially progressive (Charles Taylor and Michael Walzer) and feminist (Carol Gilligan).

Contemporary systems theory Theories of this nature analyse the ways in which complex forms of social organization function in a self-regulating manner. They restrict themselves to the perspective of an external observer who explains scientifically the anonymous operations of macro-level subsystems, such as state bureaucracies or economic markets. Their focus is on the interdependent elements of a self-maintaining system rather than on the intentions and purposes of individual participants.

Deconstruction   The term associated with the philosophy of Jacques Derrida and his strategy for interpreting texts. Deconstruction exposes the hierarchical, binary oppositions and rhetorical devices by which Western metaphysics produces an apparent 'foundation' to its claims. Philosophical arguments that present themselves as secure and fixed are thus shown to be always subject to the irreducible 'play' or movement of language.

Diachronic   The historical development of an entity (e.g. language, social structure) over time. To be contrasted with *synchronic*.

Empiricism   The philosophical theory that argues that any know-ledge we have about the world is necessarily based on experience or sense-perception. It can be contrasted with *rationalism*.

Enlightenment   A movement of political and cultural change throughout eighteenth-century Europe. Enlightenment thinkers argued for the release of human reason from the chains of prejudice, superstition and religion. They believed in human progress and, often, in human perfectibility. The Enlightenment 'project' has had an enormous impact on the social sciences, in that it advocates the view that it is possible to have a science of society.

Epistemology   The theory of knowledge. It is concerned with such questions as: 'How do we acquire our knowledge of the world?', 'What can be known?', 'Who can know?'

Essentialism   The assumption that an entity has an unchanging core or 'essence' that defines it independently of its context: for example, the idea that humans are essentially rational or have a par-ticular kind of 'nature'. Partly as a result of the development of post-structuralist theory, the term has come to have a negative, critical, connotation, and is seen to imply a disregard for both historical change and cultural difference.

Ethnomethodology   The sociological study of everyday life and activities that focuses on how the individual experiences and makes sense of social interaction. Specific attention is paid here to the ways in which individuals report on, and rationalize, their actions to others.

Frankfurt School   The persons and ideas connected with the Insti-tute for Social Research in Frankfurt (1923–50). Leading figures have included Theodor Adorno, Walter Benjamin, Max Horkheimer, Her-bert Marcuse and, most recently, Jürgen Habermas. The School argued for the necessity of providing a critical theory of Marxism; that is, for an open-ended and permanently self-critical approach. Particular attention is paid here to 'superstructural' elements, such as aesthetics (e.g. Benjamin and Adorno) or language (Habermas).

Functionalism   A sociological approach that conceives social systems as integrated wholes. It concentrates on how different parts of a social system operate to maintain and reproduce that system (or not).

Genealogy   The term used by both Nietzsche and Foucault to refer to their particular approach to history. Both rejected traditional conceptions that assumed: first, a teleological or linear structure for historical development (such as that developed by Marx or Hegel); second, the idea of a subject-centred history, where the actions of 'great' individuals were thought to shape historical development; third, the possibility of discovering the origin of any specific historical phenomenon. Instead, they argued that 'effective history' (as Nietzsche called it) is based on a struggle between competing power blocs, that it is discontinuous – that is, based on accident and chance (rather than a single design) – and that there is no single origin to historical developments, only a multiplicity of factors that converge to produce an event. The purpose of this kind of history is to fragment our understanding of the past.

Habitus   A concept employed by Pierre Bourdieu. It refers to the systematic way in which certain practices and representations are organized such that social action is oriented and directed within a particular framework. In this way, the culturally and class-specific manner in which we eat, talk, even move, is the result of our habitus.

Hegemony   A term used by Antonio Gramsci to refer to 'intellectual and moral leadership'. Gramsci claimed that the ruling class, in addition to being able to rule by coercion and economic domination, also ruled by shaping society's dominant view of the world. This dominant view is regarded by those who are subordinated as the 'normal', 'everyday' or 'common-sense' view of things. Importantly, they actively consent to it and are not simply 'brainwashed' by it.

Hermeneutics   The theory of interpretation. It aims to understand the significance or meaning of particular human actions, utterances and institutions both past and present. It asks how our present standpoint might colour our interpretation of the events of the past and whether or not an 'objective' historical interpretation is possible.

Humanism   A theoretical orientation that places humans (as opposed to, say, God or Nature) at the centre of its concerns. It contends that humans are both the key sources of knowledge about the world and the agents of historical and political progress. It assumes a subject that is unified and universal. For a contrast, see *structuralism*, which is generally regarded to be anti-humanist.

Imaginary   Lacan uses this term to refer to a belief in images and fantasies (both conscious and unconscious). It evolves from the 'mirror stage' and includes material that is pre-linguistic. It continues into adulthood through the ego and its identifications. See also *symbolic* and *real*.

Language games   According to Wittgenstein, language involves a series of social activities, all organized around distinct purposes. In this sense, there are different language games, with different conventions and rules. We employ such games, for example, when we describe the world scientifically, when we give orders or when we pray. One of the main problems with philosophy, it might be argued, is that we misunderstand these different games and assume that all language can be forced into a single pattern (or game).

Langue   Language construed within linguistics in terms of a general, or abstract, system. This system forms the unconscious underlying structure that enables speech-acts or *parole*.

Logical positivism   The theoretical approach of an influential group of philosophical empiricists working in Vienna during the 1930s. They defended the principle of verifiability, which insists that the meaning of a proposition depends upon empirical observations that can reveal whether or not it is true. It follows that any statement about reality that cannot be verified by empirical observation, such as the claim that God exists, is meaningless. In more recent decades, even committed empiricists have found this form of positivism to be indefensibly dogmatic.

Methodological individualism   The view that explanations in social science and/or history should ultimately be couched in terms of the individual; that is, in terms of particular features or qualities of, or facts about, the individual.

Ontology   The theory of the nature of being.

Ordinary language philosophy   The dominant form of Anglo-American philosophy after the Second World War, influenced in particular by Wittgenstein. It argued that the problems of philosophy were essentially ones resulting from confusions in the usage of language or philosophical terminology. These problems could be resolved by translating sentences into what they actually meant in 'ordinary language'. This produced a form of philosophy that its critics claimed was too narrow in its conception and practice. See *language games*.

Parole   In linguistics, language as demonstrated in the actual speech of individuals. It is the particular, specific, concrete speech-acts that draw upon *langue*.

Performative   An utterance that, in itself, does something rather than simply stating something that is either true or false. Thus, 'I promise to marry you' is performative (i.e. saying 'I promise' is the same as promising), while 'the sky is blue' is not.

Phallocentric   A term used by feminists to describe writing and ideas that are male-centred or patriarchal. It derives loosely from Lacan's use of the word 'phallus' to indicate a masculine style of language.

Phenomenology   Broadly speaking, a descriptive philosophy of experience concerned with the essence of meaning. In sociological terms, it has come to stand for an investigation of the assumptions underpinning everyday experience. In this context, particular attention is paid to how people think and feel about the world and their role in it.

Poststructuralism   At its simplest, a reaction against *structuralism*, in that it challenges the idea of a single hidden structure that shapes surface meaning. It rejects the fixed binary oppositions (surface/depth, event/structure, conscious/unconscious) that underpin structuralist theory. In their place, poststructuralists emphasize multiplicity, fluidity and indeterminacy (that is, they reject the idea that structures determine events, allowing for a looser relation between the two). In the context of social and political thought, and in place of an emphasis on universal structures, poststructuralists emphasize the historically specific nature of subjectivity, identity, language and so forth. Like structuralism, poststructuralism is a form of anti-*humanism*.

Rational choice theory   Now the dominant mode of explanation pursued by political scientists whose methodological assumptions are modelled on those of the natural sciences. By using a variety of tools, such as 'game theory', it seeks to offer a unified empirical theory of social behaviour that avoids the biases of a variety of ideological approaches. The fundamental unit of this form of social scientific analysis is the rational, self-interested individual who seeks to maximize expected utility. This approach has at least as many critics as it has advocates, and it continues to be the focus of much controversy.

Rationalism   The philosophical idea that our knowledge of the world derives solely from our capacity to reason. It assumes that the mind has certain innate ideas or concepts that enable it to structure its understanding of the world. It can be contrasted with *empiricism*.

Real   The term used by Lacan to refer to that which occurs outside the realm of symbols or speech. This means that it is also, formally, outside the realm of the subject, since for Lacan the subject is produced through its entry into the *symbolic* realm and into language. See also *imaginary*.

Relativism   The claim that principles, beliefs and values (especially moral ones) have no universal validity. Instead, they are specific to particular eras, cultures or groups.

Semiotics The study of the sign and symbolic systems by which humans communicate. These systems include language, music, gesture, advertisements and so on.

Sign   In the work of Ferdinand de Saussure, the sign is regarded as the union of the *signifier* and the *signified*.

Signified   The concept that is referred to by a specific sign, e.g. the *idea* of a hat invoked by the word 'hat'.

Signifier   Both the spoken sound of a sign and its written form, e.g. 'hat'.

Speech-acts   A reference to what happens when people actually speak to one another. It is mostly associated with the work of J. L. Austin. It relates, for example, to the kinds of conventions and rules on which people draw in speaking, and to how people do things with words in order to achieve particular effects.

Structuralism   This is one of the main continental philosophies of the post-war period. It is any 'scientific' approach that focuses on the hidden structures or systems that underpin and generate specific surface institutions, events, subjects or other phenomena. Thus, the structural linguistics associated with Ferdinand de Saussure takes language to be a system that produces particular relations between signs. Louis Althusser's structuralist Marxism, by contrast, asserts that human beings are not the agents of political change but the products of a system of social relations that pre-exist them. For the psychoanalyst Jacques Lacan, it is the unconscious – which is structured like a language – that shapes conscious behaviour. Structuralism is generally regarded as being anti-humanist, in that humans are regarded as being what they are as a consequence of the structures that make them such.

Structuration theory   Derived from the work of Anthony Giddens, this approach to social phenomena expresses the idea that structure and agency are mutually dependent. At the heart of the theory is an account of the 'duality of structure'. According to this idea, 'the structural properties of social systems are both the medium and outcome of the practices that constitute those systems'.

Symbolic   According to Lacan, the symbolic order refers to the realm of language and symbols. It is through entry to this realm that the subject comes into being. It relates to the domain of cultural, social and political processes. It can be contrasted with the *imaginary* and the *real*.

Synchronic   Refers to the condition of an entity (e.g. language) at a particular moment in time. As such, it does not refer either to the previous development or to the future state of that subject. See *diachronic*.

Utilitarianism   A political philosophy primarily associated with Jeremy Bentham, James Mill, John Stuart Mill and Henry Sidgwick, which assesses the rightness of any action, law, policy or decision on the basis of its capacity to maximize utility; that is, to promote the happiness of those affected by it.

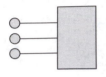

BIBLIOGRAPHY

For older pieces of work, the original date of publication is indicated in square brackets.

Ackelsberg, M. (1997) Rethinking anarchism/rethinking power: a contemporary feminist perspective, in M. Shanley and U. Narayan (eds) *Reconstructing Political Theory*. Cambridge: Polity.

Adorno, T. (1994) On popular music, in J. Storey (ed.) *Cultural Theory and Popular Culture: A Reader*. Hemel Hempstead: Harvester Wheatsheaf.

Adorno, T. and Horkheimer, M. (1972) [1947] *Dialectic of Enlightenment*. London: Allen Lane.

Alcoff, L. and Potter, E. (eds) (1993) *Feminist Epistemologies*. London: Routledge.

Althusser, L. (1971) *Lenin and Philosophy, and Other Essays*. London: New Left Books.

Althusser, L. and Balibar, E. (1970) *Reading Capital*. London: New Left Books.

Anderson, B. (1992) [1983] *Imagined Communities: Reflections on the Origin and Spread of Nationalism*, 2nd edn. London: Verso.

Anderson, R. J., Hughes, J. A. and Sharrock, W. W. (1986) *Philosophy and the Human Sciences*. London: Routledge.

Aoki, D. (1996) Sex and muscle: the female bodybuilder meets Lacan, *Body and Society*, 2, 59–74.

Arditti, R., Klein, R. D. and Minden, S. (eds) (1989) *Test-tube Women: What Future for Motherhood*. London: Pandora Press.

Arendt, H. (1956) *The Human Condition*. Chicago: University of Chicago Press.

Arendt, H. (1970) *On Violence*. London: Penguin.

Arnold, M. (1961) *Culture and Anarchy*. Cambridge: Cambridge University Press.

Austin, J. L. (1962) *How to Do Things with Words*. Oxford: Clarendon Press.

Avineri, S. (1968) *The Social and Political Thought of Karl Marx*. Cambridge: Cambridge University Press.

Bachrach, P. and Baratz, M. (1962) Two faces of power, *American Political Science Review*, 56, 947–52.

Bachrach, P. and Baratz, M. (1963) Decisions and nondecisions: an analytical framework, *American Political Science Review*, 57, 632–42.

Bacon, F. (1955) [1620] The New Organon, in H. G. Dick (ed.) *Selected Writings of Francis Bacon*. New York: The Modern Library.

Balsamo, A. (1996) *Technologies of the Gendered Body: Reading Cyborg Women*. London: Duke University Press.

Barnes, B. (1988) *The Nature of Power*. London: Sage.

Barnes, B. and Bloor, D. (1982) Relativism, rationalism and the sociology of knowledge, in M. Hollis and S. Lukes (eds) *Rationality and Relativism*. Oxford: Basil Blackwell.

Barrett, M. (1980) *Women's Oppression Today: Problems in Marxist Feminist Analysis*. London: Verso.

Barthes, R. (1972) *Mythologies*. London: Vintage.

Barthes, R. (1983) *The Fashion System*. New York: Hill and Wang.

Bartky, S. L. (1988) Foucault, feminism and the modernization of patriarchal power, in I. Diamond and L. Quinby (eds) *Feminism and Foucault: Reflections on Resistance*. Boston: Northeastern University Press.

Baudrillard, J. (1975) *The Mirror of Production*. St Louis: Telos Press.

Baudrillard, J. (1993) The evil demon of images and the precession of simulacra, in Docherty (1993).

Bauman, Z. (1992) *Intimations of Post-modernity*. London: Routledge.

Bauman, Z. (1997) *Postmodernity and Its Discontents*. London: Routledge.

Baynes, K. (1992) *The Normative Grounds of Social Criticism: Kant, Rawls, Habermas*. Albany: State University of New York Press.

Bell, R., Edwards, D. V. and Wagner, R. H. (eds) (1969) *Political Power: A Reader in Theory and Research*. London: The Free Press.

Bellamy, R. (1992) *Liberalism and Modern Society*. Cambridge: Polity.

Benhabib, S. (1992) *Situating the Self: Gender, Community and Postmodernism in Contemporary Ethics*. Cambridge: Polity.

Benhabib, S. *et al.* (1994) *Feminist Contentions*. London: Routledge.

Benjamin, W. (1973) The work of art in the age of mechanical reproduction, in *Illuminations*. London: Fontana.

Benton, T. (1984) *The Rise and Fall of Structural Marxism*. Basingstoke: Macmillan.

Benvenuto, B. and Kennedy, R. (1987) *The Works of Jacques Lacan: An Introduction*. London: Free Association Books.

Berlin, I. (1969) Two concepts of liberty, in *Four Essays on Liberty*. Oxford: Oxford University Press.

Bernstein, B. (1990) *The Structuring of Pedagogic Discourse*. London: Routledge.

Bernstein, R. J. (1976) *The Restructuring of Social and Political Theory*. Oxford: Basil Blackwell.

Bernstein, R. J. (1983) *Beyond Objectivism and Relativism*. Oxford: Basil Blackwell.

Bernstein, R. J. (1991) *The New Constellation*. Cambridge: Polity.

Bhaskar, R. (1978) *A Realist Theory of Science*, 2nd edn. Brighton: Harvester Press.

Bhaskar, R. (1986) *Scientific Realism and Human Emancipation*. London: Verso.

Bhaskar, R. (1988) *The Possibility of Naturalism*, 2nd edn. Hemel Hempstead: Harvester Wheatsheaf.

Bobbio, N. (1996) *Left and Right. The Significance of a Political Distinction*. Cambridge: Polity.

Body and Society (1995) *Cyberspace, Cyberbodies, Cyberpunk: Cultures of Technological Embodiment* (special issue).

Bordo, S. (1990) Material girl: the effacements of postmodern culture, *Michigan Quarterly Review*, Fall.

Bordo, S. (1993) *Unbearable Weight: Feminism, Western Culture, and the Body.* Berkeley: University of California Press.

Bordo, S. (1997) *Twilight Zones: The Hidden Life of Cultural Images from Plato to OJ.* Berkeley: University of California Press.

Boulding, K. E. (1989) *Three Faces of Power.* London: Sage.

Bourdieu, P. (1977) *Outline of a Theory of Practice.* Cambridge: Cambridge University Press.

Bourdieu, P. (1978) Sport and social class, *Social Science Information,* 17, 819–40.

Bourdieu, P. (1984) *Distinctions: A Social Critique of the Judgement of Taste.* London: Routledge.

Bourdieu, P. (1990) *The Logic of Practice.* Cambridge: Polity.

Bourdieu, P. (1991) *Language and Symbolic Power.* Cambridge: Polity.

Bourdieu, P. and Darbel, A. (1992) The love of art, in F. Frascina and J. Harris (eds) *Art in Modern Culture: an Anthology of Critical Texts.* London: Phaidon Press in association with the Open University.

Bowie, M. (1991) *Lacan.* London: Fontana.

Braidotti, R. (1991) *Patterns of Dissonance: A Study of Women in Contemporary Philosophy.* Cambridge: Polity.

Butler, J. (1990) *Gender Trouble: Feminism and the Subversion of Identity.* London: Routledge.

Butler, J. (1991) Imitation and gender insubordination, in D. Fuss (ed.) *Inside/Out: Lesbian Theories, Gay Theories.* London: Routledge.

Butler, J. (1993) *Bodies that Matter: On the Discursive Limits of Sex.* London: Routledge.

Butler, J. and Scott, J. (eds) (1992) *Feminists Theorize the Political.* London: Routledge.

Carver, T. (ed.) (1991) *The Cambridge Companion to Marx.* Cambridge: Cambridge University Press.

Chadwick R. (ed.) (1987) *Ethics, Reproduction and Genetic Control.* London: Routledge.

Chalmers, A. F. (1978) *What Is This Thing Called Science?* Milton Keynes: Open University Press.

Chodorow, N. (1978) *The Reproduction of Mothering.* Berkeley: University of California Press.

Cixous, H. (1980a) The laugh of the Medusa, in E. Marks and I. de Courtivron (eds) *New French Feminisms.* Hemel Hempstead: Harvester Wheatsheaf.

Cixous, H. (1980b) Sorties, in E. Marks and I. de Courtivron (eds) *New French Feminisms.* Hemel Hempstead: Harvester Wheatsheaf.

Clegg, S. (1989) *Frameworks of Power.* London: Sage.

Cohen, J. and Arato, A. (1992) *Civil Society and Political Theory.* Cambridge, MA: The MIT Press.

Condorcet, Marquis de (1955) [1795] *Sketch for a Historical Picture of the Progress of the Human Mind.* London: Weidenfeld and Nicolson.

Connolly, W. E. (1983) *The Terms of Political Discourse,* 2nd edn. Oxford: Martin Robinson.

Connolly, W. E. (1991) *Identity/Difference: Democratic Negotiations of Political Paradox.* London: Cornell University Press.

Conway, D. (1996) *Nietzsche and the Political.* London: Routledge.

Corea, G. (1985) *The Mother Machine: Reproductive Technologies from Artificial Insemination to Artificial Wombs.* London: The Women's Press.

Couvalis, G. (1997) *The Philosophy of Science: Science and Objectivity*. London: Sage.

Crenson, M. A. (1971) *The Un-politics of Air Pollution: A Study of Non-decision-making in the Cities*. London: Johns Hopkins Press.

Cronin, C. (1996) Bourdieu and Foucault on power and modernity, *Philosophy and Social Criticism*, 22, 55–85.

Crossley, N. (1995) Merleau-Ponty, the elusive body and carnal sociology, *Body and Society*, 1, 43–63.

Crowley, T. (ed.) (1991) *Proper English? Readings in Language, History and Cultural Identity*. London: Routledge.

Culler, J. (1985) *Saussure*. London: Fontana.

Dahl, R. (1957) The concept of power, *Behavioural Science*, 2, 201–15.

Dahl, R. (1961) *Who Governs? Democracy and Power in an American City*. New Haven, CT: Yale University Press.

Daly, M. (1979) *Gyn/Ecology: The Meta-ethics of Radical Feminism*. London: The Women's Press.

Daly, M. (1984) *Pure Lust: Elemental Feminist Philosophy*. Boston: Beacon Press.

Davis, A. (1982) *Women, Race and Class*. London: The Women's Press.

Davis, K. (1991) Remaking the she-devil: a critical look at feminist approaches to beauty, *Hypatia*, 6, 21–43.

Davis, K. (1995) *Reshaping the female body: the dilemma of cosmetic surgery*. London: Routledge.

Davis, K., Leijenaar, M. and Oldersman, J. (eds) (1991) *The Gender of Power*. London: Sage.

de Lauretis, T. (1987) *Technologies of Gender: Essays on Theory, Film, and Fiction*. Basingstoke: Macmillan.

Deleuze, G. (1988) *Foucault*. Minneapolis: University of Minnesota Press.

DeNora, T. (1997) Music and erotic agency – sonic resources and social-sexual action, *Body and Society*, 3, 43–65.

Derrida, J. (1973) *Speech and Phenomena, and Other Essays on Husserl's Theory of Signs*. Evanston, IL: Northwestern University Press.

Derrida, J. (1986) *Memories for Paul de Man*. New York: Columbia University Press.

Derrida, J. (1994) *Specters of Marx: The State of the Debt, the Work of Mourning and the New International*. London: Routledge.

Descartes, R. (1984) [1641] Meditations on first philosophy, in J. Cottingham, R. Stoothoff and D. Murdoch (eds) *The Philosophical Writings of Descartes, Vol. II*. Cambridge: Cambridge University Press.

Dews, P. (1987) *Logics of Disintegration: Poststructuralist Thought and the Claims of Critical Theory*. London: Verso.

Dews, P. (1988) The return of the subject in the late Foucault, *Radical Philosophy*, 51, 37–41.

Dobson, A. (1995) *Green Political Thought*, 2nd edn. London: Routledge.

Docherty, T. (ed.) (1993) *Postmodernism: A Reader*. Hemel Hempstead: Harvester Wheatsheaf.

Dreyfus, H. and Rabinow, P. (1982) *Michel Foucault: Beyond Structuralism and Hermeneutics*. Hemel Hempstead: Harvester Wheatsheaf.

Dunn, J. (ed.) (1992) *Democracy: The Unfinished Journey, 508 BC to AD 1993*. Cambridge: Cambridge University Press.

During, S. (ed.) (1993) *The Cultural Studies Reader*. London: Routledge.

Eco, U. (1976) *A Theory of Semiotics*. Bloomington: Indiana University Press.

Eco, U. (1993) The city of robots, in Docherty (1993).

Elliot, G. (1987) *Althusser: The Detour of Theory*. London: Verso.

Elshtain, J. B. (1981) *Public Man, Private Woman*. Princeton, NJ: Princeton University Press.

Elshtain, J. B. (1992) The power and powerlessness of women, in G. Bock and S. James (eds) *Beyond Equality and Difference: Citizenship, Feminist Politics, Female Subjectivity*. London: Routledge.

Engels, F. (1978) [1883] Speech at the graveside of Karl Marx, in R. Tucker (ed.) *The Marx–Engels Reader*. New York: Norton and Company.

Featherstone, M. (1991) *Consumer Culture and Postmodernism*. London: Sage.

Featherstone, M., Hepworth, M. and Turner, B. S. (eds) (1991) *The Body: Social Process and Cultural Theory*. London: Sage.

Feyerabend, P. (1993) *Against Method*, 3rd edn. London: Verso.

Fine, R. and Rai, S. (eds) (1997) *Civil Society: Democratic Perspectives*. London: Frank Cass.

Finlayson, A. and Martin, J. (1997) Political studies and cultural studies, *Politics*, 17, 183–9.

Firestone, S. (1976) [1970] *The Dialectic of Sex: the Case for Feminist Revolution*. London: Virago.

Fiske, J. (1989) *Understanding Popular Culture*. London: Unwin Hyman.

Fiske, J. (1991) *Reading the Popular*. London: Routledge.

Flammang, J. A. (1990) Feminist theory: the question of power, in J. Scott (ed.) *Power: Critical Concepts, Vol. I*. London: Routledge.

Flax, J. (1990) *Thinking Fragments: Psychoanalysis, Feminism and Postmodernism in the Contemporary West*. Oxford and Berkeley: University of California Press.

Foucault, M. (1965) *Madness and Civilisation: A History of Insanity in the Age of Reason*. London: Routledge.

Foucault, M. (1970) *The Order of Things: An Archaeology of the Human Sciences*. London: Routledge.

Foucault, M. (1972) *The Archaeology of Knowledge*. London: Routledge.

Foucault, M. (1977) *Discipline and Punish: The Birth of the Prison*. London: Penguin.

Foucault, M. (1978) *The History of Sexuality, Volume 1: An Introduction*. London: Penguin.

Foucault, M. (1980) *Power/Knowledge: Selected Interviews and Other Writings 1972–1977*. C. Gordon (ed.). Hemel Hempstead: Harvester Wheatsheaf.

Foucault, M. (1984) Nietzsche, genealogy, history, in P. Rabinow (ed.) *The Foucault Reader*. London: Penguin.

Foucault, M. (1985) *The Use of Pleasure: The History of Sexuality, Volume 2*. London: Penguin.

Foucault, M. (1986) *The Care of the Self: The History of Sexuality, Volume 3*. London: Penguin.

Foucault, M. (1988) The ethic of care for the self as a practice of freedom, in J. Bernauer and D. Rasmussen (eds) *The Final Foucault*. Cambridge, MA: MIT Press.

Fraser, N. and Bartky, S. L. (eds) (1992) *Revaluating French Feminism: Critical Essays on Difference*. Bloomington: Indiana University Press.

Freud, S. (1986) [1933] *The Essentials of Psychoanalysis: the Definitive Collection of Sigmund Freud's Writings*. Selected, with an introduction and commentaries by A. Freud. London: Penguin.

Friedan, B. (1965) *The Feminine Mystique*. London: Penguin.

Frith, S. (1996) *Performing Rites*. Oxford: Oxford University Press.

Frosh, S. (1987) *The Politics of Psychoanalysis: An Introduction to Freudian and Post-Freudian Theory*. Basingstoke: Macmillan.

Gadamer, H.-G. (1989) *Truth and Method*, 2nd edn. London: Sheed and Ward.

Gallie, W. B. (1955/6) Essentially contested concepts, *Proceedings of the Aristotelian Society*, 56, 167–98.

Gamble, A. (1981) *An Introduction to Modern Social and Political Thought*. Basingstoke: Macmillan.

Garfinkel, H. (1967) *Studies in Ethnomethodology*. Englewood Cliffs, NJ: Prentice Hall.

Gibbons, L. (1996) *Transformations in Irish Culture*. Cork: Cork University Press.

Giddens, A. (1968) 'Power' in the recent writings of Talcott Parsons, *Sociology*, 2, 257–72.

Giddens, A. (1971) *Capitalism and Modern Social Theory: An Analysis of the Writings of Marx, Durkheim and Weber*. Cambridge: Cambridge University Press.

Giddens, A. (1977) *Studies in Social and Political Theory*. London: Hutchinson.

Giddens, A. (1979) *Central Problems in Social Theory: Action, Structure and Contradiction in Social Analysis*. Basingstoke: Macmillan.

Giddens, A. (1984) *The Constitution of Society*. Cambridge: Polity.

Giddens, A. (1991) *Modernity and Self-identity: Self and Society in the Late Modern Age*. Cambridge: Polity.

Giddens, A. (1994) *Beyond Left and Right: The Future of Radical Politics*. Cambridge: Polity.

Gilligan, C. (1982) *In a Different Voice*. Cambridge, MA.: Harvard University Press.

Gitlin, T. (1978) Media sociology: the dominant paradigm, *Theory and Society*, 6, 205–53.

Goffman, E. (1959) *The Presentation of the Self in Everyday Life*. London: Penguin.

Goffman, E. (1963) *Behaviour in Public Places: Notes on the Social Organization of Gatherings*. New York: The Free Press.

Goffman, E. (1968a) [1963] *Stigma: Notes on the Management of Spoiled Identity*. London: Penguin.

Goffman, E. (1968b) [1961] *Asylums*. London: Penguin.

Goffman, E. (1972) *Interaction Ritual: Essays on Face-to-face Behaviour*. London: Penguin.

Gramsci, A. (1971) *Selections from the Prison Notebooks*. London: Lawrence and Wishart.

Grosz, E. (1990a) Contemporary theories of power and subjectivity, in S. Gunew (ed.) *Feminist Knowledge: Critique and Construct*. London: Routledge.

Grosz, E. (1990b) *Jacques Lacan: A Feminist Introduction*. London: Routledge.

Grosz, E. (1994) *Volatile Bodies: Toward a Corporeal Feminism*. Bloomington: Indiana University Press.

Habermas, J. (1974) The classical conception of politics, in *Theory and Practice*. London: Heinemann.

Habermas, J. (1984) *The Theory of Communicative Action, Volume 1: Reason and the Rationalization of Society*. Cambridge: Polity.

Habermas, J. (1986) Hannah Arendt's communications concept of power, in S. Lukes (ed.) *Power*. New York: New York University Press.

Habermas, J. (1987a) *The Theory of Communicative Action, Volume 2: the Critique of Functionalist Reason*. Cambridge: Polity.

Habermas, J. (1987b) *The Philosophical Discourse of Modernity*. Cambridge: Polity.

Habermas, J. (1989) *The Structural Transformation of the Public Sphere*. Cambridge: Polity.

Habermas, J. (1990) *Moral Consciousness and Communicative Action*. Cambridge: Polity.

Habermas, J. (1992) *Postmetaphysical Thinking: Philosophical Essays*. Cambridge: Polity.

Habermas, J. (1996) *Between Facts and Norms*. Cambridge: Polity.

Hall, S. (1988) *The Hard Road to Renewal: Thatcherism and the Crisis of the Left*. London: Verso.

Hall, S. (ed.) (1997) *Representation: Cultural Representations and Signifying Practices*. London: Sage.

Hall, S. and Gieben, B. (eds) (1991) *Formations of Modernity*. Cambridge: Polity.

Hall, S. *et al.* (1978) *Policing the Crisis: Mugging, the State and Law and Order*. Basingstoke: Macmillan.

Haraway, D. (1991) *Simians, Cyborgs and Women: The Reinvention of Nature*. London: Free Association Books.

Harding, S. (ed.) (1987) *Feminism and Methodology*. Milton Keynes: Open University Press.

Harding, S. (1991) *Whose Science? Whose Knowledge? Thinking from Women's Lives*. Milton Keynes: Open University Press.

Hargreaves, J. (1997) Women's boxing and related activities: introducing images and meanings, *Body and Society*, 3, 33–49.

Hartsock, N. (1990) Foucault on power: a theory for women?, in L. J. Nicholson (ed.) *Feminism/Postmodernism*. London: Routledge.

Harvey, D. (1990) *The Condition of Postmodernity: An Enquiry into the Origins of Cultural Change*. Oxford: Basil Blackwell.

Hawkes, T. (1977) *Structuralism and Semiotics*. London: Methuen.

Hayek, F. A. (1963) *The Constitution of Liberty*. London: Routledge and Kegan Paul.

Hegel, G. W. F. (1991) [1821] *Elements of the Philosophy of Right*. Cambridge: Cambridge University Press.

Held, D. (1989) *Political Theory and the Modern State*. Cambridge: Polity.

Held, D. (ed.) (1993) *Prospects for Democracy: North, South, East, West*. Cambridge: Polity.

Heller, A. (1991) The concept of the political revisited, in D. Held (ed.) *Political Theory Today*. Cambridge: Polity.

Hindess, B. (1996) *Discourses of Power: From Hobbes to Foucault*. Oxford: Basil Blackwell.

Hobbes, T. (1991) [1651] *Leviathan*. Cambridge: Cambridge University Press.

Hodge, R. and Kress, G. (1993) *Language as Ideology*, 2nd edn. London: Routledge.

Hollis, M. (1994) *The Philosophy of Social Science: An Introduction*. Cambridge: Cambridge University Press.

Hollis, M. and Lukes, S. (eds) (1982) *Rationality and Relativism*. Oxford: Basil Blackwell.

hooks, b. (1984) *Feminist Theory: From Margin to Centre*. Boston: South End Press.

hooks, b. (1992) Is Paris burning?, in *Black Looks: Race and Representation*. Boston: South End Press.

Horkheimer, M. and Adorno, T. (1973) [1944] *Dialectic of Enlightenment*. London: Allen Lane.

Hoy, D. C. (ed.) (1986) *Foucault: A Critical Reader*. Oxford: Basil Blackwell.

Hoy, D. C. and McCarthy, T. (1994) *Critical Theory*. Oxford: Basil Blackwell.

Hughes, A. and Witz, A. (1997) Feminism and the matter of bodies: from de Beauvoir to Butler, *Body and Society*, 3, 47–60.

Hume, D. (1978) [1739] *A Treatise of Human Nature*. Oxford: Clarendon Press.

Ignazi, P. (1997) New challenges: postmaterialism and the extreme right, in M. Rhodes, P. Heywood and V. Wright (eds) *Developments in West European Politics*. Basingstoke: Macmillan.

Inglehart, R. (1977) *The Silent Revolution*. Princeton, NJ: Princeton University Press.

Irigaray, L. (1985) *The Sex Which Is Not One*. Ithaca, NY: Cornell University Press.

Jaggar, A. (1983) *Feminist Politics and Human Nature*. Totowa, NJ: Rowman and Allanheld.

Jameson, F. (1991) *Postmodernism, or the Cultural Logic of Late Capitalism*. London: Verso.

Jenkins, H. (1992) *Textual Poachers: Television Fans and Participatory Culture*. London: Routledge.

Jenkins, R. (1992) *Pierre Bourdieu*. London: Routledge.

Johnson, C. (1997) *Derrida: The Scene of Writing*. London: Phoenix.

Jordan, T. (1995) Collective bodies: raving and the politics of Gilles Deleuze and Felix Guattari, *Body and Society*, 1, 125–44.

Kant, I. (1964) [1785] *Groundwork of the Metaphysic of Morals,* translated and analysed by H. J. Paton. New York: Harper and Row.

Kant, I. (1991) [1784] An answer to the question 'what is enlightenment?', in H. Reiss (ed.) *Kant: Political Writings*, 2nd edn. Cambridge: Cambridge University Press.

Kant, I. (1993) [1781] *Critique of Pure Reason*. London: Everyman.

Keane, J. (1988) *Democracy and Civil Society*. London: Verso.

Kearney, R. and Rainwater, M. (eds) (1996) *The Continental Philosophy Reader*. London: Routledge.

Keat, R. and Urry, J. (1982) *Social Theory as Science*, 2nd edn. London: Routledge and Kegan Paul.

Kelly, M. (ed.) (1994) *Critique and Power: Recasting the Foucault–Habermas Debate*. Cambridge, MA: MIT Press.

Klein, R. D. (ed.) (1989) *Infertility: Women Speak out about Their Experiences of Reproductive Medicine*. London: Pandora Press.

Kristeva, J. (1986) *The Kristeva Reader* (ed. T. Moi). Oxford: Basil Blackwell.

Kroker, A. and Kroker, M. (eds) (1987) *Body Invaders: Panic Sex in America*. Basingstoke: Macmillan.

Kroker, A. and Kroker, M. (eds) (1993) *The Last Sex: Feminism and Outlaw Bodies*. Basingstoke: Macmillan.

Kuhn, T. (1970) *The Structure of Scientific Revolutions*, 2nd edn. Chicago: University of Chicago Press.

Kumar, K. (1995) *From Post-industrial to Post-modern Society: New Theories of the Contemporary World*. Oxford: Basil Blackwell.

Lacan, J. (1977) *Ecrits: A Selection*. London: Tavistock Publications.

Laclau, E. (1996) *Emancipation(s)*. London: Verso.

Laclau, E. and Mouffe, C. (1985) *Hegemony and Socialist Strategy*. London: Verso.

Laclau, E. and Mouffe, C. (1990) Post-Marxism without apologies, in E. Laclau *New Reflections on the Revolution of Our Time*. London: Verso.

Lakatos, I. (1970) Falsification and the methodology of scientific research programmes, in I. Lakatos and A. Musgrave (eds) *Criticism and the Growth of Knowledge*. Cambridge: Cambridge University Press.

Lakatos, I. and Musgrave, A. (eds) (1970) *Criticism and the Growth of Knowledge*. Cambridge: Cambridge University Press.

Laqueur, T. (1990) *Making Sex: Body and Gender from the Greeks to Freud*. Cambridge, MA: Harvard University Press.

Larrabee, M. J. (1993) *An Ethic of Care: Feminist Interdisciplinary Perspectives*. London: Routledge.

Lash, S. and Urry, J. (1987) *The End of Organized Capitalism*. Cambridge: Polity.

Lefort, C. (1986) *The Political Forms of Modern Society*. Cambridge: Polity.

Lenin, V. I. (1973) [1902] *What is to be Done?* Peking: Foreign Languages Press.

Lévi-Strauss, C. (1963) *Structural Anthropology*. New York: Basic Books.

Lloyd, G. (1993) *The Man of Reason: 'Male' and 'Female' in Western Philosophy*, 2nd edn. London: Routledge.

Lloyd, M. (1996) A feminist mapping of Foucauldian politics, in S. Hekman (ed.) *Feminist Interpretations of Michel Foucault*. Philadelphia: Penn State Press.

Lloyd, M. (1996) Feminism, aerobics and the politics of the body, *Body and Society*, 2, 79–98.

Locke, J. (1988) [1690] *Two Treatises of Government* (ed. P. Laslett). Cambridge: Cambridge University Press.

Longino, H. (1990) *Science as Social Knowledge*. Princeton, NJ: Princeton University Press.

Lorde, A. (1984) *Sister Outsider: Essays and Speeches*. Freedom, CA: The Crossing Press.

Lukes, S. (1974) *Power: A Radical View*. Basingstoke: Macmillan.

Lukes, S. (ed.) (1986) *Power*. New York: New York University Press.

Lyotard, J.-F. (1984) *The Postmodern Condition: A Report on Knowledge*. Manchester: Manchester University Press.

Lyotard, J.-F. (1988) *The Differend: Phrases in Dispute*. Manchester: Manchester University Press.

McCarthy, T. (1984) *The Critical Theory of Jürgen Habermas*. Cambridge: Polity.

McCarthy, T. (1991) *Ideals and Illusions: on Reconstruction and Deconstruction in Contemporary Critical Theory*. Cambridge, MA: MIT Press.

Macey, D. (1988) *Lacan in Context*. London: Verso.

McGuigan, J. (1992) *Cultural Populism*. London: Routledge.

Machiavelli, N. (1988) [1513] *The Prince*. Cambridge: Cambridge University Press.

MacIntyre, A. (1988) *Whose Justice? Which Rationality?* London: Duckworth.

MacIntyre, A. (1990) *Three Rival Versions of Moral Enquiry*. London: Duckworth.

McLuhan, M. (1974) *Understanding Media*. London: Abacus.

McNay, L. (1992) *Foucault and Feminism: Power, Gender and the Self*. Cambridge: Polity.

McNay, L. (1994) *Foucault: A Critical Introduction*. Cambridge: Polity.

Macpherson, C. B. (1963) *The Political Theory of Possessive Individualism: Hobbes to Locke*. Oxford: Oxford University Press.

Marcuse, H. (1964) *One Dimensional Man: Studies in the Ideology of Advanced Industrial Society*. London: Routledge and Kegan Paul.

Markula, P. (1995) Firm but shapely, fit but sexy, strong but thin: the postmodern aerobicizing female bodies, *Sociology of Sport Journal*, 12, 424–53.

Marsh, D. and Stoker, G. (eds) (1995) *Theory and Methods in Political Science*. Basingstoke: Macmillan.

Marshall, T. H. (1992) *Citizenship and Social Class*. London: Pluto Press.

Marx, K. (1977) *Karl Marx: Selected Writings* (ed. D. McLellan). Oxford: Oxford University Press.

Marx, K. (1996) *Later Political Writings* (ed. T. Carver). Cambridge: Cambridge University Press.

Meehan, J. (1995) *Feminists Read Habermas: Gendering the Subject of Discourse*. London: Routledge.

Metz, C. (1982) *Psychoanalysis and Cinema: The Imaginary Signifier*. Basingstoke: Macmillan.

Miliband, R. (1972) The capitalist state: Reply to Nicos Poulantzas, in R. Blackburn (ed.) *Ideology in Social Science: Readings in Critical Social Theory*. London: Fontana.

Mill, J. S. (1972) [1859] 'On liberty' in *Utilitarianism, On Liberty and Representative Government* (ed. H. B. Acton). London: Dent.

Mill, J. S. and Taylor Mill, H. (1983) [1859] and [1851] *The Subjection of Women and the Enfranchisement of Women*. London: Virago.

Moore, H. (1994) 'Divided we stand': sex, gender and sexual difference, *Feminist Review*, 47, 78–95.

Morgan, K. P. (1991) Women and the knife: cosmetic surgery and the colonization of women's bodies, *Hypatia*, 6, 25–53.

Mouffe, C. (1993) *The Return of the Political*. London: Verso.

Mouffe, C. (ed.) (1996) *Deconstruction and Pragmatism*. London: Routledge.

Mulhall, S. and Swift, A. (1996) *Liberals and Communitarians*, 2nd edn. Oxford: Basil Blackwell.

Muller, J. P. (1983) Language, psychosis and the subject in Lacan, in J. H. Smith and W. Kerrigan (eds) *Interpreting Lacan*. New Haven, CT: Yale University Press.

Mulvey, L. (1989) *Visual and Other Pleasures*. Basingstoke: Macmillan.

Navari, C. (1981) The origins of the nation-state, in L. Tivey (ed.) *The Nation-state: The Formation of Modern Politics*. Oxford: Martin Robertson.

Nicholson, L. J. (ed.) (1990) *Feminism/Postmodernism*. London: Routledge.

Nietzsche, F. (1909) [1883] *Thus Spake Zarathustra*. London: T. N. Foulis.

Nietzsche, F. (1954) [1873] On truth and lies in a non-moral sense, in W. Kaufman (ed.) *The Portable Nietzsche*. New York: The Viking Press.

Nietzsche, F. (1968) [1909] *The Will to Power*. New York: Vintage Books.

Nietzsche, F. (1969) [1887] *On The Genealogy of Morals and Ecce Homo*. New York: Vintage Books.

Nietzsche, F. (1972) [1886] *Beyond Good and Evil*. London: Penguin.

Nietzsche, F. (1994) [1878] *Human, All Too Human*. London: Penguin.

Norris, C. (1987) *Derrida*. London: Fontana.

Norval, A.J. (1996) *Deconstructing Apartheid Discourse*. London: Verso.

Nozick, R. (1974) *Anarchy State and Utopia*. New York: Basic Books.

O'Brien, M. (1981) *The Politics of Reproduction*. London: Routledge and Kegan Paul.

O'Neill, S. (1997) *Impartiality in Context: Grounding Justice in a Pluralist World*. Albany: State University of New York Press.

O'Sullivan, N. (1997) Difference and the concept of the political, *Political Studies*, 45, 739–54.

Outhwaite, W. (1987) *New Philosophies of Social Science: Realism, Hermeneutics and Critical Theory*. Basingstoke: Macmillan.

Outhwaite, W. (ed.) (1996) *The Habermas Reader*. Cambridge: Polity.

Parsons, T. (1963) On the concept of political power, *Proceedings of the American Philosophical Society*, 107, 232–62.

Parsons, T. (1990) The distribution of power in American society, in J. Scott (ed.) *Power: Critical Concepts, Vol. III*. London: Routledge.

Pateman, C. (1988) *The Sexual Contract*. Cambridge: Polity.

Petchesky, R.P. (1986) *Abortion and Woman's Choice*. London: Verso.

Phillips, A. (1993) *Democracy and Difference*. Cambridge: Polity.

Pierson, C. (1986) *Marxist Theory and Democratic Politics*. Berkeley and Los Angeles: University of California Press.

Pierson, C. (1996) *The Modern State*. London: Routledge.

Popper, K. (1957) [1945] *The Open Society and Its Enemies*, two vols. London: Routledge and Kegan Paul.

Popper, K. (1970) Normal science and its dangers, in I. Lakatos and A. Musgrave (eds) *Criticism and the Growth of Knowledge*. Cambridge: Cambridge University Press.

Popper, K. (1994) [1934] *The Logic of Scientific Discovery*. London: Routledge.

Poulantzas, N. (1972) The problem of the capitalist state, in R. Blackburn (ed.) *Ideology in Social Science: Readings in Critical Social Theory*. London: Fontana.

Poulantzas, N. (1973) *Political Power and Social Classes*. London: New Left Books.

Rabinow, P. (ed.) (1984) *The Foucault Reader*. London: Penguin.

Radtke, H. L. and Stam, H. J. (eds) (1994) *Power/Gender: Social Relations in Theory and Practice*. London: Sage.

Radway, J. A. (1984) *Reading the Romance: Women, Patriarchy, and Popular Literature*. Chapel Hill: University of North Carolina Press.

Rawls, J. (1972) *A Theory of Justice*. Oxford: Oxford University Press.

Rawls, J. (1993) *Political Liberalism*. New York: Columbia University Press.

Rich, A. (1977) *Of Woman Born*. London: The Women's Press.

Rorty, R. (1989) *Contingency, Irony and Solidarity*. Cambridge: Cambridge University Press.

Rorty, R. (1990) *Objectivity, Relativism and Truth: Philosophical Papers, Vol. 1*. Cambridge: Cambridge University Press.

Rose, J. (1986) *Sexuality in the Field of Vision*. London: Verso.

Rousseau, J.-J. (1968) [1762] *The Social Contract*. London: Penguin.

Russell, B. (1938) *Power: A New Analysis*. London: Allen and Unwin.

St Martin, L. and Gavey, N. (1996) Women's bodybuilding: feminist resistance and/or femininity's recuperation, *Body and Society*, 2, 45–57.

Sandel, M. J. (1982) *Liberalism and the Limits of Justice*. Cambridge: Cambridge University Press.

Sandel, M. J. (1992) The procedural republic and the unencumbered self, in S. Avineri and A. de-Shalit (eds) *Communitarianism and Individualism*. Oxford: Oxford University Press.

Sapir, E. (1949) *Selected Writings in Language, Culture and Personality* (ed. D. G. Mandelbaum). Berkeley: University of California Press.

Sarup, M. (1992) *Jacques Lacan*. Hemel Hempstead: Harvester Wheatsheaf.

Saussure, F. de (1960) [1916] *Course in General Linguistics*. London: Peter Owen.

Sayer, A. (1984) *Method in Social Science*. London: Hutchinson.

Sayers, J. (1982) *Biological Politics: Feminist and Anti-feminist Perspectives*. London: Tavistock Publications.

Schattscheider, E. E. (1960) *The Semisovereign People*. New York: Holt, Rinehart and Winston.

Schmitt, C. (1996) [1932] *The Concept of the Political*. Chicago: University of Chicago Press.

Schutz, A. (1972) *The Phenomenology of the Social World*. London: Heinemann.

Schutz, A. (1982) *Life Forms and Meaning Structure*. London: Routledge and Kegan Paul.

Scott, A. (1990) *Ideology and the New Social Movements*. London: Unwin Hyman.

Scott, J. (ed.) (1994) *Power: Critical Concepts*, three vols. London: Routledge.

Sedgwick, P. (ed.) (1996) *Nietzsche: A Critical Reader*. Oxford: Basil Blackwell.

Seidler, V. (1989) *Rediscovering Masculinity: Reason, Language and Sexuality*, London: Routledge.

Seidler, V. J. (1994) *Unreasonable Men: Masculinity and Social Theory*. London: Routledge.

Seiter, E. (1992) 'Semiotics and Structuralism', in R.C. Allen (ed.) *Channels of Discourse, Reassembled*. London: Routledge.

Seligman, M. (1992) *The Idea of Civil Society*. New York: The Free Press.

Sheridan, A. (1980) *The Will to Truth*. London: Tavistock Publications.

Shilling, C. (1993) *The Body and Social Theory*. London: Sage.

Simons, J. (1995) *Foucault and the Political*. London: Routledge.

Simpson, P. (1993) *Language, Ideology and Point of View*. London: Routledge.

Skinner, Q. (1979) *The Foundations of Modern Political Thought*, two vols. Cambridge: Cambridge University Press.

Skinner, Q. (ed.) (1985) *The Return of Grand Theory in the Human Sciences*. Cambridge: Cambridge University Press.

Skinner, Q. (1990) The republican ideal of political liberty, in G. Bock, Q. Skinner and M. Viroli (eds) *Machiavelli and Republicanism*. Cambridge: Cambridge University Press.

Smith, A. M. (1994) *New Right Discourse on Race and Sexuality: Britain, 1968–1990*. Cambridge: Cambridge University Press.

Staten, H. (1985) *Wittgenstein and Derrida*. Oxford: Basil Blackwell.

Storey, J. (1993) *An Introductory Guide to Cultural Theory and Popular Culture*. Hemel Hempstead: Harvester Wheatsheaf.

Storey, J. (ed.) (1994) *Cultural Theory and Popular Culture: A Reader*. Hemel Hempstead: Harvester Wheatsheaf.

Street, J. (1997) *Politics and Popular Culture*. Cambridge: Polity.

Strinati, D. (1995) *An Introduction to Theories of Popular Culture*. London: Routledge.

Taylor, C. (1985) *Philosophical Papers*, two vols. Cambridge: Cambridge University Press.

Taylor, C. (1989) *Sources of the Self: the Making of the Modern Identity*. Cambridge: Cambridge University Press.

Taylor, C. (1992) The politics of recognition, in A. Gutmann (ed.) *Multiculturalism and 'The Politics of Recognition'*. Princeton, NJ: Princeton University Press.

Tester, K. (1992) *Civil Society*. London: Routledge.

Thompson, J. B. (1984) *Studies in the Theory of Ideology*. Cambridge: Polity.

Trigg, R. (1985) *Understanding Social Science*. Oxford: Basil Blackwell.

Turner, B. S. (1984) *The Body and Society*. Oxford: Basil Blackwell.

Turner, B. S. (1991) Recent developments in the theory of the body, in M. Featherstone, M. Hepworth and B. S. Turner (eds) *The Body: Social Process and Cultural Theory*. London: Sage.

Turner, B. S. (1992) *Regulating Bodies: Essays in Medical Sociology*. London: Routledge.

Turner, G. (1990) *British Cultural Studies: An Introduction*. London: Unwin Hyman.

Viroli, M. (1992) *From Politics to Reason of State*. Cambridge: Cambridge University Press.

Wacquant, L. (1995a) Why men desire muscles, *Body and Society*, 1, 163–79.

Wacquant, L. (1995b) Pugs at work: bodily capital and bodily labour among professional boxers, *Body and Society*, 1, 65–93.

Walzer, M. (1983) *Spheres of Justice: A Defence of Pluralism and Equality*. Oxford: Basil Blackwell.

Walzer, M. (1987) *Interpretation and Social Criticism*. Cambridge, MA: Harvard University Press.

Walzer, M. (1989a) *The Company of Critics*. London: Peter Halban.

Walzer, M. (1989b) Citizenship, in T. Ball *et al.* (eds) *Political Innovation and Conceptual Change*. Cambridge: Cambridge University Press.

Warner, M. (1994) *Managing Monsters: Six Myths of Our Time. The 1994 Reith Lectures*. London: Vintage.

Weber, M. (1947) *The Theory of Social and Economic Organisation*. London: Routledge and Kegan Paul.

Weber, M. (1978) *Economy and Society*. Berkeley: University of California Press.

Weber, M. (1991) [1948] *From Max Weber: Essays in Sociology* (ed. H. H. Gerth and C. Wright Mills). London: Routledge.

West, D. (1996) *An Introduction to Continental Philosophy*. Cambridge: Polity.

White, S. K. (1988) *The Recent Work of Jürgen Habermas: Reason, Justice and Modernity*. Cambridge: Cambridge University Press.

White, S. K. (1991) *Political Theory and Postmodernism*. Cambridge: Cambridge University Press.

Whorf, B. L. (1954) *Language, Thought and Reality* (ed. J. B. Carroll). Cambridge, MA.: MIT Press.

Williams, R. (1961) *The Long Revolution*. London: Chatto and Windus.

Williams, R. (1981) *Culture*. London: Fontana.

Williams, R. (1988) *Keywords: A Vocabulary of Culture and Society*. London: Fontana.

Williams, R. (1989) *The Politics of Modernism. Against the New Conformists*. London: Verso.

Williamson, J. (1978) *Decoding Advertisements. Ideology and Meaning in Advertising*. London: Boyars.

Wilson, B. R. (ed.) (1970) *Rationality*. Oxford: Basil Blackwell.

Winch, P. (1972) Understanding a primitive society, in *Ethics and Action*. London: Routledge and Kegan Paul.

Winch, P. (1990) *The Idea of a Social Science and Its Relation to Philosophy*, 2nd edn. London: Routledge.

Wittgenstein, L. (1967) [1953] *Philosophical Investigations*. Oxford: Basil Blackwell.

Wittgenstein, L. (1994) [1921] Tractatus logico-philosophicus, in A. Kenny (ed.) *The Wittgenstein Reader*. Oxford: Basil Blackwell.

Wollstonecraft, M. (1975) [1792] *Vindication of the Rights of Woman*. London: Penguin.

Woodward, K. (ed.) (1997) *Identity and Difference*. London: Sage.

Wrong, D. (1979) *Power: Its Forms, Bases and Uses*. Oxford: Basil Blackwell.

Yeatman, A. (1997) Feminism and Power, in M. L. Shanley and U. Narayan (eds) *Reconstructing Political Theory*. Cambridge: Polity.

Young, I. M. (1990) *Justice and the Politics of Difference*. Princeton, NJ: Princeton University Press.

INDEX

DATE DUE